RIGHT HERE IN RIVER CITY

RIGHT HERE
IN RIVER CITY

A Portrait of Kansas City

TRACY THOMAS
AND WALT BODINE

Doubleday & Company, Inc., Garden City, New York, 1976

Library of Congress Cataloging in Publication Data

Thomas, Tracy.
  Right here in river city.

  1. Kansas City, Mo.—Description. 2. Kansas City, Mo.—History. I. Bodine,
Walt, joint author. II. Title.
F474.K2T45   977.8′411
ISBN 0-385-00713-2
Library of Congress Catalog Card Number 73-21156

To Jerry Jette, K.C.'s spartan sage,
in appreciation

INTRODUCTION

It is a formidable task to undertake to write a book about a city. Especially this book and this city. This volume seeks to be more of a here-and-now book than a redo of Kansas City history. After all, there are already several excellent histories of Kansas City. A. Theodore Brown, Darrell Garwood, Richard C. Fowler, Henry Haskell, Jr., and others have done first-rate jobs of pulling together the city's beginnings. The late Bill Reddig's *Tom's Town* updated that history by chronicling the Pendergast era.

So this will be a book that talks more about the present—the exciting birth of a "New Kansas City," the flavor and FEEL of such a place. History will be here more as a flashback.

Just as there are two Kansas City's (Missouri and Kansas), there are two authors to this book. Tracy Thomas, president of NEXUS Corporation, is a business consultant and conceptual designer who uses a palette of words and pictures to convey ideas. Walt Bodine, a journalist and regional director of the National Conference of Christians and Jews, has spent most of a lifetime here. He loves Kansas City as one loves a woman—trying not to make too much of her faults and failures—and wanting to believe the promise in her eyes.

This book is subjective, especially when we come an experiment—emotional maps of Kansas City, Missouri, and the surrounding areas. These sketches are meant to catch the spirit and flavor of various towns and neighborhoods. Others may see them differently—and fair enough.

It takes some kind of gall to set out on such a project when there are so many others who could also write this book and perhaps better than we. But in this we repair to the feeling Harry Truman had about the Presidency; there might be a million other people who could do that job better, but he was the one who had the job to do.

And that too in spite of what so scholarly a book reader as Clifton Fadiman said, "Writing about most American cities is like writing a life of Chester A. Arthur. It can be done, but why do it?"

Our hope is that this book will not be like a life of Chester A. Arthur. If it must be like someone's life, our own Missouri President will do. For like Kansas City, Truman broke upon the country as hopelessly Midwestern and basically uninteresting. In a few short years, he managed to make them all know better than that. Kansas City is doing the same thing right now. Maybe this book will help.

Tracy Thomas
Walt Bodine

CONTENTS

RIGHT HERE IN RIVER CITY

1. HOW NOW, COWTOWN?

From the first day when the first explorer looked at the river front and contemplated the chances for a town, Kansas City has suffered from image paranoia.

Kansas City has been counted out time after time. In its earliest years, it was counted out as a presumptuous upstart by the much more promising cities of Independence, St. Joseph, Leavenworth, and Atchison. Later it had to survive outbreaks of cholera and being torn apart by the Civil War—the very rope itself in a life-and-death tug o' war.

Later it was to be written off as a wild, crude cattle town whose idea of culture was a piano in a whorehouse. Again it was counted out when the great political machines of the twenties and thirties came crashing down—and the Pendergast machine was one of the most powerful of all.

Since then, various self-appointed coroners have declared Kansas City dead just from its past reputation, then from being in a location remote from the two coasts, where every good and perfect thing must be; to some it seemed for years to be dead of an overdose of civic righteousness and business conservatism.

And when that malady finally seemed to be passing—and the victim was once more respirating a little—a deadening construction strike shut down everything in sight for months on end. Some Kansas Citians believed the entire nation was watching this deadlock and passing negative judgment on the city. These same people continue, year after year, to shift the blame for almost anything unfortunate that may occur to the effects of "the construction strike."

The same worriers are convinced that it is still very much on the mind of all America—ranking right up there with Watergate, the Middle East, airline hijackings, and the oil crisis as a coast-to-coast concern. It would seem as if some persons need to have some kind of ongoing shame to feel regretful about.

In reality, that wasn't the trouble at all. Kansas City has suffered from being ignored coast to coast—from being immaterial to any discussion of anything. Like a Russian politician who falls from grace and becomes a nonperson, Kansas City has really suffered from being a nonplace.

If Kansas City has any image at all, it is not as a center of industrial strife . . . many Americans would be ready to swear there isn't that much industry or construction in Kansas City to fight over. And the image is not one of a great "sin city" as the post-Pendergast fretters are convinced. It might give a boost to the growing tourist trade if that impression *were* abroad. Las Vegas is not running scared.

The truth is that Kansas City nationally for many years had the pale image of a great-aunt; not much known about her, and no great urgency for finding out. Today the young are more likely to be interested in what Great-Auntie was like, and to be delighted if they find out she was quite a magnificent old party with just a touch of indiscretion in her past—and a certain free and open style in her manner.

That is what young people find out when they come to Kansas City. The word has gone around the youth culture that K.C. is not a bad town. There are places to be and things to do. The other thing the kids discover which is truly one of the great assets of the city is a spirit of live and let live. To some degree, politicians despair of it. People in Kansas City rarely respond to a crusader. They have seen too many to become excited.

It is a favorite stop-off for those who are out to rally America. The radical on the road—whether an American Nazi, a Reverend Jesse Jackson or a Grand Dragon of the Ku Klux Klan—will be able to speak a piece in Kansas City without fear of violence. Even a protest, when it occurs here, tends to be muted and low-key. If you are far out enough, you might be picketed a little.

Here and there, someone might shout at you. But more likely, if you leave Kansas City in despair, it will not be because you ran into a wall of repression or a flame of resentment. It will be because you shouted and shouted and there wasn't much coming back to you but an echo. The audience is not sullenly unresponsive. It sits out there and looks pleasant enough. But it doesn't really do anything pro or con. It does the most damnable thing of all to the rabble-rouser; it regards him or her as interesting.

Some call it apathy; some call it Midwestern conservatism. But Kansas Citians call it a very healthy kind of live-and-let-live spirit. It is open-minded enough to want to hear you and what you say. But it is self-possessed enough to be able to tell any passing Joan of Arc that it was nice to meet her, but that until the voices begin to speak up so the rest of us can hear them, we will just have to wish her luck.

The positive self-image of Kansas City is a development of the 1970's. Cities, like people, have varying degrees of desire for survival. Kansas City's instinct is newly sparked, oddly enough by the expressions of confidence by newcomers, visitors, and outside investors.

If there was one city which used to provoke Kansas City into rivalry—the full body press of resentful, combatively fierce fighting—it was St. Louis. For a hundred years, St. Louis was the popular, cultured, attractive older sister in William Inge's play, *Picnic*, while Kansas City was the clutzy tomboy younger sister . . . always second best, and only then by default. For years, Kansas City and St. Louis legislators were so locked in coy combat that rural interests waltzed off with the state's General Assembly in tow.

Then, people began to notice that as subtly as puberty, Kansas City was growing up and getting it together. The 1970 census revealed that St. Louis City was landlocked, forcing the population to spread to St. Louis County and beyond. The census further whispered that Kansas City, with vast areas available for expansion and growth, was the *next* largest city in Missouri. By 1980, Kansas City may surpass St. Louis City in population.

The mark of a great politician is the ability to appease both sides of any issue. Like an astute father who is proud of both daughters, Senator Tom Eagleton began to refer to Missouri as "the home of St. Louis—the last great city of the East, and Kansas City—the first great city of the West." Like unwashed Levi's, it is an image that Kansas City is just beginning to feel comfortable in.

The 1970's sparked a major public relations program, Prime Time, which had a clever boomerang effect on Kansas City. Too broke to buy ads in major national magazines and newspapers, the Chamber of Commerce of Greater Kansas City encouraged news stories about "one of the few liveable cities left."

Prime Time had three effects. One, it attracted interest from other cities, encouraging tourism, business investment, and migration of families on the move. Two, these good vibrations boomeranged on people already living in Kansas City, who began to believe it because they read it in the New York *Times*. Third, it taught a lot of grammarians and public relations experts that liveable is not only difficult to define, it is difficult to spell. According to Merriam-Webster's, it is either *livable* or *liveable*.

Kansas City in the 1970's has struggled with multiple images . . . cowtown, in its Western flavor; cartown, in its Los Angeles-like absolute dependence on the automobile to get around; and nowtown, in the expectations of its business investors and civic boosters.

After the adrenalin boost of Prime Time, Kansas City pursued the Alternative Futures program, which was a governmental planning session keyed to the comments of civic leaders. Federal dollars financed a statistically quantified game of "You tell me your dream, I'll tell you mine." While some thought it an expensive way of stating the obvious, most agreed that it was good therapy. In transactional analysis terms, Kansas City grew from a not-OK-child into a multifaceted OK-adult.

The Alternative Futures report listed seven areas where Kansas City will continue to grow in the next thirty years and have national or international impact:

1. as a national/international distribution center
2. as an international agribusiness center
3. as a national convention center
4. as a regional health center
5. as a regional service and governmental center

6. as a scientific and technological research center

7. as a model of a liveable city

In addition to an exploration of Kansas City's current assets, several prime movers are pushing to discover what Kansas City needs to grow even more, in both a quantitative and qualitative sense. The concept that is developing is an elastic one similar to Kansas City's relaxed social sense of give and take.

Kansas City is pulsing with energy. With centrifugal force, its central location as a transportation and distribution center shoots the seeds of growth outward to the boundaries of American society. All those corny sayings about "The breadbasket of the nation and the hub of the system" cannot diminish Kansas City's ability to supply the great quantity of resources which are needed by people on both coasts.

Conversely, with centripetal force, Kansas City also pulls in— selecting quality in ideas and people who are attracted back to the heart of a society which with a little luck, a little rain, and a sense of humor will make it to the next generation.

Business leaders are manifesting their new-found pride in Kansas City by expanding their scope of vision. In addition to the building boom, there is an intensity of purpose on the leaders' faces. It is as if they are saying, "Well, let's settle down and get to work. We're no longer just playing at being a great city."

When St. Louis built the arch, many Kansas Citians were incensed. In the first place, St. Louis was never the "Gateway to the West." It was Kansas City, the last westward stopping point on the Missouri River before embarking by wagon train for California. And in the second place, the arch posed a challenge of vision and leadership, commitment and action that Kansas City wasn't ready at the time to meet.

Today, Kansas City's leadership is exploring plans for a major exhibition which will focus the world's attention on both the present and the potential qualities of Kansas City. It is a concept which would have been inconceivable ten, even two years ago.

2. SURPRISE CITY

Kansas City is a matter of opinion; it is either out in the middle of nowhere geographically—or it is right in the middle of everywhere. This attitude divides the optimists and pessimists the way the old test did, in which a person would say a drinking glass was half empty or half full.

For several years now Kansas City has been in a period of change. And this is nowhere more evident than in the self-image of the city. For years, the local pessimists dominated the scene saying that here was a town that only a yahoo could love. But for some time now, such negative forces have been falling back in retreat. The optimists—not mindless Babbitt-like civic boosters, but people with a quiet confidence and an exciting dream—have taken over the scene.

This will come as a genuine surprise to a great many people who have been observing the city over the years. For decade upon decade it seemed as if Kansas City had decided to settle for being comfortably dormant. A West Coast broadcasting executive who used to make regular trips into Kansas City said he would look out the window of the airport limo at the same buildings and the same traffic, and he could only conclude that "Nothing is happening here."

And yet, after all of those years of municipal dawdling along, a dramatic change has taken place. A newsman who pessimized with the best of them commented recently, "By God, I never thought I'd see it; but the old girl is coming to life!"

Today, for the people who live in Kansas City, and for the occasional visitor merely viewing the city casually, Kansas City is full of surprises. It is, in fact, the Surprise City of the American nation.

Only now are the coastal regions beginning to rediscover it. The great journalistic thought leader, the New York *Times*, has written about the rebirth and general upgrading of the city.

The Surprise City is truly that for people who view it from afar. To people sitting in New York or Los Angeles, Kansas City may seem to be a nowhere sort of place. One looks at its remote land location, surmises that it is some kind of expanded Dodge City with buildings, and one wonders why anyone would want to live in a place like that. The word "Kansas", in the city's name, reinforces that image of a prairie cowtown, plunked down in the center of endless flatland wheat fields, beaten unmercifully by a relentless sun in summer and blizzard winds in winter. The streets, one would imagine, are wide but dusty, with diagonal parking and a hell of a crowd on Saturday nights when the farmers come to town. One might assume that the people there would be honest but square, virtuous but crude—and that the local girls would have the rosy look of being "corn fed and hand spanked" as an old hillbilly comic used to say.

That perhaps is where the thought of Kansas City ends with millions of Americans. All of us go about dismissing distant places with which we have no personal involvement or interest with a fleeting impression. We dream up a quick mental picture of the distant place as we casually suppose it to be; then we freeze frame that picture and file it in our minds, and that's that.

The first-time visitor to Kansas City is invariably surprised at just how far off the prejudgment has been. If middle-aged or older, he or she may best remember Kansas City as a place that had a mighty political machine—a wide open city whose gambling and red-light activities made it the Las Vegas of another generation. A politically oriented visitor may recall that good old Harry Truman came from around here someplace. The visitor may also arrive with some notion that this is a town with a sports tradition of major league baseball, football, basketball, and hockey.

Any or all of those things might be in the mind of the new arrival and not a lot else. So from there on in, it is surprises almost all the way.

The first astonishment of the arrivee may be the fantastic new Kansas City International Airport, with its three gigantic circular terminals (any one of which might pass for all the airport building an average city would need). The airport seems to have been built not to dwarf people but to serve them.

Outside, a visitor will make first contact with one of the country's best freeway and interstate highway systems. And one may wonder at the expectation that he or she would be going down some country lane.

Instead, in the fast speed but relatively safe traffic flow, a visitor will see evidence of a bustling metropolis where one and one-third million people live, work, and play every day. And that's not counting the thousands of daily visitors or the large numbers of conventioneers (favored with the vast and elaborate new Bartle Convention Center completed in 1976). It also does not include all those families from the large and prosperous trade area who descend daily upon the city for shopping, shows, or sports events. Swelling the local population daily is a healthy stream of visiting business and sales executives who are drawn to Kansas City because of its role as a vigorous regional and national distribution, manufacturing, and home-office center. It is a good town to do business in—competitive but in a relaxed and confident manner. It's the kind of a town where a person's word still means something, and where a handshake on a deal can be relied upon.

Just ten minutes or so after being seated on the nation's most luxurious airport bus, the visitor comes into view of the majestic skyline of downtown Kansas City. The skyscrapers of downtown, impressive enough in their own right, loom even taller because the main business district is located atop the high bluffs overlooking the Missouri and the Kansas rivers. As the bus speeds along, the traveler also begins to realize that the place he or she thought would be a flat plain is in fact a city built on a whole series of hills in the manner of, though not as steep as, those of San Francisco.

If traveling through a good part of the city to one of the new hotels, the newly arrived visitor will be impressed with some other things. Kansas City is in the middle of a construction boom unequaled by any comparable city in the country—a $3.4 billion building surge. In one year alone (1973), just in the downtown area, eleven new buildings valued at more than $145 million were either under construction or about to begin.

But despite that, the visitor finds surprisingly a city that doesn't put its greatest store in shiny new skyscrapers or public buildings. Instead, the accent in Kansas City, in the very time of its rebirth, has been not so much on seeing how big the city can become, but rather on seeing how good it can become. Liveability is emphasized.

True enough sometimes, liveability and mammoth construction projects go hand in hand. The city's new Royals baseball stadium is acknowledged universally as the finest baseball stadium in the world—with unbelievable facilities and comforts for the fans. Located just next to it in the Harry S. Truman sports complex is the vast Arrowhead Stadium where the K.C. Chiefs play. Kansas Citians have a wholesome and overwhelming interest in sports; this is in evidence everywhere one turns in the city. It can be read in the attendance figures which have always made Kansas City a dear, dear place to the officials of the major leagues. The devotion of its armies of sports fans has made Kansas City the home of major league teams in baseball, football, hockey, and basketball. The new Kemper Arena for the hockey and basketball teams and the annual American Royal livestock and horse show round out the sports picture.

But liveability amounts to more in Kansas City than a lively sports life. The visitor is struck, as every preceding visitor has been, by the biggest surprise of all—the beauty of the place.

Yes, there are some flat and dreary streets and there is an inner city with some tragic pockets of poverty. But these are exceptions to the rule of natural and man-made beauty that has stopped many wayfarers in their tracks.

For here is a city in love with nature, with green rolling hills and lines of stately trees at streetside. Parkways abound, planted with flowers and attractive shrubs, with wading ponds for children often a part of them.

Even where poverty exists at its worst big city level, it is only a walk of a few short blocks to a green space where nature offers some respite.

Green grass is encouraged everywhere. The city has more parks and areas of green space than any other U.S. city. They range from tiny vest-pocket-size urban parks a half block to one block in size, to the larger neighborhood parks with tennis courts (some operating twenty-four hours), picnic tables, and ovens —and sometimes a lake or a formal garden.

The greatest of these parks is Swope Park, second largest municipal park in America, covering over 1,750 acres. Swope Park includes one of the nation's most innovative zoos stressing the display of animals in natural settings. The park also includes a large lagoon with boating, a fishing lake, and one of the nation's largest outdoor theaters, Starlight Theater, where the big names in show business and the musical world appear all summer long to large and appreciative crowds.

Throughout Kansas City the visitor notices the gentle winding boulevards—more miles of them than in that city of boulevards, Paris. Again, the boulevards may be lined with impressive churches, public buildings, apartments, and homes. But whatever else they have, they first of all have more of those magnificent trees. Kansas City has been described as a "city within a forest."

Some of the most beautiful residential areas in all the world help to complete the picture of a lovely and liveable place.

One is struck by something else—the preoccupation of this city with beautiful fountains. Among all the cities of the world, only Rome can rival Kansas City in the number of graceful fountains. They are found everywhere, even in the heart of downtown and in parts of the inner city.

Fountain fanciers should be careful not to miss the dramatic J. C. Nichols Memorial Fountain at Forty-seventh Street and Nichols Road. At that busy intersection, it catches the glimpse of almost everyone passing by. And in the evening little family groups and hand-holding couples are seen walking around it or sitting on the benches which surround it.

Another "must" for the appreciator of fountains is located at Volker Park. It was the last great work of the famed sculptor Carl Milles, and depicts St. Martin of Tours giving his cloak to a beggar. One of the interesting curiosities about it is the wrist-watch-wearing angel who looks on. Volker Park is located in the center of the vast lawns which extend from the Nelson Gallery of Art on the north, to the Midwest Research Institute and the University of Missouri at Kansas City on the south. In this same park each Sunday during the summer, thousands of young people from Kansas City mingle and talk and listen to the music of a rock band provided by the city's Parks and Recreation Department.

All of this instead of the flat dusty cowtown one might have expected; no wonder it is America's "surprise city."

Liveability in surroundings seems also to produce a kind of liveability in relationships of human beings with each other. That may be the nicest surprise of all. For there is not a friendlier city on the face of Mother Earth than Kansas City. Ask a citizen for street directions and that person will stop everything to help. People who come from a more reserved section of the country are startled at first when perfect strangers smile at them when passing on the sidewalk or toss them a cheery hello. But that is how things are done here. There is a basic live-and-let-live attitude and assumption that the next person is a pretty good person unless proved otherwise. Some visitors are startled by the openness of the people toward each other—but essentially it is a society that is still built more upon trust than upon fear. How many American cities can say that today?

So it is a surprise city—and a very pleasant surprise at that.

3. RIVER CITY

It all begins with a river; the Missouri, the wide Missouri, the Mighty Mo, or, as the Indians called it before the first paleface ever worried about water purity, the Big Muddy.

People in Kansas City today forget the river is there. Yet its presence is felt in many ways and its contribution to the life of the city is very great indeed.

Thousands of people pass over the Missouri each day on one of the several bridges that connect downtown Kansas City, Missouri (the original city located south of the Missouri River), with the "Northland."

Those thousands commuting across the river each day can spare the Missouri River only a fleeting glance, if that.

One reason is that the river and its bridges constitute a major hurdle on the daily obstacle course known as rush-hour traffic. The Northlander, like all people, has his or her share of life's travails—but none are more consistently vexing than the chore of getting to and from work each day over the Paseo Bridge, the Broadway, the ancient ASB, or the Chouteau on the far east side.

So much a part of life is this bridge bottleneck that it is a ready-made political issue. Having been closely associated with several political campaigns, the authors have seen candidates for offices ranging upward from city council to the governorship going before audiences north of the river to promise them another bridge over the Missouri. Neither the candidate nor the listener really believes the promise. It is just a nice way to commiserate and indicates that the candidate knows a little about the area. And who knows?—If candidates keep talking about it . . . well, Missourians are used to playing political long shots, and maybe one day the much-needed new bridge or bridges will be built by the Missouri Highway Department.

One thing is sure, old man river will just keep rolling along. And as it does, most of those who spare it a quick look in passing will tend to see what they expect to see . . . a wide, muddy stream (about the color of a good chocolate malted without too much chocolate). They expect it to look like that, and that is what they see. One frustrated Clay County farmer described the Missouri as too thin to plow, too thick to drink.

Yet many people see the river as something else. For that river, historically the mother of this metropolis, has stories to tell those who look toward her with a closer and more loving eye. At one time the Mighty Mo is telling about floods and hard times upstream. She holds up tree limbs, boards, and other debris that tell of floods in northern Missouri, Nebraska, or Montana. The very swiftness with which these objects bob into view and move past tells also of the push, the power, and the speed of that famous stream. Another time finds the Missouri filled with enormous chunks of ice. A view of the skyline from the water's edge reveals a bartender's dream—a whole city on the rocks. Those great globs of ice tell of a hard, cold winter in the midlands. Sometimes enormous ice jams have been known to occur upriver in the Missouri, cutting the usual heavy water flow past Kansas City so drastically as to imperil briefly the intake of water at the electric power stations.

Nor is that all the wise old Missouri is willing to confide. In years of drought, river watchers see her shrink. And here and there a normally submerged sand bar will be visible as a temporary island.

All of that, drought, floods, hard winters, may make the Missouri sound unappealing. But those are the exceptional times. On ordinary days those who look and really see the river behold a lady of changing moods and great beauty. At dawn there seems to be a quietness about the river—even though its currents move no less swiftly then. At another time, under another sky, she will seem to be gray blue—like a great inlet of the Atlantic Ocean.

And then—and only those who really know and love the Missouri will believe it—the Missouri River can be magically transformed at dusk. On the right day, and at the right time, around sundown, crossing the Broadway Bridge and looking westward toward Kansas, the Missouri River and all its muddiness can look as blue as the blue Pacific.

At night, the traveler coming upon the river may find it a mirror of the lights of Kansas City's impressive downtown skyline. But it is more moving—with an ominous kind of beauty—when seen from a downtown skyscraper. (The thirtieth floor of the Commerce Tower is one excellent perch.) From up there the river is not really visible, it is implied. In an unending vista of twinkling lights there is but one break. Looking like a great spill of black ink on a field of diamonds, the river winds into view from the Fairfax district, around to where it is joined by the Kansas, or Kaw, River, and then sweeps along beside the high bluffs where the towers of downtown are built.

And still this is only the look of the river. Before leaving that aspect, the San Benito Marina in eastern Jackson County comes highly recommended as a place to really get acquainted with the river. For here the river watcher can park, walk, and picnic right at the water's edge, dip a toe into the Big Muddy or even launch a motor boat from a special ramp for that purpose.

Three things will strike any newcomer to the Missouri: the width of the river (which only a fool among fools would attempt to swim across); the swiftness of its currents (which can be truly appreciated only when viewed in this way at a right angle to the river; and the silence of it. It is always moving to see great power that makes no boastful sound. Down by the Missouri River one must go very close to hear so much as a splash. From a grassy bank a hundred feet away all that massive movement is experienced without hearing it make a single sound.

The Missouri, like many rivers, has more effect upon the life styles on its two sides than its physical width would indicate. It is a line of separation of human attitudes and states of mind. In a later chapter the reader will find an effort to draw a psychological map of Kansas City, outlining the emotional topography in various parts of the city. The powerful influence of the river as a divider will re-emerge there.

The oft-forgotten river is vital to Kansas City today. It provides an excellent water supply; helps produce electric power; serves as a highway for commerce on river barges; provides a living to commercial fishermen; offers recreation to boaters and outdoor lovers; and helps industry (within proper ecological bounds).

In the beginning it was the river that gave Kansas City its first breath of life as a community.

As the river has always been important to Kansas City, so also Kansas City marks an important point in the river's own existence. It is here that the Missouri River, after coursing southward for hundreds of miles, changes direction. This is what is called "The Great Bend of the Missouri"—and at this place the Missouri swings eastward to cross the state that bears its name and join the Mississippi River at St. Louis.

This bend was a great spot for farming and trapping. The Indians found that out long ago. For years after the white man had reached the New World, the Indians were undisturbed and unchallenged in this area. There was, as a matter of fact, so much to explore on this continent in the late 1700's that the early inhabitants were kept busy. And what they didn't get around to they, for a time, wrote off.

So it was that the Kansas City area was part of a section of Missouri which was widely held to be almost useless. If there had been a Gallup poll in those days, it might have shown that a majority of Americans considered Missouri as "a jungle." And as to the country to the west, from Kansas on out, someone named it "The Great American Desert." In other words, for a time the area had about as much real estate attraction as today's American might feel toward parts of Alaska, Siberia, or the back country of South America. Who needed it?

Eventually somebody did. Politically it fell under the French flag at first, after France claimed the whole wilderness for its own. The French eventually gave way to the British in the New World, so the Spanish took it over—only to hand it back later to Napoleon. And finally it went to the United States, which paid $15 million for it.

In those early times, a few explorers came through the area. They were fascinated with the territory and impressed with the fertility of the land. But in the East, people didn't want to be confused with the facts. They had already decided that the territory was afflicted with poor soil. They entertained stories of fierce wild animals and equally fierce Indian tribes, perhaps even cannibals.

So, the enthusiastic talk of these first French and Spanish explorers fell on deaf ears. It was only when the Lewis and Clark Expedition had pushed into the area that a few minds began to open up, as the territory itself was opened up to the white man.

Incidentally, the area now known as Jackson County, Missouri —where the heart of Kansas City is—was granted early exemption from the "Great American Desert" title. Instead, the people who came into it found reason to call it the Big Blue Country . . . blue skies, blue streams, and the blue mist seen against the hillsides near daybreak and dusk made a profound impression. And that will explain why the word Blue has been so well thought of and retained; Blue River, Blue Valley, Blue Hills, and Blue Springs are all with us today as a result. It may even have influenced the selection of the name of the city's old minor league baseball club, known as the Kansas City Blues.

The blue skies over Jackson County still impress the visitor. Recently a young woman who had worked in Kansas City and then returned to her native California wrote back to say, "How I miss that wonderful big blue sky of yours, with its fluffy clouds."

Not only were the early Americans outside the area wrong about it being a wilderness. They were also wrong about the Indians. The first explorers were received by the red man with friendly curiosity.

As others arrived, a lively trade in furs began with Indians furnishing many of the hides and other kinds of goods to supplement what the French trappers were bringing in. Many of them also embraced the white man's religion, as taught by Christian missionaries as time went on. So it was a beginning without bloodshed.

One of the principal tribes in the immediate area contributed the name for the city and for a state, the Kanza, or Kansas, Indians.

Far from living up to the Eastern rumor of bloodthirsty and

cannibalistic savages, the Kansas Indians were a gregarious lot who got along by farming, fishing, and trapping. But what they really liked was to have big get-togethers with plenty of food. These occasions also called for dancing, speechmaking, and gambling. The Kansas Indians even produced a native poet or two, and it was one such poet who said the real meaning of "Kansas" was "People of the South Wind."

Their eventual fate is a familiar story because these gentle and fun-loving people were no match for the white man's progress. Today a few members of the tribe survive and were last reported living in Oklahoma. The spirit of Wounded Knee came far too late for them.

Explorers came and went for a while, but an explorer and a settler are two different kinds of people. The first real settlers were the group of French traders from St. Louis, which included François Chouteau and his family, who settled in 1821 around a trading post near where the Kaw River empties into the Missouri. They made a few roads, such as they were, and they built rough log cabins to live in. And that was the settlement. Around it some farms began to take shape, cultivated by Americans, Frenchmen, Germans, and Belgians. What all of these people did in that place was what thousands of others would be doing in place after place as the white man moved into, settled, and conquered the American West.

But to conquer it, one had to reach it. And like everything else the pioneers faced, it was not easy.

At the time, the most practical way was for the settlers to come as far as they could by river boat, and that was to the landing at Independence, Missouri. From there the people and goods could disembark and begin the overland trek to the West.

Two towns preceded Kansas City because of this. Independence, of course, and the town of Westport, four miles inland from where Kansas City was to be. Westport had set up shop as a rival to Independence as a trail town.

And here emerges the real father of Kansas City. Picture John C. McCoy, the practical and material-minded son of a famous Baptist missionary to the Indians. Mr. McCoy was described as a square-cut sort of fellow.

He had ample sideburns which would make him look at home

in the Westport of today (centered around Westport Road and Broadway in midtown K.C.). McCoy, who in today's world would probably be known as a hard-hitting real estate developer, had established Westport in 1833. He had trained as a surveyor and had graduated from Transylvania University in Kentucky. McCoy set up a store in Westport where he could conduct trade with the Indians.

But getting supplies for his store was another thing. To do so, he had to use an ox team, spending an entire day bringing the goods to Westport from the landing at Independence.

To a mover and doer like McCoy, that was a terrible waste of time and effort. One day while he was down visiting the Chouteau post, he saw something that made his eyes open a little wider.

For there, just next to the trading post area, was a nice flat rock that jutted outward into the river, big enough and flat enough to serve as a natural levee from which a steamboat could unload passengers and cargo. In that brief moment, when an idea clicked in the head of John McCoy, Kansas City's future was assured; that moment sealed a decline in the fortunes of Independence as *the* jumping-off place for the West, and set in motion forces which would one day make Westport not a town but just a neighborhood of Kansas City.

McCoy decided to have the steamboat deliver his next order of merchandise, not to the Independence landing, but here . . . here at . . . well, call it Westport Landing.

And in 1834—whatever McCoy had to do to convince the steamboat people they should come up the river another fourteen miles—the steamer pulled up beside McCoy's flat rock and dropped his supply of goods overboard to John McCoy, on the rock.

There was still the matter of getting the merchandise from the landing to Westport. But in today's parlance, McCoy was a fellow who didn't fool around. He loaded his wagon and headed south. A four-mile run was ahead of him. But he had found a route, mostly through a ravine which is now downtown. Here and there some underbrush had to be chopped away and a tree or two had to be cut down. But McCoy did it.

John McCoy knew he had done more than shorten his own

trip to the river. He had opened up a new path toward the West —fourteen miles of additional distance that could be covered for the westward-bound pioneer by river boat rather than on land. Besides, those landing at Independence had been plagued with problems from several streams in the area which could not be forded whenever the waters were swollen by rain.

Within a very short time, Independence had been supplanted as the head of the Santa Fe and the Oregon trails. But as this came to pass, McCoy and other observers also came to another realization. Every sign they could see pointed to the fact that Westport Landing was really where the action would be—more than Westport itself, and more than anywhere else in the area. John McCoy and some other people of ambition and vision began to focus upon the landing, thinking of it as not just a landing but also a town.

Their vision was to come true—with a comic overtone or two, in a relatively brief period of time.

4. THE LANDING AND THE BRANDING

Naming things has always been a big hangup in Kansas City. The phenomenon goes back to the Year One of Kansas City, when the early pioneers had a spirited meeting on the subject of a name for the city. It was the forerunner of many more to come. Kansas City seems to be a city that can build some remarkable public facilities without too much sweat. Ah, but naming them . . . there is a real challenge. Tempers have been lost and voices have become hoarse in many an encounter over semantic designations. But the very first one on this soil was probably the wildest.

It all took place back in November of the year 1838. The locale was the cabin of a grizzly old party whose own given name eludes most historians. Instead, they tend to favor the designation the early residents gave him: One Eyed Ellis. Mr. Ellis was, on the respectable side, a justice of the peace. And on the more profitable side he sold whiskey to the Indians, which was described by one resident at the time as "remarkably bad whiskey" at that. He was the town oddball. But he was to have his moment of glory that day . . . a moment that would thrust him briefly into the very heart of what passed at the time for the "establishment." For this honor he could thank the blustery and chilling weather outside—and the fact that he was a man who always kept a big hickory fire going in the fireplace of his cabin on cold days.

But first, one must look to another scene not far away. There a small crowd had gathered—twenty-five or thirty people—dressed to withstand the weather in boots, fur caps, and heavy coats. The occasion was the auctioning off of the property of their late fellow townsman, farmer Gabriel Prudhomme. The property, which joined up with the site of the river-boat landing, was ideal for a townsite.

It was with this goal in mind that John McCoy and thirteen other men had formed something called the "Kansas Town Company." A Westport squire, George W. Tate, was the auctioneer. He worked from a makeshift platform. Some boards had been laid across the rails in a cattle pen. The Kansas Town Company had chosen one of its members, Captain Bill Sublette, a skillful trapper and a widely known mountain man, to do its bidding. The captain was an impressive six feet two inches in height and bore a lengthy scar on his chin which had won him the title from the Indians of "Cut Face." The bidding moved along, with Captain Sublette raising his big hand in the air several times to enter bids. In the end he made the winning bid. He bought the 271-acre Prudhomme farm for $4,220. In terms of today's Kansas City streets, he was buying the area from the river, south as far as Independence Avenue, and from Broadway to Troost.

The bidding and the consummation of the purchase took time, and a cold north wind blowing in over the river left everyone chilled through. And here One Eyed Ellis comes into the picture. The nearest place where the members of the new company could sit down and talk things over was Ellis' nice warm cabin.

Ellis, it is said, used to stand around the doorway a lot, watching for Indians interested in his brand of firewater. Now and then he would engage in a little traffic in stray horses, too. But this day, as Ellis watched from his door, the leaders of the community could be seen making a brisk approach. They greeted Ellis, came into the welcome warmth, and took up seats around the room so as to get on with their business.

These fourteen men, the founders of Kansas City—perhaps to repay his hospitality and perhaps because he was known as a justice of the peace and a "writing man"—designated One Eye as chairman of the session. The principal business of this session was to select a name for the new town.

As it turned out, one of their number had been thinking about that. And now he was ready to offer his suggestion. His name was Abraham Fonda and he not only affected a tail coat but, when required to list his occupation, would put it down in one word: "Gentleman." It was his feeling that Port Fonda was a nice name for a town. But as it happened there was bad blood between Mr. Fonda and another member of the group, Henry Jobe. Taking note of Fonda's pretensions in listing himself as "gentleman," Jobe put his occupation down simply as "farmer." He also put his foot down resoundingly on "Port Fonda" as a name.

One Eyed Ellis, unaccustomed to such important goings on, was doing what he could to help things along. He passed around a jug. One hopes it was something better than he reserved for his Indian customers, a type of joy juice purchased wholesale for fifteen cents a gallon.

He also tried to spur the deliberations a bit by getting out his old spelling book and looking through it to see if any words appropriate for a town title might be in it. No luck.

By this time, and with the Port Fonda flare-up disposed of, the conferees were getting warmed up, inside and out. The groping for a name was getting a little wild, too.

"How about Rabbitville?" a trapper offered. The matter was thoughtfully considered, debated for a spell and then put to a vote. Rabbitville was out.

"Alright, I'll tell you a good name," another settler declared. "And that's Possum Trot. What do you think of that?" The group thoughtfully sent the jug around again, and as time wore on the name Possum Trot was starting to look good to them. Understandably no precise minutes were kept, but one historian's version holds that Kansas City missed being called Possum Trot by a single vote.

In the end, saner heads prevailed. The Indian word Kansas seemed to have universal appeal. And so the final decision was "Town of Kansas," which was later switched around to become "Kansas City."

There is an interesting matter of timing here, too. It is commonly held that for some reason Kansas City was named after the State of Kansas. This of course isn't so. The State of Kansas did not exist at that time. There was only the Kansas territory, which did not qualify for statehood, not entering the federal union until 1861. So there was a Kansas City in Missouri before there was ever a state of Kansas.

That first naming session in One Eyed Ellis' cabin was prophetic, however, of repeated traumas over name designations—persisting until this day.

For one thing, people in Kansas City seldom leave a name alone. Sometimes it seems that names of things in the city should be written on blackboards, the easier to change them.

Linking the downtowns of Kansas City, Missouri, and Kansas City, Kansas, is the Intercity Viaduct, as generations knew it, now dubbed the Lewis and Clark Freeway. Whatever its name, it leads to the Sixth Street Expressway, formerly just plain old Sixth Street. It is the principal thoroughfare on the onetime "north side" now "River Quay."

But that brings to mind Fifteenth Street and the saga of its renaming. If one follows Fifteenth Street far enough to the east, ten miles or more, it will eventually deliver the driver to an intersection with Delaware Street in Independence.

At that corner stands a famous old white frame house—a big place, surrounded by an iron fence—which once decorated the covers of national magazines. It was the home of President Harry S. Truman and his widow, Bess, who lives there still.

When Harry Truman first took over the office of President upon the death of Franklin D. Roosevelt, there was a feeling among some in Kansas City (a metropolitan area that had not produced a President before) that the community should take note by naming something—a street, a highway, a bridge—after Harry Truman.

But it was an idea born too soon. The local Republicans were not all that thrilled that what they considered a "product of the Pendergast machine" was now sitting in the White House. The fat cats who gathered each day at the exclusive Kansas City Club were not dancing in their thick-carpeted hallways over it either.

And so the idea went glimmering. Maybe if Harry Truman turned out to be a very good boy and surprised everyone by becoming a marvelous President, well, then we'd see about naming something after him in Kansas City, Missouri.

Among Democrats, the only one who agreed with that was Harry S. Truman himself. He steadfastly maintained then—and many times thereafter—that it was not a good thing to name anything important after a man who was still alive. The inference was that such an honoree might still mess up and disgrace whatever was named for him.

But in 1948, after his stunning upset of the "unbeatable" Thomas E. Dewey, the local Democratic faithful were no longer to be denied. It was then that Fifteenth Street was at last renamed by the City Council, becoming "Truman Road."

By now, Kansas City has done a little better by the late President. There is a Truman Bridge; the vast football and baseball stadiums are located in what is officially designated as the Harry S. Truman Sports Complex. And most fitting of all, for a man who demonstrated deep interest in the health care systems of his country, the new hospital for the University of Missouri School of Medicine—replacing Kansas City's old General Hospital—is named the "Harry S. Truman Medical Center."

There is another Kansas City hospital which has changed its name. A recent patient at Research Hospital asked a doctor, "What kind of research goes on here?" "None," was the doctor's reply. "But what would *you* have done during World War I if your name was German Hospital?"

The what'll-we-name-it hangup has persisted even when the name is purely geographical. What is today known as Kansas City International Airport started out being called the Platte County Airport for the not illogical reason that it was located in Platte County. Then it picked up the title Mid-Continent Airport and that, in turn, was amended to be Mid-Continent International. An old Kansas City watcher would not begin to give odds that Kansas City International, the present title, will still be the name of the local airdrome, say, four or five years from now. There is a sizable body of opinion in the city favoring naming the $250 million facility for Mr. Truman. They cite the tendency in other cities to name airports after people; O'Hare in Chicago, Dulles in Washington, and Will Rogers in Oklahoma City. For the moment these forces are in retreat, but, knowing Kansas City, it is best to think of them as regrouping.

Today's namers of things seem to be a more practical lot than some of our colorful old-timers. These were the people who named Eleventh Street downtown, with its many women's shops and quality stores, "Petticoat Lane." Ironically, no one is trying to change the name of Petticoat Lane, even though the lane itself has changed in nature. The attrition to the shopping center has cut down seriously the number of petticoats swirling up and down the lane each day; the places to shop have likewise thinned out somewhat. Today Petticoat Lane looks to happier things, however. Mercantile Bank erected a major office building on the lane at Walnut Street, and the new H. Roe Bartle Convention Center a few blocks away will add a daily contingent of conventioneers. So Petticoat Lane is far from finished.

In keeping with Kansas City's naming syndrome, the Park Board has added a few puzzles of its own. Troost Park is not on Troost Avenue, but on Paseo Boulevard at Thirty-first Street. (The area was originally an amusement park opened by the Kansas City Cable Company about 1888, with free admittance to all patrons of the nearby Troost Avenue Cable Line.)

Columbus Square, in the North End, was called Washington Square until 1926. In that year, an equestrian statue of President George Washington was placed in the park adjacent to Union Station. The statue's rider took his name with him, so the square at Missouri and Holmes avenues was renamed in honor of the resident Italian population's hero, Christopher Columbus.

The ultimate in name-dropping in Kansas City, however, is the underground movement to change the name of Kansas City, Missouri. And there *is* such a serious movement (as yet unnamed, of course) to rename the city. The reasoning is described in typical businessese by the Chamber of Commerce as "Business Loss and Image Damage." It means there's no zing to it, and even if there were, it's only a nice place to be from if you're from Kansas—not Missouri.

And so the search is on. Everyone agrees Kansas City isn't the best name; all that's needed is a good alternative. It would be nice if it had the same initials, some add. After all, "K.C." is how everyone already knows the place, thus conversion would be much simpler.

A good obvious solution—a familiar name, with the same initials as our nickname, and one of a kind, would be simply "K.C.," Missouri. It's not short for anything. It's just "K.C.," which surely would be one of the briefest municipal handles in all the world.

Kansas City, Kansas, could keep its name and be prouder of it. Besides, they stole it from Kansas City, Missouri, years ago, to capitalize on the business trade already associated with Kansas City, Missouri. They rejected the name of the resident Indians, the Wyandots, in favor of the more natural Kansas City, Kansas. They counted on enough people getting confused that business would drift their way, and some of it did.

For those who need more convincing, "K.C." is quicker and easier to pronounce. Some Midwesterners have such a nasal twang that "Kansas City" comes out sounding like "Can City" or "Kent City" (which doesn't exist but if it did it would be where Nancy Drew would live).

But the real attraction is that it's fun to say. Just try it a few times, K.C., K.C. It has a swagger to it, the kind of name people like to drawl as they board airplanes to fly there. "Ah think ah'll fly on up to ole K.C. for a few days." It's the kind of name people could get homesick for.

5. BUILT IN BEAUTY

One way to feel a city's pulse is to study its architecture, for it invariably reflects the values of the people who build there. Kansas City is fortunate in having a broad spectrum of architecture still standing, a blessing attributable to several seemingly negative factors. For one thing, a corrupt political machine took kickbacks for a quarter of a century from the construction industry. A principal firm in that industry was the Pendergast-owned Red-D-Mix Concrete Company. However, they built incredibly durable buildings which are still functional today.

A second blessing in disguise was the conservatism of Kansas City bankers, who were notoriously reluctant to loan money for construction and redevelopment. This has been a Kansas City "tradition" since 1888, when Arthur E. Stilwell had to go to Philadelphia and finally to Amsterdam to finance the forerunner of the great Kansas City Southern Railroad. Many post-Stilwell developers have not been as persistent, and have given up in the face of the Kansas City bankers' opposition to their removal and reconstruction plans. Several areas of architectural heritage have narrowly missed the bulldozer of progress because of this conservative banking attitude.

Visitors from barren and "modernized" cities of the sixties such as Atlanta and Dallas are amazed at the number of old buildings in Kansas City, such as the great New York Life Building, at 20 West Ninth Street. Perhaps through delays and red tape, Kansas City has "Magoo'd" its way through the era of land clearance for redevelopment to a realization that historically preserved buildings can be functional; that in fact their personalities add a measure of economic feasibility to this city. In order to attract some of the truly creative, think-tank industries, a city must provide a character, which is most tangibly demonstrated by its architecture.

The Bicentennial thrust toward historic preservation adds momentum to this trend. This is fortunate, since, according to the patron saint of architectural criticism, Ada Louise Huxtable, America can no longer afford to build great buildings. High construction costs, rule by committee, and a shift from aestheticism to materialism have almost wiped out quality in new architecture. Thus forewarned, here is a quick tour of Kansas City's architectural heritage while it's still standing.

The first case in point of preservation due to conservatism is the River Quay. Most certainly, if a Kansas City developer had found the financing during the 1950's and '60's, that area would have been bulldozed for a money-making tower of glass and steel. Instead, the area sat around gathering blight and bums, until Marion Trozzolo pioneered the restoration of the area to its early fame as the river-front heart of the city.

Trozzolo began by putting his plastics company in the original Board of Trade Building; he then invited others, especially artists, to move into the warehouse-type buildings and renovate the interiors. The artists got out their sanders, chemicals, and toothbrushes and discovered some great brick under the layers of plaster. Larger business interests have now moved into the area, but the commitment to preservation is still paramount; they've discovered that the old buildings' charm is an economic plus. The high ceilings offer a striking display space for merchandise. And the architecture is amenable to many period décors, providing variety for the many bars and restaurants.

While there are many significant structures throughout Kansas City, Tracy Thomas has a favorite worth describing. That old New York Life Building, at 20 West Ninth Street, is the kind of landmark that dim memories are made of. Only those few people born before 1890 will remember when it wasn't standing there like a proud fortress barricading the north end of Baltimore Street.

The best approach to it is driving north from Truman Road on Baltimore. As the Louis Saint-Gaudens eagle comes into view, there is an emotional sense of having arrived in the downtown area. The sights and sounds of commerce—flashing stock market reports, bell tower chimes, honking horns—completely inundate the visitor. Hovering above is a bronze symbol of protection. Beneath the twelve-foot wing span, a snake is clamped in the eagle's claws, barely out of reach of two anxious eaglets.

At the time it was built, the New York Life Building was twice as tall as any other in Kansas City, approaching the maximum possible for masonry-bearing walls. The lobby floor is a complex serpentine mosaic, which was laid by the hands of an Italian work crew. None of the crew spoke English, and they traveled around to various U.S. cities to create works of art underfoot.

Several other old downtown masterpieces still stand, including the Folly Theatre at Twelfth and Central, which is reverting from its burlesque past to community use. The Folly Theatre opened as the Standard Theatre in 1900, and hosted such stars as Gypsy Rose Lee, Tempest Storm, Rose La Rose and Peaches Browning. It is still noted for its perfect acoustics and sight lines and for its Louis Curtiss design, which gives it a Greek or Roman look, similar to Jefferson's Monticello. All three factors are appropriate to its location near the new convention center, which is viewed by many as the key to the renaissance of downtown Kansas City.

Farther west on Twelfth Street is the gold-domed Cathedral of the Immaculate Conception, near the old Quality Hill section on the west bluffs. Now a somewhat run-down area for the down and out, Quality Hill was developed a hundred years ago by Kersey Coates as a plush haven for Northerners and Easterners after the Civil War. Main Street served as a sort of Mason-Dixon line then, and people of Southern sympathies moved to the eastern and southern parts of Kansas City. Some of Kansas City's finest homes were built on the West Side, on old Quality Hill. Pennsylvania Street has several good examples, some of them recently converted to use as architects' offices.

Other historic buildings in downtown Kansas City are more fully covered by the tours of the American Institute of Architects (check with the Convention and Visitor's Bureau), but three are worth mentioning for their political significance. Thanks to his financial holdings in the Red-D-Mix Concrete Company, boss Tom Pendergast took a great interest in civic building projects. It's a fact that his concrete was the best in the area—even Johnson County projects used it. But it also happened to be in great demand for any and every use imaginable in Jackson County, Missouri.

During the Great Depression of the 1930's, Kansas City built six major structures downtown, three of them city- or county-financed. These were the Jackson County Courthouse, Municipal Auditorium, and City Hall. They are magnificent structures with great attention to detail and incorporating much artwork. Flimsy they aren't, and each one offers something special.

The Courthouse, named after Andrew Jackson, who rides in bronze out front, houses a jail on the top five floors. Municipal Auditorium's Music Hall sports a grand staircase reminiscent of the old Ziegfeld Follies movies, when hundreds of sequined and ostrich-plumed couples sang and danced in extravagant routines. Finally, the City Hall lobby showcases friezes of various professions, plus a huge city seal in the floor. The elevator doors are of hand-polished brass. The observation deck is reached via the twenty-ninth floor and offers one of the finest panoramas of Kansas City.

Immediately south of the central business district but still a part of the downtown area is the Crown Center complex, flanked by Hospital Hill and the Liberty Memorial. Catty-corner is the Pershing Square development, enveloping the Union Station. Jarvis Hunt's 1914 neoclassic Union Station was one of the last great train stations, built when trains were fashionable and when people had the time to enjoy a mammoth waiting room's pleasures. At one time, almost forty-thousand train depots dotted the American landscape. Kansas City's hope for saving the Union Station is to utilize it as a museum.

Neighboring Crown Center once was an ugly mottle of billboards known as Signboard Hill, now memorialized in one of the hotel's bars. In its place, Hallmark's Joyce Hall built a fantasy complex, right out of Disneyland. It is strikingly done yet beset with problems. Unless one drives a very tiny car or a medium-sized motorcycle, Crown Center has the world's worst parking garages. Yet, it is staffed by the world's friendliest security force, dressed like Canadian mounties riding orange steel horses.

The fantasy land continues as the hotel doorman, dressed as a Russian Cossack, directs visitors to the Polynesian restaurant a hundred feet away, or across the psychedelic carpet to the five-story waterfall. In the gay and noisy cafeteria area dotted with real trees, one can choose from seven international food lines. Shoppers may want to get a directory and wander through the West Village, a psychedelic maze of narrow steel steps connecting tiny multilevel exposed boutiques, witchcraft supply stores, and ski shops, etc. Resident artists and craftspersons have studios throughout.

The Crown Center Square just outside is superb . . . lots of grass, umbrellas, and a Calder stabile, *Shiva.* The Crown Center Corporation is very community oriented and sponsors many community programs, concerts, and festivals on the square.

Overlooking the square are the Crown Center offices, which are very sleek and plushly decorated. Tenants there all seem to have good taste. And yet, at least one visitor has had the sensation of looking at a life-size version of all the buildings she built with her childhood Lego blocks. The Crown Center complex is very "Kennedy Center"—larger than life but lifeless when empty. It's a great improvement over Signboard Hill.

Heading south, one can't help but see the KCMO-TV5 tower at Thirty-first Street: the world's tallest free-standing antenna, 1,042 feet. A firm from Topeka has made a family business out of changing the light bulbs on the tower.

Just west of Broadway on Westport Road is another small restoration project, Westport Square. Nestled among the San Francisco skylights and cosmopolitan shops is Kelly's Westport Inn. Kelly's is the watering hole for those people who still like conversation. Housed in the oldest building in Kansas City, Kelly's started out as Colonel Albert G. Boone's trading and outfitting post for the Santa Fe Trail. Some people claim it was also the site of a slave market. A model of a mangy Confederate peers out at passers-by from a second-floor window.

The next architectural cluster is the Country Club Plaza, the world's first shopping center. Let it be noted that running through the plaza is the world's only paved creek. In a creative fit of flood control, T. J. Pendergast poured his Red-D-Mix concrete the two-mile length of Brush Creek, at a depth of eight inches and at times a width of seventy feet. It is absolutely undocumented that Brush Creek's banks are lined with his political opponents.

Just east of the plaza on Forty-seventh Street, fronted by a great expanse of lawn, is the stone and marble Nelson Gallery. Architecturally, the Nelson Gallery is about as warmly inviting as when Dorothy tiptoed up to the smoke-belching castle to visit the Wizard of Oz. In both cases, it's what's inside that counts. Still, the imposing building which houses Kansas City's great art might scare off the faint of heart.

However, the design is probably just what Colonel Nelson would have wanted. In his will, Nelson stipulated that his money could not be used for any works unless the artist had been dead for thirty years. In that sense, the frequent description of the Nelson Gallery as a mausoleum is really apropos.

Nearby, in the 500 block of Pierce Street, is a row of stone houses built by Nelson for his Kansas City *Star* staff executives. Always the patriarch, Nelson provided for his own, but in a close-knit way. Today, no company would think of having its employees live together in one neighborhood, for it would be viewed as communist domination. But in those days, housing was viewed as a fringe benefit. The stone homes are no longer exclusively for *Star* employees but are still highly sought after by the general public. With the probable arrival of the UMKC Center for the Performing Arts as their next door neighbor, the stone homes may be moved to a nearby location or destroyed.

South of the Nelson Gallery, at Fifty-second and Troost, is a striking example of what's right with modern architecture. St. Francis Xavier Church is not the typical inverted Noah's ark design, but a Christian symbol of love. "The Fish Church," as it is known by most people, was designed in 1947 by Barry Burn of Chicago. The windows are of deep indigo glass, which gives the worshipers, many of them students at nearby University of Missouri at Kansas City, a violet hue. This church inspired one Christian to exclaim, "Holy mackerel. A house of cod."

Most of the homes south of the plaza from Troost to State Line Road and beyond, including the lush Ward Parkway, were built by J. C. Nichols. These homes are a mixed bag, architecturally, from Tudor to colonial, linked by good landscaping and $1 million worth of stone cupids and vases. Nichols' genius was in building everyone's dream castle starting at a middle-class price range.

Across State Line Road in Johnson County, Kansas, is the Beverly Hills-like Mission Hills. From there, more Nichols homes wind on endlessly, few with architectural merit.

In the middle of this suburban sprawl is old Shawnee Mission, an 1830's Methodist school and farm for the Indians. It's interesting to tour the excellently preserved buildings there, built by Kansas City pioneer brothers Thomas and William Johnson. Yet, it's sad to realize that Kansas City had no Wounded Knee; instead, we "civilized the savages" by sending them to school in Shawnee Mission, Kansas.

Our tour now loops around Kansas City to the east, where Independence has several landmarks. The Truman home, at 219 North Delaware, has always looked like a postcard, with its immaculate white-painted walls surrounded by the black wrought-iron fence.

RLDS Auditorium, world headquarters for the RLDS church, is located at River and Walnut streets in Independence. The huge auditorium seats almost 6,000 people and is most famous for the organ concerts given there on the outstanding Aeolian-Skinner organ, with its 6,334 pipes. Another Independence favorite is the Old Stone Church at 1012 West Lexington.

Returning to Kansas City, Missouri, the old Northeast section offers the greatest architectural variety in the city. Gladstone Boulevard is outstanding, including the R. A. Long home (now Kansas City Museum) and the Scarritt mansion, 3500 Gladstone, which is the family home of the late political leader Bill Royster. Jim Ryan, Kansas City Museum curator, is the expert on this area's architecture, and occasionally leads walking tours.

Tracy Thomas's favorite Northeast home, at 512 Benton Boulevard, exemplifies how a person's house was once his or her art form—an expression of self. This home was built by a couple who shared an interest in Assyrian art. Supporting one corner of the porch is a copy of a temple guard from an Assyrian tomb.

The retaining walls surrounding this house have water-spouting gargoyles, in the European tradition of frightening away evil spirits. And there's not another house on the block like it!

Eighteen miles north of downtown Kansas City is the new airport, Kansas City International, or KCI. It was designed by Kivett and Myers in the days before the energy crisis, when cars and the green express busses whizzed out there at seventy-five miles per hour. When the energy crisis reduced speeds to fifty-five miles per hour, the public turned to Clarence Kivett, expecting him to repeat Colonel Swope's famous mutterings, "Too far out, too far out."

But Clarence Kivett is an optimist. He believes the city will grow to reach the airport, just as it did Swope Park. "Besides," Kivett explains, "we included the tall grass prairie concept in our landscape design, and the drive out there is a nice break from the clutter of the city."

Aside from its debatable location, the airport itself is a superior modern design. Kivett describes the unique "drive to your gate" concept as "about as close to the ideal of driving right onto the plane as we can get at this time." The interior has clean lines and is on a human scale. In keeping with the best traditions of architecture as an art form, KCI is really a sculpture that people walk through.

And now for the bad news. Every city has its black sheep, and Kansas City's is a black sheep of design. Alex Barkett, self-made man, entrepreneur, and banker, is making a reputation for himself as the patron of questionable taste. His many business ventures are housed throughout downtown, and in each building, Mr. Barkett seldom seeks an architect's advice, preferring to make most design decisions himself. This is unfortunate, since he is the "architect" of a great fortune. One striking example of his work is the garish gold Twelve Grand Building.

But "Baa Baa" Barkett's *pièce de résistance* is the rejuvenated old Southwestern Bell Telephone Building. This stately Neo-Gothic structure at Eleventh and Oak was bought by Barkett for office use. Rather than clean the ornate stonework which ran up the length of the building, he chose to strip off the sculptured ornamentation which gave the building its character. In its place, he put white paint with electric blue racing stripe high-

lights. Midway through the project, Barkett changed his mind.
He then replaced the electric blue with fake gold tin grillwork.
Perched on top of the building is a monstrous communications
system which is visible for miles around. This system is used by
the building's top floor tenant, American Telephone and Tele-
graph. Apparently this system cannot be screened or removed to
a site away from the downtown skyline, so Barkett convinced the
phone company to give it a fresh coat of white paint in the
remodeling process.

On the positive side, these peculiarities of design judgment
have become a source of unification for the many who appreciate more aesthetic surroundings. If, as noted architect Richard
Saul Wurman recommends, we are to view the city as one giant
"learning resource," then these artistic choices have taught Kansas City a great lesson.

Kansas City in the seventies has undergone a tremendous
building boom, not only of new buildings but also of remodeling
and restoration. Some of the city's oldest buildings—some landmarks, some eyesores—have been removed, making way for
major developments with a new style and élan. It will be fun to
watch the blending of such varied architectural periods and see
the new landmarks distinguish themselves. Hopefully, this building boom will produce more and more building owners who will
come to realize that quality architecture is important to Kansas
City as an important and functional attraction for quality people.

As her own personal contribution to historic preservation, Tracy
Thomas headquarters her advertising and consulting firm,
NEXUS Corporation, at 1908 Main Street. Her office was formerly that of Boss Tom Pendergast, and the back room used to
serve in the twenties and thirties as the meeting room of his Jackson Democratic Club. In those days, the office was open from
6:00 A.M. to noon. In the afternoons, Tom dispatched his precinct captains to the "field" to solve the day's problems while he
called the race tracks throughout the country, and placed his
bets. (The great state of Missouri, famous for breeding race
horses, has no track.)

Daily a stream of citizens—rich, poor, ward bosses, jobless fathers and mothers, and perhaps half of what is today Kansas
City's business leadership, waited in the back room for a five-

minute visit with Boss Pendergast. They asked for jobs or favors or food. In return, Tom asked that his friends register to vote and remember who had helped them. In that office, Harry Truman was dissuaded from running for Jackson County collector (the job was already promised) and encouraged to run for the poorer-paying job of U.S. senator.

1908 Main still holds mementoes, including the interoffice buzzer from aide Bernie Gnefkow's office to Tom's. Recently, a sign fell from its position covering a ceiling vent. The aging message of those wonderful full employment years read, "All job applicants must check with the precinct captain in the ward in which they live."

6. THIS IS THE HUB, BUB

As the real gateway to the west, Kansas City has long been known as the embarkation point for a number of trails, including the Santa Fe, the California, and the Oregon. Today there are enough Santa Fe Trail markers in Kansas City to rival the claims in the Holy Land to authentic relics of the true cross. By plotting all the Santa Fe Trail markers on a map, one discovers the possible evolution of a famous wagon trail concept of protection, that of drawing the wagons into a circle. Contrary to the notion that the migration westward was an orderly single-file march, the trail tends to wander around Kansas City a bit before angling southwestward.

Today in Kansas City, the decision-making processes of the city's movers and shapers tend to emulate the Santa Fe pattern. Several people, all going in the same general civic direction, will plot their own courses and amble along individually. Eventually they may run into one another, and only then determine that the journey will be easier if attempted co-operatively.

Kansas City still attracts the individualist; it is a city free enough in its thinking to allow a person to seek a solution or a fortune or a life-style. And if those individualists occasionally collaborate, then all to the benefit of Kansas City.

Such was the case with the planning of the city's street system. City lovers who take the time to wander about Kansas City (perhaps looking for those Santa Fe Trail markers), are treated to a beautiful journey.

As early as 1856, Kersey Coates, a Pennsylvania Quaker, envisioned a boulevard system connecting the parks of Kansas City. After twenty-five years of dreaming, he teamed up with William Rockhill Nelson. In 1881, as editor of the year-old Kansas City *Star*, Nelson trumpeted the need for parks as a source of recreation. The third individual who catalyzed the parks and boulevard plan was August R. Meyer. In addition to the emphasis on transportation and recreation needs, Meyer stressed the business attitude of development and "urban" renewal. Meyer dreamed of developing the city's northern bluffs, clearing out the shanties on Vinegar Hill (Penn Valley Park), and constructing a grand boulevard to rival Mexico City's Paseo.

These three dreamers collaborated in passing a special tax assessment to pay for the parks and boulevards, which were designed according to the plans of landscape architect George E. Kessler. Today it is possible to travel over 140 miles of boulevards maintained by the Parks and Recreation Department of Kansas City, Missouri. These boulevards are linear parks in their own right and are often graced with sculptures contributed by the students of the Kansas City Art Institute.

One sad note is the fate of scenic Kersey Coates Drive, which ran along the west bluffs in West Terrace Park overlooking the Kaw River. This drive, named for the first person in Kansas City to campaign for a boulevard transportation system, was eliminated to make room for a freeway.

The parks system in Kansas City, which was also part of the Meyer/Kessler plan of 1893, got off to a slow start. Land developers so opposed parks that the first three park property donations were rejected by the city. So much for the civic altruism of planning and zoning committees. The first park accepted by the city, Dripps Park at Sixteenth and Belleview, totaled only .16 acre of land. It is smaller than many traffic islands.

However, from that little acorn of land, the idea grew quickly. In 1896, Colonel Thomas H. Swope, formerly an opponent of "all that park foolishness," gave the city a park with 1,331 acres. Swope was a rather crazy old bachelor who refused to sit on the dais during the Swope Jubilee dedication, preferring to wander amid the public, listening to their comments.

After all, Colonel Swope hadn't really intended to give the city

THIS IS THE HUB, BUB

a park; his original goal was to help the poor. He thought of building a public library, but a day spent on the steps outside the existing library convinced him that library patrons were quite well dressed, needing little help.

Swope, described as a "wealthy, dyspeptic recluse," had originally opposed the park system because it threatened to increase real estate taxes. Swope had made his fortune in real estate. In the 1850's, when Swope bought the land between the present Ninth and Twelfth streets, a neighboring newspaper editor commented, "The fools are not all dead. One has just paid $250 an acre for a cornfield near Kansas City."

Colonel Swope, feeling a bit guilty about his fortune, which he claimed he made without ever having done a day's work, was finally moved by the writing of William Rockhill Nelson. The *Star* decried the "pinching enonomy, the picayunish policy, the miserable parsimony which characterize our city government." The result of Nelson's tirade on Swope's conscience was the second largest park within any American city, now over 1,750 acres. In these days of public apathy, when the news tends to numb people, it is almost inconceivable that anyone was so affected by reading the *Star* that he was inspired to change his opinion.

While there are great parks all over Kansas City, several have a historic heritage. Loose Park was the site of the Civil War's Battle of Westport, known as the Gettysburg of the West. The Union soldiers, led by General Curtis, charged south across Brush Creek (then unpaved) and up the ravine which today is Sunset Drive. Near what is now Loose Park, Curtis's men confronted General Sterling Price's Confederates. Price was assisted by the infamous guerrillas, Quantrill's Raiders, whose members included Frank and Jesse James.

The Confederates had just skirted Jefferson City in favor of taking Kansas City. The pursuing Union soldiers from Jeff City finally caught up to Price's rear guard just west of the Big Blue River (north of Swope Park), forcing Price to fight unsuccessfully in two places at once. It was perhaps a foreshadowing of political things to come. Much of the strength of the Union Army was actually from Kansas, and it required the co-operation of Jefferson City to "save the day" for Kansas City.

The Battle of Westport was bloody, and many of the wounded

were removed to the John Wornall home, at what is now Sixty-first Terrace and Wornall Road. It has been restored and is open for guided tours. Several of the old homes near Loose Park have been known to contain cannon balls. Today, families stroll calmly around the lake or through the Rose Garden there, and occasionally a loving couple, seeking a few moments of privacy, will urge their children to charge over the next hill in search of Civil War relics. The Loose Park Rose Garden, by the way, is such a popular public wedding site that it is booked up three months in advance during the summer months.

With all the parks available for naming in Kansas City, a case can be made to show that justice has been twice blind. Nothing in Kansas City is yet named for Louis Hammerslough, a merchant who served on the Park Board with August Meyer, William Glass, Simeon Armour, and Adriance Van Brunt. The authors recall the state of extreme depression described in *Pilgrim's Progress*, the Slough of Despond, which was a deep bog into which Christian fell on the way from the City of Destruction. In Bunyan's allegory, Help saved him; the authors wish the same for Louis Hammerslough.

Second on the list of *causes célèbres* is Delbert J. Haff. Few in Kansas City realize that he was the aristocratic bearded lawyer who wrote the crucial amendments to the city charter providing for the tax assessments which paid for park acquisitions. Haff's amendments were challenged in the Missouri Supreme Court by the park opposition forces, tagged by William Rockhill Nelson as the "Hammer and Padlock Club. With hammers they attacked civic improvements; with padlocks they kept their money to themselves." For a time, Colonel Swope was a friend of theirs.

It was Delbert J. Haff who wrote the law which withstood their haranguing. True, at present there is a Delbert J. Haff fountain at the entrance to Swope Park. But it would seem only fitting to honor him, at least for a few years, by also naming a *park* after him. Certainly a park named Haff, or half a park, is better than none.

Finally, any wandering around Kansas City will reveal the beauty of its many fountains. To keep up the good work, the goal of the newly formed City of Fountains Foundation is to build one fountain per year.

Fountains, like music, may be classified according to purpose. First, there are the roadside drive-by kind, like the downtown Muse of the Missouri and the Sea Horse Fountain in Meyer Circle on Ward Parkway. This one is sometimes lit with colored lights, all the better to allure the viewer's eyes as he or she drives slowly by. Many Johnson County commuters advocate moving this fountain elsewhere, so fountain admirers can be allured on their own time, leaving Ward Parkway as a straightaway to the suburbs.

Next, there are people fountains, in peripatetic settings, where one almost participates in all that cavorting of water and statuary. William Volker Fountain in the Theis Memorial Mall, south of the Nelson Gallery, and the J. C. Nichols Fountain on the Country Club Plaza are two favorites.

Finally, just as Hollywood has its superstars, the City of Fountains has its superfountains. The Crown Center Hotel has a running waterfall five stories high, right inside the main lobby. Another, the Alameda Plaza hotel's waterfall, is on the corner of Wornall and Ward Parkway. The water rushes downward from the pool area above it. On a hot summer day, the viewer sometimes gets the impression that a sunbather is about to tumble over the falls, chaise lounge and all, into the outstretched arms of the ever-waiting statuary.

But the most unbelievable fountain is the water spectacular in the Royals' stadium at the Truman Sports Complex. Royals-owner Ewing Kauffman built it, for a mere $750,000, to accompany his $2 million twelve-story scoreboard. The computer-programmed fountain can flow through eight shows of lights and water without repetition. And in a 1984-version of audience participation, one water jet is programmed to spurt upward in relation to the level of the crowd's cheers.

Someone once claimed that Kansas City was "behind the times" because people spent countless years figuring out where they were. In other cities, that telltale bulge in someone's pocket might mean a flask of whiskey. In Kansas City, it's as likely to be a map or a regional guide to municipalities and districts.

Certainly there is strength in diversity. Kansas City's economy is the perfect example, never so heavily pegged to one industry that a failure or weakness destroyed everything else. Kansas City has made diversity an art form . . . here regionalism is the newest industry. "Getting it together" is a full-time job for hundreds of people.

Almost everything overlaps here, but not exactly. One may live in Kansas City, Missouri, and have children in the school district of North Kansas City, Missouri. Or one might live in Independence and have children in the Kansas City, Missouri, School District.

North Kansas City is a separate city, but Kansas City North and Kansas City South are "areas," larger than most neighborhoods, which are part of Kansas City, Missouri. And Kansas City North is *north* of North Kansas City. The post office for the city of Shawnee is Shawnee Mission, Kansas. The post office for the city of Mission is Shawnee Mission, Kansas. Yet, there is no city named Shawnee Mission, though many people will tell you they live there.

Relatively few people live and work in the same city. Wyandotte County, Kansas, estimates a three-way split: one-third live and work there, one-third live there but work elsewhere, and one-third live elsewhere but work there.

The national political problem of a low awareness of voting districts and representatives is acute in Kansas City. Those people who do find their way to the polls are frequently amazed to learn which public school, junior college, city council, and state legislative districts they live in. One woman emerged from a voting booth during a recent election, grinned widely, and exclaimed, "I didn't even know I'd get to vote against that creep!"

So when people speak of Kansas City as a surprise city, it is just as true for the residents as for the visitors. And when someone wants to know "where you're coming from," it is often meant literally.

From a business and cultural standpoint, the central identity of Kansas City is in Jackson County, the original part of Kansas City, Missouri. The newer parts of Kansas City, Missouri, are in Clay and Platte counties, north of the Missouri River. They were annexed in the 1950's during the hungry reign of Mayor H. Roe Bartle.

When people speak of Greater Kansas City, it's important to determine just how much Greater they mean. The five-county designation would include Jackson, Clay, and Platte in Missouri, Wyandotte and Johnson counties in Kansas. The Standard Metropolitan Statistician Area (SMSA) adds Cass and Ray counties in Missouri. And the Mid-America Regional Council (MARC) identifies an eight-county area, counting Leavenworth County, Kansas. This eight-county MARC region numbers 109 municipalities.

There are lots of complex metropolitan setups in the United States, but there is no question that the one and one-third million residents of metropolitan Kansas City are faced with one of the most perplexing of all. Down-to-earth attempts to do such things as provide a uniform kind of emergency medical service, top flight police protection (through the Metro Squad), good solid mass transportation (through the Area Transportation Authority)—all of these face massive problems. Funding is like asking 109 mommies and daddies for an allowance.

Some of the problems have been solved, some not. MARC is struggling at this writing to effect sometime in the reasonable future the 911 emergency telephone service for the metro area—a system that has been accomplished in many a less governmentally tangled community.

And the good news is that governmental leaders for the most part are convinced that new standards of intergovernmental cooperation are a must, and that MARC is here to stay.

School districts in Missouri have a history all their own. Districts have grown in their own ways for their own reasons, while the municipalities around them have changed and expanded for other reasons.

Thus, the Independence School Board does not supervise all of the schools in Independence. Some fall into the Kansas City, Missouri, School District. And the Kansas City School Board doesn't control all the schools in its area. In fact, there are thirteen distinct school districts within the city limits of Kansas City, Missouri. There is the North Kansas City district to the north, while in the far south side of the city, some schools are under the jurisdiction of the Center School District. Worse yet, Center is not in the center of the city at all; Center, from the standpoint of city geography, is well off-center.

People who find the modern tendency toward standardization

boring will never find city and county government in this area boring. For example, in some of the eight counties, the familiar governmental leaders are commissioners . . . a group of elected officials who constitute a sort of combination legislative and executive branch. Johnson and Wyandotte counties in Kansas have this setup.

But in Missouri, some counties have what is called a County Court. And the people who would be called commissioners elsewhere are called Judges of the County Court. Often it is a three-way split—two judges being elected geographically, for example, Western Judge and Eastern Judge, with a third or Presiding Judge being elected by the entire county. The county court system often must get approval from the state legislature in order to take necessary steps in local government.

In Jackson County, the voters made the decision to switch in 1973 from just such a county court system to a county charter government, giving the local government more autonomy. Now Jackson County, Missouri, is unlike all the other counties in the area. There is an elected county executive with wide powers who works with a county legislature of fifteen members, which makes laws and sets policy.

So much for counties. As for all those cities, one can find just about every variety of city or town council, and mayors who range in responsibility from ceremonial figureheads to mayors with plenty of power.

Depending upon the vantage point, then, Kansas City is either a mishmash of overlapping authorities or the quintessence of diversity. There is good reason to focus on the second interpretation, for Kansas City is home to about one hundred national associations, as well as many regional ones.

The national associations range from the Veterans of Foreign Wars to the National Egg Council. The international headquarters of People to People is here, as is the American Goat Society. The American Hot Rod Association supervises drag racing from Kansas City, while the American Dehydrators Association oversees the dehydrating of alfalfa for livestock and poultry feed. And right here in River City we have the International Brotherhood of Boilermakers, Iron Shipbuilders, Blacksmiths,

Forgers and Helpers. That's not bad for being over seven hundred miles from the nearest ocean.

With over a thousand churches and synagogues in Kansas City, it's natural that several religious organizations are headquartered here. These include the Church of the Nazarene, Unity School of Christianity, Defenders of the Christian Faith, and the Ratisbonne Center, which promotes understanding between Christians and Jews.

Independence, Missouri, is world headquarters for the Reorganized Church of Jesus Christ of Latter Day Saints, or RLDS. They are the descendants and followers of Joseph Smith, Jr., son of the founder of the Mormon Church. Before he was shot to death, Joseph Smith had declared Independence, Missouri, as the true home of the church, and ordained his son to carry on his work there. Others chose to follow another Mormon, Brigham Young, to Salt Lake City, Utah. The Brigham Young followers do not use the title "Reorganized," instead calling their denomination the Church of Jesus Christ of Latter Day Saints.

In addition to these national headquarters, Kansas City is a regional capital, often serving the four-state area of Missouri, Kansas, Iowa, and Nebraska. Kansas City is one of ten cities in the United States designated as a headquarters for a standard federal region. The federal government maintains many offices here, scattered in at least ten buildings throughout the city. Just one of those, the Federal Building at 601 East Twelfth Street, employs over five thousand people.

Other regional groups include the Mid-America Arts Alliance, the Big Eight Conference (collegiate athletics), and the Heart of America Council of the Boy Scouts of America.

In business, Kansas City is often known as a branch office city. While more than half of the Fortune 500 firms maintain regional offices or distribution centers here, only a handful of those are national headquarters. Kansas City plays second fiddle to many important industries, including automobiles, wheat flour, and garment production. This regional office phenomenon has a few drawbacks but offers a remarkable measure of diversity and back seat strength.

True enough, Kansas City is a stopping-off point for many people who are en route to somewhere else. Topographically,

Kansas City is a plateau, not a pinnacle. And that is pleasant enough for most people who value the measured sense of being able to survey the nearby terrain with few surprises. Historically, Kansas City has always been a stopping-off point—a place for people to take stock of their lives and settle down or embark on an unknown journey—perhaps over the Santa Fe Trail.

Sociologically, there is still a strong sense of nativity in Kansas City. It permeates the power structure and the social structure. Kansas City is not like Washington, D.C., or New York or Los Angeles, where almost everyone is a newcomer, so no one bothers to determine origins.

Kansas City is a chauvinistic city in which 99 per cent of all new acquaintance encounters include the studied inquiry, "Are you *from* here?" Strange accents are immediately suspect. Anything north of the Missouri/Iowa border draws raised eyebrows, and a Boston or Brooklyn accent will lead to a slowly straightened spine and a queerly intent stare at the speaker's moving lips, lest anything weird escape the listener's ears. When Chief Joseph McNamara replaced Clarence Kelley as Chief of Police, the social flutter centered on the idea that "I'm sure he'll do fine at police work if he can just lose that New Yawk accent."

7. PICKING THE BONES OF
THE BODY POLITIC

Jerry O. Jette, a lifelong Kansas City Irish politician, describes the treacherous and complex business of politics thus: "Political science is to politics what botany is to neurosurgery." Knowing limited amounts about all four subjects, the authors decided that a vivid description of Kansas City politics is best painted by a local working politician, and Jerry Jette agreed to assist. A Democratic party dragon, Jette is a veteran of a fistful of successful campaigns who also served for four years as administrative assistant to the Mayor of Kansas City. He is currently a free-lance marketing consultant. The authors met with Jette in the back booth of a typically smoke-filled restaurant to learn more about the subject he savors.

As one attempts the dissection of the body politic, an instinctual wariness sets in. All sizes of red flags go afluttering, and there are visions of the yawning jaws of personal political exile springing open to devour one who would make a careless observation about an individual or organization. Risking the inevitable chastisement of friends and fools, Jette plunged ahead with what he believed to be an accurate if foolhardy account of metropolitics right here in River City.

While the body politic of greater Kansas City covers a two-state, five-county, ten-major-city area, Jette chose to focus the chapter except where otherwise noted on city politics meaning Kansas City, Missouri, and county politics, meaning Jackson County, Missouri. As the largest and most locally discussed of all political entities involved, these deserve the most attention.

About ten years ago, Democratic politicians began to take a long, covetous look at some political real estate that had been denied them for the previous twenty-five years, City Hall. Now city elections under the charter are nonpartisan, yet this locale is so actively political that party labels are virtually inescapable. The Citizens Association, originally a reform group, swept in during the 1940's on the heels of Tom Pendergast and a scandalous gangster-ridden succession of administrations. Over the years, the Citizens Association allied itself closely with the establishment. The Kansas City *Star*, offered such respectable candidates, supported them down the line and elected them to the mayor's office and the City Council again and again.

As is inevitable with all reform groups, the Citizens Association began to sour. During this Citizens Association reign of City Hall politics, Democratic politicians had been restricted to Jackson County matters. Few non-Citizens Association politicians and/or elected officials today did not cut their teeth on county politics before attempting to enter city politics with any hope of success. In the late 1960's, the public became restless for change. The first inkling of their restlessness was the response to a major capital improvement bond issue offered in 1969 by the Ilus Davis administration. The bonds were totally defeated. The public seemed to be saying, "We want a change."

Change came dramatically when two years later a popular Western Judge (commissioner), named Charles Wheeler, of the Jackson County Court, defeated a favorite Citizens Association son for mayor. Wheeler was the first mayor in thirty years who had not been endorsed by the Citizens Association and the Kansas City *Star*. At last, county politicians saw an opportunity to once more take a shot at entering City Hall through the voting booth.

Modest councilmanic gains were made in the 1971 city elections as well. Later gains were made in the 1975 city races, with the addition of at least three non-Citizens Association councilmanic seats and the re-election of the Democratic, county-apprenticed mayor.

As evidenced by the plurality given the incumbent Mayor Wheeler, the public respected and liked a return to more colorful politics. Color was not a substitute for corruption but meant simply color. When former county politicians turned to city posts, many of the rural-oriented areas welcomed them and gave them necessary pluralities since they knew them from the county and had close ties with friends and associates. Conversely, the Citizens Association seemed to have painted itself into a small area of the city and lost its former widespread base of support. The Kansas City *Star* picked up on this shifting in the 1975 city elections. For the first time, it endorsed persons who had never enjoyed *Star* support in the past.

As in every major city's political community, there exists without exception certain groups who are best described as "claim agents"—political brokers who allude to nonexistent precinct captains and loyal voting constituents. One club in particular resembles a geriatric convention whose members continually mutter things like "If Mayor Brown was still around, things would be a lot better" (Darius Brown—turn-of-the-century Kansas City mayor). A safe assumption is that pre-Pendergast loyalists have limited viability.

A discernible dash of the old West resurfaces as Kansas Citians play politics. Traditionally a rough-and-tumble brand is intensely played, and as recently as the last city elections in Kansas City, Missouri, a punched nose or two were in evidence on election day. Overall, candidates of the GOP can be counted on to refer to their Democratic opponents as faction-influenced gangsters. In turn, they are lashed as being stuffed shirt hypocrites and/or pawns of the Kansas City *Star*. Over the years, Kansas City voters have become so accustomed to mudslinging that they are indifferent to political charges and countercharges. Rhetoric is viewed as the coming of spring.

One story that made the rounds for years involved a once active political figure, long deceased, who earned his livelihood as a funeral director. Without going into gory details, it will suffice to say many a person went to their reward unclothed, which should account for that politician's club being one of the better dressed groups of their day.

Many old line politicians of the Democratic stripe have a propensity to live in areas other than what is required by residency laws. This causes the courts, the Board of Election Commissioners, and the newspaper great concern, although the particular area's constituency seems largely indifferent. In the 1975 elections, one city council candidate was accused of having lived in Johnson County, Kansas, shortly before filing for office in Kansas City, Missouri. This prompted his opponent to privately describe the alleged wrongdoer as "the man who knows Kansas, Kansans know"—a widely publicized slogan used in a previous Kansas governor's race. Then there was the one about a certain Democratic state senator who preferred to live in a more affluent home than those available within his district. Yet, he was so oblivious to the residency requirements that even though he owned a motel located within his district he didn't bother to check in.

The pendulum of political style runs the gamut from old party machine to reform groups and back. The once dour Citizens Association which has dominated city politics for thirty-odd years appears to be losing its voter appeal to a more independent, lighthearted political force. A great deal of grave spinning has undoubtedly been going on as the deceased political reform patriarchs view this shift in Kansas City politics, whether from overhead or from wherever.

The Kansas City *Star,* guardian of the City Charter and keeper of the biggest political shillelagh in town, continues to be the single most potent opinion shaper around when it comes to the body politic. From time to time even a flash of humor comes through its editorial page. As political campaigns ebb and flow and different personalities vie for office, the *Star* manfully bears the brunt of charges of favoritism and editorializing. But in all fairness such charges roll exclusively off the tongues of those failing to be endorsed by the newspaper with monotonous regularity. The Kansas City *Star,* at times arrogant, at times moralistic, has nevertheless over the years always been counted upon by the more sophisticated Kansas Citians as the single most positive factor in the healthy development of a great city.

Kansas Citians take their politics seriously and campaign for their favorites with ingenuity and vigor. In the 1971 mayoral race between Charles Wheeler and Dutton Brookfield, the Democratic Good Government Association, a Northeast political club, backed Charles Wheeler. The DGGA reprinted a clipping from the Kansas City *Star* which was an endorsement of Brookfield by the former mayor, Ilus Davis, and passed it door to door in the three Northeastern wards. Knowing that area's dislike for the *Star* and the Citizens Association, the DGGA added a bold red stamp across the face of the endorsement, bearing the message, "If you like the Kansas City *Star* and Ike Davis, you'll love Brookfield!" The Brookfield forces countered this approach by reproducing the DGGA's sample ballot on election day, but substituted Brookfield's picture and name for Wheeler's. Brookfield workers passed this doctored ballot at the polling places hoping to trade in on the DGGA's political clout with area residents.

Various novel political strategies have been in evidence in other neighborhoods. A state representative race in the southern and eastern parts of the city took a low road approach when one candidate printed flyers with a false picture of his opponent, portraying him to be black.

Black politics in Kansas City can also be a lesson in roughness. The 1975 City Council races pitted two black women against one another. Zealous supporters of one candidate distributed flyers headlined "the great *white* hope," charging her opponent with tokenism and an Uncle Tom background. The "great white hope" candidate lashed back before election day charging that her female opponent was not a member of the black race!

Kansas City's political complexion changes from area to area. It is interesting to note the differences in voting patterns and profiles. The Country Club district extends south from the Plaza to near Eighty-fifth Street, west to State Line, east to Holmes Street. Within this zone is the city's affluent residential population. Traditionally Republican with strong strains of Independent voting tendencies, the Country Club area is the bastion of the Citizens Association; concurrently, it has the heaviest voting percentage in the entire city. Appropriately, the Country Club area is described as the silk stocking district. Regardless of one's particular base of political support, being out of voter favor in this particular area is the kiss of death. School bond issues as well as general obligation capital improvement issues do well here, a testimonial to the civic commitment of the residents of the Country Club area. Voter density reflects itself strongly when one considers the Country Club area occupies only 20 per cent of the number of city wards yet produces as much as 33 per cent of the total vote.

Contrary to reported national trends, lawyers in the metro-politic area do not predominate the field from an elective nor at the political-decision-making level. Rather, the leadership is a composite of business and professional people which creates a healthy representative mix. While new people filter through the political community from time to time, a cardinal rule is to have earned one's leadership spurs through the heat of many an in-tensely waged campaign. Hard work is a prerequisite in this ball park, and exhaustive effort at the top level is taken for granted. To identify some of the faces at the top level, one must learn to separate the men from the boys. And, just as importantly, one must separate the men from the women; since the beginning of time women have done most of the day-to-day political work that ever got done right. Mrs. Dutch Newman is a testimonial to that fact. Dutch's club, the Westport Landing Democratic Club, is an active, working, vote-producing group which does yeoman work in the city's midtown wards. Dutch's personal following and pop-ularity play a major role in the organization's effectiveness on any election day.

Younger faces promise to play an ever-increasing role in future political strategy. Newly elected city councilperson Joe Serviss brings to the political mainstream strong personal relationships with the state and county legislatures. Serviss, who chairs the powerful Finance and Audit Committee, symbolizes the new smart elected official of the future and is the comer from western Missouri for whatever the future holds.

With an average of a dozen years of solid political grooming and experience, the new pols are introducing a more sophis-ticated style than did their sometimes rowdy fathers and grand-fathers. A classic example of new politics is James Nutter, suc-cessful businessman and political heavyweight. A long-time outspoken advocate of "open door" politics, Nutter is qualitative in his approach to screening and candidate selection. He demands that those who receive his support have a firm grasp of important issues. An officer of the Committee for County Prog-ress, Nutter exerts his influence in the heavy-voting Country Club wards; he is regarded by many political observers as a major force on the scene.

One new leader who was groomed by Jim Nutter is Mike

White. As Jackson County Executive, White must be considered at the top of local political leadership. The youthful former county legislator whose baptismal election was won by a one-vote plurality is widely respected. White's style matured in a landslide county executive race, a smooth launch for his political future.

Mayor Charles Wheeler is one extraordinary person and vote getter from the Country Club district. Having regularly violated practically every rule of politics ever written down, he continues like old man river getting elected and re-elected over and over. Wheeler is impatient at times with endless political jockeying and prefers dealing directly with the people. He generally avoids getting too personally involved in party decisions. The mayor's political future is not known by anyone at this time, but a political analysis without Charles Wheeler is unthinkable. Highly gregarious and equally a tireless campaigner, Wheeler has captured the present voters' devotion yet uniquely appears just short of indifferent to the political community around him. An in joke told to the writer by someone who should know claims privately Wheeler is called Mr. McGoo, after the cartoon character whose unconscious luck saves him time after time from certain disaster. Ability and luck have lavished their sought-after favors on Charles Wheeler.

Even though metropolitics is tipped heavily in favor of the Democrats, GOP's Richard Berkley, mayor pro tem, is widely respected and liked by both sides of the aisle. The former Republican state chairman brings a freshness and human professionalism to the political arena, and can be counted upon to play a key role in his party's progress with the people being the winner.

The so-called "inner city" occupies roughly eight wards bounded by the river on the north, extending in an egg shape in the city's center to the south. The inner city filters south to Eightieth Street with Troost its western boundary and Jackson Street its eastern edge. Black residents almost exclusively occupy this area. Low registration and residency requirements plague the black political leadership in this political entity. The latest census indicates an approximate black city population of 23 per cent, yet voting figures reflect a loose average of under 15 per cent voting in a given election.

The dominant black political organization, Freedom, Inc., presses continually for greater voter registration and organization within the inner city wards and plays a key role as a decisive balance in many elections. The former president of Freedom, Inc., Bruce Watkins, displays a sign on his office desk, "Don't talk politics in this office if you're not REGISTERED TO VOTE."

With few exceptions Freedom, Inc., is the political voice of the black community; judged in light of its successes, it serves its people satisfactorily. It is to the credit of the people in all areas of Kansas City that black representation is evident at municipal, county, and state governmental levels. The caliber of black officials, both elected and appointed, has been outstanding over the years and continues to provide valuable input and insight into the complexities of urban life on the political scene.

Black is beautiful to some, but a frequent complaint by a few white political cronies is that Freedom, Inc., has changed that phrase to "Green is beautiful." Charges of Freedom being for sale arose during the years the organization really became a major force in Kansas City politics. As with all things, somewhere between jealousy and imprudence lies the real story.

Certain black religious and civic leaders have opposed Freedom from time to time; by and large they have been unsuccessful. Aggressiveness is part of this ball game, and Freedom's leadership has mastered the most basic tenet of politics, survival. On the other hand, the notion that the black community has one large deliverable vote is not documented. The black community no more votes in concert on given issues than does the white community. To suggest that it does is insulting as well as factually in error.

An example of successful representation by factors outside of Freedom was the election of Joanne Collins to the City Council. Ms. Collins is a bright woman who defeated Freedom's candidate, Mamie Hughes, the dynamic county legislator, in a hotly contested at-large race. The leadership from the black community also includes Harold (Doc) Holliday, Jr., another county legislator who is a master of the legislative process. As president of Freedom, Inc., he will continue in a dominant position aided by a low-key, high-level performer, Charles Hazley, who is chairman of the Plans and Zoning Committee of the City Council.

The west side has served as the city's stage for an ongoing David and Goliath political struggle, with the west side as David. One of the city's oldest sections is now the contemporary setting for the west side residents' struggle for solidarity and recognition. Naturally enough, with unity and organization has come the sought-after political recognition. It was not until the 1970's that the west side gained elected representation on the City Council, Jackson County Legislature, and State Legislature. The west side houses virtually all of the city's Mexican-American population, yet has an over-all population mix evenly divided ethnically a third white, a third black, and a third Mexican-American.

While individual temperaments run high at times, the community as a whole gets along quite well in dealing with racial differences. However, a political plague seemed to be present for years within the Mexican-American portion of the west side in the form of bitter personal in-fighting. The victor of such encounters appeared too hopelessly exhausted for further political battles outside the community. Rivalries ran deep and lengthy, spilling over into ecclesiastical and educational areas. It was said at one time that when west side political leaders ordered a firing squad they formed a circle!

Bilinguality and cultural differences prevented the surfacing of political leadership for many years when the west side was considered a factional adjunct to the heavily Italian-populated North End. These two neighborhoods constitute one city council district. The void of political leadership on the west side is mirrored in the physical scars of trafficways and high traffic arteries that slash through and isolate the community from downtown and neighboring Westport. The addition of new political personalities from the west side has proven to be an asset to the city as a whole. Robert Hernandez, an upset victor in a councilmanic race in 1975, clearly demonstrated what youthful, well-organized planning and shoe leather can accomplish. Hernandez is the first Mexican-American member of the City Council in the city's history and should be considered from now on as the spokesperson for the once voiceless west side.

"Little Italy" once described the colorful section of the city directly north of downtown. No other part of the city's seventy-five identifiable neighborhoods has been the subject of more controversy than the North End. One can practically see the pseudosinister gangster ghosts of the thirties prowling the quiet streets of the city's eleventh ward. It is a matter of public record that the North End has one of the lowest crime rates in the city. Architecturally, a European flavor dominates the scene, and behind many plain-appearing two-story flats exist small, attractive courtyards where area residents exchange recipes and gossip. A high percentage of elderly still live in the North End; they are visited regularly on weekends by children and grandchildren who have prospered and moved far to the south of their immigrant parents.

A stronger Democratic area could hardly be envisioned. It is rumored that the Italian Republican Committeeman has the loneliest job in North America. The North End in the past provided the heart of machine and patronage politics and has therefore produced more than a few capable, hard-working officials, much to the surprise and disapproval of the Kansas City *Star* and the Citizens Association. Johnny Lazia, onetime gangster leader and political enforcer for the infamous Pendergast machine, singlehandedly over the years created a type of "spaghetti curtain" with which concerned Italian Americans continually must deal. A type of siege mentality can be observed as one talks with residents and civic neighborhood influentials.

Party loyalty is still much in favor as every other summer (during election years) political rhetoric abounds in Little Italy. A good-natured poke at the Kansas City *Star* still can be counted upon to bring nods of approval from the North End's constituency. A story once went around that in the city election of 1936, a Republican received eleven votes out of 389 cast in one North End precinct. The machine's precinct captain was told he was losing his grip and asked to explain where the eleven votes came from!

"Out northeast," as it is described by Kansas Citians, can always be counted upon as one of the city's most politically active areas. Political highjinks are the order of the day as the city's twelfth, thirteenth, and fifteenth wards go about their business of electing officials. At one time these three wards produced for a major candidate of their choice over ten thousand votes! Northeast citizens are conservative and are fiercely proud of it. Although an uneasy truce exists today between them and their black political counterparts to the west, racial overtones can still be detected in subtle ways. The independent nature of the northeast section lends itself to loud criticism of the Kansas City *Star* and its favorite political sons. Some political influentials imply that a conspiracy between the *Star*, City Hall, and the Citizens Association works against them in terms of recreational and capital improvement projects for this area. Northeasterners are quite sensitive to this so-called "silk stocking" rule.

The late William Royster, state representative and political leader of the northeast during the sixties and early seventies, played a major role by the force of his magnetic personality in making the northeast a political force with which to deal. He was one of the last strong political bosses in the old sense of taking care of "his people" and being able to deliver a sizable vote. Royster, a former city councilman, excelled at political organizing and took a satanic delight in jabbing relentlessly at what he termed "those tuxedo bandits at the Kansas City *Star*." Royster recognized the importance of party discipline and hard precinct work before and on election day. To the dismay of the *Star*, the people of the northeast delighted in electing Royster again and again with huge majorities until his death from cancer in 1972.

An interesting sidelight about Royster was that although he chose to strongly identify with the conservative blue-collar worker, he was himself from the manor born, being the grandson of the wealthy pioneer William Scarritt. Ironically, the dominance of Royster's personality was precisely responsible for the now-existing political vacuum in northeast politics. To be sure, the area will never lose its intense political interest, but it remains to be seen if strong unified leadership will emerge. Younger, more conciliatory personalities seem to be developing, yet the controversial legacy of Bill Royster still prevails. While spirited intradistrict rivalries flourish, a type of last minute unity seems to surface along strict party lines on election days. Struggling to fill the leadership vacuum left by Bill Royster's death, several northeast leaders have been sparring and commanding respect, including Mary Gant, the first woman state senator in Missouri's history, and Virgil Troutwine, a county legislator with supersavvy political instincts.

The east side is far and away the most intentionally unorganized political section of the city. It appears to be the somewhat, sometime domain of Jackson County politicians and/or Independence, Missouri, city politicians rather than Kansas City, Missouri, city politicians. The city's east side has a rural flavor to it and a virtual indifference to what goes on at City Hall. The low residential density dotted with industrial parks and heavy industrial complexes projects a political prognosis of unpredictability. The vote is light on the city's eastern edge, which undoubtedly accounts for a lack of political interest at the ward and precinct level there. Aside from an occasional homeowners' association blast at a City Hall proposal, the east side lies politically isolated and indifferent by choice.

Eastern Kansas City politics takes what nod it ever takes from anyone or anything from Armco Steel Corporation. As one of the city's largest manufacturing concerns, politics is not beyond Armco's grasp. The personnel rolls of Armco reflect a deep interest in politics at all local levels. Arthur Asel, respected City Council member and assistant works manager at Armco, heads the list of its elected officials which also includes a county legislator, Democratic committee people, and a state legislator or two. The corporate giant, Armco, is certainly not unmindful of the body politic to date; its contribution at both the civic and political levels has been dimensional and impressive. Touching base with Armco should be on the agenda of any aspirant pol who wishes to be in the winning column on election night.

Leon Brownfield, City Council member and chairperson of the city's Legislative Committee, reigns supreme in the eastern parts of Kansas City. Rumor has it that Brownfield may have an eye for a statewide office in the foreseeable future. He enjoys a solid base of both civic and plain people support as a springboard for any unannounced adventures.

The city's southeast section is known for its Southern flavor. Stark conservatism served liberally with dashes of rural southern Missouri ideology is the bill of fare for this heavily populated section of the city. The southeast grew into existence at the close of World War II and has since chosen a course of small-townism in preference to big-cityism. Strictly middle class, on a clear day, one can almost hear the Platters or the Four Freshmen from the 1950's rocking and rolling through the Ruskin Heights Shopping Center. Like the east side, the southeast appears more interested in county and township politics than city politics. At times residents seem alarmed if overtures are made to involve this community in urban problem solving. The term "down in Kansas City" is not infrequently heard, suggesting a lack of involvement in city life. Although it is heavily populated, the southeast area's voter registration is not heavy and the voting turnout is comparatively light. The area's political leadership addresses itself most intensely to school bond issues and strictly provincial matters, although it turns out infrequently in respectable numbers for a popular state representative or two. Left-of-the-roaders are uncomfortable here, and candidates exhibiting liberal tendencies best find other pastures. Goldwater, Wallace, and Nixon did well here in past elections, which tended to establish a "circle the wagons" pattern.

Kansas City's far south side is one of the more affluent communities which seems to be progressing aggressively well in the political arena. The voter in this area is independent, affluent, and well educated. In spite of a transient population, voter registration is stable and voter turnout is heavy. One observer claims, "If a line could be drawn from State Line Road east to Grandview, Missouri, only four elected Democratic officials would live south of that line." The south side appears not to be anti-Democratic nor pro-Republican, necessarily. Rather, it is unquestionably independent. New political organizations from both the major parties can be seen working hard to court this voting segment. Both have their work cut out for them. Residential density is light in terms of yard size, which makes traditional door-to-door precinct work extremely difficult. Well done media campaigning has its effect in this area over traditional methods of canvass campaigning. Political clubs take on a social facet in the far south side. The traditional political gathering place, the smoke-filled room, has been replaced here with smoke-filled barbecue pits in well-manicured back yards. Harry Gallagher, former state representative and a political leader in this neighborhood, claims every election is a new ball game because party ties are fragile at best.

Kansas City, Missouri, is unique in being a city within a three-county jurisdiction. Two of the three counties, Clay and Platte, are north of the Missouri River. Politically, they comprise the huge twenty-first ward, with approximately 31,000 registered voters. Not long ago, Clay County, the larger of these two counties, was described as the most Democratic county in the entire state of Missouri. This description is changing, and while state Democratic politicians were secure there, city elections rarely reflect a major party dominance.

The Missouri River not only drives north-of-the-river citizens mad with traffic frustrations due to the lack of an additional bridge connecting them with the center of the city, but it actually serves as a psychological barrier between city south and city north residents. The result is unmasked resentment and at times open distrust of city politics and politicians. It is suspected by more than one person that city bond issues are joyfully voted down with consistency north of the river as tangible evidence of their frustration and hostility toward City Hall. Over twenty years ago, a large amount of land was annexed by Kansas City, Missouri, bringing these residents under city rule—and they have never gotten over it to this day. They feared they would be paying city taxes but not receiving their share of basic city services. Frankly, they weren't too far wrong in their fears. But in all fairness, with the opening of the new airport and recent major street improvements, the city government is making strong overtures to its city residents north of the river.

Fierce north-of-the-river political rivalries spring up with the advent of any election. While general party lines are warily observed, northlanders are always treated to a free-swinging, emotion-charged campaign regardless of who is running for what. Due to the heavy Democratic plurality in the area, state and county campaigns are primary fights with a pantomime general election. On the other hand, the bipartisan city elections keep northlanders interested and active through the general elections.

A real challenge faces those nonnatives seeking political support for themselves or their candidates in this section. Fighting among officers of individual clubs is a favorite intramural political pastime which leaves the hat-in-hand political hopeful confused and depressed. A combination of rural conservatism blended with a history of (self-described) disfranchisement makes the traditional urban issues treatment largely irrelevant. Northlanders often prefer discussions of strictly local provincial matters by office seekers appealing for their support. Candidates are well advised to make the complete political rounds when garnering support in northland because feelings are easily hurt and mistakes never forgotten. Political plain talk is the only acceptable language and a too generous sprinkling of baloney is viewed with hostility as city slickerism.

As a result of a weird state statute, the city of Gladstone, population 23,422, is required to hold city elections every year. Continual campaigning reigns in this northland community. Mike Mardikes, Assistant Dean for the Conservatory of Music at the University of Missouri at Kansas City, is one of the political "maestros" orchestrating the activity through the Gladstone Citizens Club. Getting the nod from the Gladstone Club gives a candidate a strong foothold in his or her quest for a warm Clay County welcome. Candidates so favored have received vote pluralities of 80 and 90 per cent! An obvious testimonial to the popularity and respect Mardikes and company command. Gladstone pols are a joy to work with, possessing those rare qualities of genteel deliverance and thoughtful leadership. Ed Bauman, Presiding Judge of the Clay County Court and former Mayor of Gladstone, is an excellent example of the type of leadership Gladstonians produce.

The affluent bedroom community of Johnson County, Kansas, southwest of Kansas City, has always played a key political role in metropolitics. Many opinion shapers and moneyed influentials live in Johnson County while earning their livelihood or directing their financial empires in Kansas City. This situation has not been overlooked by various Kansas City, Missouri, politicians who regularly charge that Johnson Countians are carpetbaggers and meddling do-gooders. Every campaign since Lewis and Clark dragged their canoe ashore at Possum Trot has included charges of Johnson County interference favoring certain candidates. Frankly, considering the amount of wealth and influence many Johnson Countians exert, it would be inconceivable to observers of the body politic that the jayhawkers would not take a keen interest in their Missouri neighbors' political jockeying.

Johnson County is rock-ribbed GOP land. Political wags claim that when Roosevelt swamped Alf Landon, Landon carried only the state of Maine and Johnson County, Kansas. Republican majorities dominate the political scene at all levels. It has been rumored that a Democrat in Johnson County has a type of lighthouse keeper's existence. From time to time, certain popular Missouri politicians have enlisted residents of Johnson County to slip over State Line Road to act as neighborhood volunteers in their campaigns. The reverse is also true, with Missouri volunteers posing as "neighbors from down the street" in a door-to-door canvass. The exceedingly high transience, with most families moving every six months to two years, has made this cross-pollination possible. Who knows a neighbor these days?

A philosophical tug of war is waged in Kansas City, Missouri, between those who would or would not penalize Johnson Countians for their affluent flight to suburbia. Those who charge that Johnson County robs the city of taxes and resources were successful in passing an earnings tax to partially cover the city's expenses in serving nonresidents. The opposition argues that Johnson Countians make an invaluable contribution to the city's growth by providing jobs and industrial expansion.

Kansas City, Kansas, is to Wyandotte County what Phoenix City is to Alabama. The third largest city in the state has a stormy recent past of political highjinks and corruption, with much attention paid to massage parlors and private clubs with late hours. When the political pundit crosses the Kaw River into Kansas City, Kansas, he enters a bewildering foreign country. When compared to Kansas City, Missouri, whose political players are identifiable most of the time, Kansas City, Kansas, politicians and clubs seem for the greater part to be invisible and impermanent. Yet, the municipal government is highly sensitive and responsive politically; the patronage rolls silently testify to this. It is incredible but true to this writer that these two sister cities' political personages and organizations are total strangers to one another. A week after the Wyandotte County elections in 1975, not one Kansas City, Missouri, political leader or activist could even name the three Wyandotte County commissioners.

This is partially the case because the city's major newspaper, the *Star*, publishes different editions for different cities or neighborhoods. Thus, news of supposedly local interest reaches only those living in that locality. Obviously, the *Star* has studied the reading interests of its public and has determined that the state line is indeed an interest barrier.

A blue-collar mixed ethnic population ghettoizes the constituency of Wyandotte County to a great extent and has resulted in the loose federation of meaningful political organizations. County and city politics are conducted most of the time in an incestuous fashion where selection rather than election is the name of the game. Provincialism is obvious as one watches Kansas City, Kansas, campaigns develop. The record shows a tendency for Democratic officials to be elected, although gains are being made by the Republicans in the county's more affluent western edge. Kansas City, Kansas', heavy minority population should lend itself to the future formation of influential political groups which will direct the thrust of city and county policies.

Finally, a word about parish politics. In an overview of metropolitics, Irish names abound; behind each one is a story in itself which the writer cannot tell in this short chapter. The family names would include the colorful controversial Joe Shannon, Truman's sidekick Tom Gavin, the Donnellys and the Hugheses, the McKeevers and the Gallaghers, the McDonnells and the Ryans, the Morans and the Gormlys. The list goes on and on, interlaced with events both political and civic which developed a small prairie town into an exciting city.

A flash of Irish humor surfaces from time to time as opponents are described as spending too much time with their friends meeting at the Cotton Mather Room of the Kansas City Club. Of course, no such room exists but an impish implication of this type can always be relied upon to brighten up a potentially drab campaign. When reaching for the city's sizable Catholic vote, it is not uncommon for a candidate to refer tongue in cheek to his own campaign photograph apologetically as his first communion picture.

The Irish seem to be drawn to the political scene like the proverbial bee to honey. Didn't someone once say about the Irish that "One Irishman is a faction, two Irishmen are a caucus, and three a third party"? Even today in analyzing a given campaign projection or result, Kansas City's Irish politicos will describe the seventh ward as St. Peter's parish. Speculation about the chances of one's favorites is described "If Sweeney loses St. Augustine's, breaks even in St. Thomas More, and closes strong in St. Elizabeth's, he's a winner." A serious breach of political etiquette is an alert candidate who fails to "work the masses" on the Sunday before a Tuesday election. One successful public official could always be counted upon to be listed in that Sunday bulletin with a mass being offered for a "special intention." As in the timeworn stories of Boston campaign techniques, the Kansas City Irish candidate would be remiss in not attending a rosary or two at McGilley's funeral parlor right before election day.

The Ancient Order of Hibernians, a social group whose parents were born in Ireland, is a political force in Kansas City which at times is mistakenly not courted by budding candidates. One popular young Irishman who ran for mayor by the name of Shaughnessy fell into disfavor when it was called to the Hibernians' attention by another Irishman of a different persuasion that it was a pity Shaughnessy chose orange for his campaign color. With names like Reardon, O'Brien, Kearney, Deming, and Flanigan serving as pastoral shepherds, is it any wonder that healthy political activity is encouraged in Kansas City parishes? State Representative Thomas Ryan, veteran legislator and campaigner extraordinaire, was once quoted in a speech before an admiring group of the "Irish Mafia." In a burst of political fervor, Ryan vowed, "I was a Democrat even before I was a Catholic!"

And that is a political dissection by Jerry O. Jette, an Irish politician who has been through the wars of Kansas City's political fortunes.

8. CITIZEN NUMBER ONE:
HARRY TRUMAN

Harry S. Truman of Independence was a surprise to the nation, but not to Kansas City. His courage, his scrappiness, his dedication to seeing a job through no matter what, and his ability to shrug off harsh criticism and do what he thought was right—all of these qualities a lot of people in Kansas City knew all about.

President Truman, as he first took office in 1945, was a shock to the American people. For more than twelve years, Americans had been accustomed to the smooth style and cultured oratory of Franklin D. Roosevelt. FDR had it all, style, pizazz, class. Suddenly he was gone, and in his place stood a man with a Missouri twang, not the trace of showmanship in his delivery, and an appearance that suggested at best a superintendent of schools. When people were flocking to Capitol Hill to hear Truman's first words to Congress, one House of Representatives guard tried to discourage them, saying, "You don't really want to hear him. He's only Coolidge with glasses."

The nation regarded Truman at first with a mixture of dismay and sympathy, wondering if he could do the job. Being an excellent senator and a capable no-favorites investigator didn't seem like much of a background for the Presidency, with the top leadership role in a global war. In time, people came to know Harry S. Truman as a fighter, a man with a salty delivery of down home Missouri phrases, and a stubborn leader. He followed the dictates of his conscience and his common sense, no matter how many people screamed at him, no matter for how long or how loud. His famous firing of General MacArthur proved that.

But there are plenty of books already in print, including Mr. Truman's own memoirs, to tell the story of his life in Washington and his years as the thirty-second President. This chapter deals more with Harry Truman as Citizen Number One of Independence and Kansas City.

Potomac Fever is a disease not easily cured in men and women who have tasted power and high office. The tendency is to not want to return to the old home town. Most who are retired or ejected from office jump at the chance to remain in Washington in some capacity, or to settle in New York, or perhaps to pick up a college presidency in the Ivy Leagues.

This was not so of Bess and Harry Truman, for Harry didn't really want to be President, and Mrs. Truman was delighted to shed the title of First Lady.

Harry Truman was always that practical kind of man who knew when he had had enough. The night he announced he would not run again for the Presidency (he had served almost two full terms but was entitled to a second elective term), HST laid it on the line in his characteristic plain language. "In my opinion, eight years as President is enough and sometimes too much for any man to serve in that capacity. There is a lure in power. It can get into a man's blood just as gambling and lust for money have been known to do."

It seemed like a private comment on his old friend and political supporter, Tom Pendergast, who fell victim to gambling on horses and vote fraud in his insatiable quest for political control. Truman had learned a lesson from his old Kansas City friend.

Kansas City has produced its fair share of famous people, but very few cities have been able to claim an ex-President in residence. And since Mr. Truman lived in Independence, Kansas City adopted a proprietary feeling toward him too. So he was often referred to, in the broad metro sense, as Kansas City's first citizen.

From 1953—after he rode down Pennsylvania Avenue in the tight-lipped politeness that masked very strained relations with President-elect Dwight Eisenhower—until the time of his death in 1972, Mr. Truman once more became a part of the Kansas City and Independence scenes.

From the pinnacle of world power to Independence, Missouri,

is quite a transition for anyone. But Harry and Bess Truman made it, and with visible relief. They seemed to relish all the little everyday things that they could once more take part in.

For a time, it appeared they would be frustrated in that desire. The combined press, radio, and TV of the world were reluctant to give up the colorful Missourian who had been good for so many headlines and who was the best source since General George Patton of unprintable quotes.

All the same, the simple homey touches of a regained ordinariness soon were evident. Randall Jessee, then a TV newsman, recalls the Truman's first morning back at 219 North Delaware. Jessee was with the large press detachment which set up shop on the sidewalk just outside the gate in the iron fence surrounding the house. The press was there to cover the first full day back home, as ordinary citizens, of a President and his wife (assuming that people can be ordinary citizens and have NBC, CBS, and ABC in the front yard).

The door opened and Mrs. Truman walked out onto the front porch, pointedly ignoring all the hubbub on the sidewalk. Poking around in some bushes at the edge of the porch, she leaned forward into one bush and came up with something. It was her folded copy of the Kansas City *Times*, (the morning Kansas City *Star*). The press heard Mrs. Truman mutter, "Seven years and that fool kid still hasn't learned how to throw the paper on the porch."

For weeks after that, Harry Truman was accompanied by a small army of press every time he went out for one of his early morning walks. Traffic would jam as the circle of men walking would come into view. In the center of all the commotion would be the jaunty HST, walking at a brisk clip and throwing oneliners over his shoulder—many of them unprintable and the rest often off the record.

Mr. Truman seldom used the phrase "off the record." He would simply talk to reporters directly in a fashion that was so offhand that one knew it was off the record.

Harry Truman was a no-fooling walker, and if a reporter couldn't keep up with him the hard luck was all his. Walt Bodine remembers one NBC cameraman, Johnny Dial, who was twenty years or more Truman's junior.

In those first few weeks after Truman's return, John would struggle along each morning, carrying his heavy equipment and battery back pack. John would go as long as he could, then he would keel over on somebody's lawn, gasping. Mr. Truman would take note of it with mock dismay, and after a comment on the softness of the American press, would walk on. Somewhere on the way back, the pack of reporters would pick up John, and the former President would give a stern lecture on John's bad habit of chain smoking.

In 1953, Harry Truman wanted nothing more than to settle down and be a private citizen. One of the things the President resumed doing for himself almost immediately was driving a car. Not that he drove all that well. He had rather bad luck colliding with things in his new Dodge sedan. It didn't seem to upset him too much, though it was usually traumatic for the other driver.

Until the Truman Library was completed, HST drove into Kansas City each morning to an office in the Federal Reserve Bank Building at Tenth and Grand. One of those mornings, Randall Jessee was waiting on Grand Avenue with a question on behalf of NBC news. Mr. Truman approached, carrying a small metal file box, and Randall reached out toward it saying, "Let me take that for you, Mr. President."

"Randall," Harry Truman replied, "before we left Washington, Bess and I resolved that when we got back home we were going to do everything possible for ourselves. That includes carrying this case."

In time everything changed. After a few weeks, the press contingent for the daily early morning walks began to thin out. There were some good reasons. One was that it was terribly early, and visiting press in a town are inclined toward late nights and revelry. For another, it became apparent that to see one "120 paces a minute press conference," as Truman called them, was to see them all. The most promising avenue of inquiry for newsmen was always fruitless, namely a request for comment on what the new President, Dwight Eisenhower, was doing.

"I know what it is to be in that job," Truman would always reply, "and I am not going to second-guess the President of the United States." He stuck by his rule for years, despite his pronounced personal dislike for Eisenhower. It was years later, when Joyce Hall got them together for an evening in Kansas City, that the two men finally shook hands and made up. Being the strong characters that they were, no one pushed the reconciliation much beyond that. The evening ended on a handshake and the friendship remained formal, a slight improvement over frosty.

At home again in her family home in Independence, Mrs. Truman emerged as the dominant force in Truman's life. According to Randall Jessee, Bess didn't take highly to drinking, so Mr. Truman was somewhat of a secret nipper, concealing a pint of bourbon behind the toilet near his office. He wasn't one to overindulge, however, generally limiting himself to two shots.

Rita and Thomas Hart Benton were close friends, and the four visited frequently. One evening, Rita tried anxiously to get her husband to tone down his cussing, but Mrs. Truman said, "Don't worry about that. You can't have lived with Harry Truman as long as I have without hearing everything there is to hear."

The Trumans' relationship was warm, though curiously matter-of-fact, rather Midwestern. On a visit to the Randall Jessees' home, Mrs. Jessee escorted Mrs. Truman to the bathroom. Mrs. Jessee reached into the dark room to pull on the light, and gasped at discovering Harry Truman with his back turned. Mr. Truman explained, "I couldn't find the light."

Mrs. Truman chided, "Well, weren't you about through anyway, Harry?"

Some favorite Kansas City luncheon spots in the Truman retirement years were Dixon's Chili, Bretton's Restaurant, and the Kansas City Club.

For entertainment, the Trumans enjoyed the Kansas City Philharmonic and especially the musical theater at Starlight Theater. In fact, the first time Truman was taken ill, he was at the Starlight, preparing for his walk-on part in *Call Me Madam*.

Spina's Barbershop was a frequent afternoon stop. Truman liked to tease short Frank Spina cornily that God must have sawed him off at the knees.

Truman rented a room at the Pickwick Hotel as a reading retreat. Ever since his youth, when he read every book in the Independence library, Truman maintained the habit of reading one book per day.

One of Truman's favorite places was the Oakwood Country Club, where he played poker and reminisced with his old haberdashery partner, Eddie Jacobsen, about the 1948 whistle-stop campaign. Truman especially loved to tell stories about the people he was with at the time. At Oakwood, Truman would beam proudly, declaring, "I've always been fond of my Jewish friends here in Kansas City. Without them, I would never have been reelected. Eddie Jacobsen saved my neck during the campaign. Those railroad men were going to kick me off the train in Oklahoma if I didn't pay my bills. Eddie, here, met with ten Jews in Kansas City who each put up $1,000 to keep the train rolling. Without my Jewish friends, I'd have been kicked off at one of my whistle stops."

Truman's financial situation was almost as bleak when he retired. At the time, there was not yet a pension, and Truman once remarked that he had to hurry up and finish his memoirs so he'd have a little spending money. The serialization of his memoirs in *Life* magazine was thought to be his greatest single source of income.

The completion of the Truman Library was a great source of pride for him. He especially liked to take children through on tours, pointing out his favorite parts. Truman used these tours to comment about the people he'd known. He disliked Richard Nixon and would remark, "That man once called me a traitor."

On those library tours, Truman would always point out the Eisenhower memoirs autograph. "Look at there, what that fellow said about me." Truman would then walk off while the visitor read the inscription, "I will always be indebted to the man who helped me so much in my career."

Stopping in front of the painting of the Potsdam Conference, Truman reminisced, "I was surprised at Stalin's stature. He was not over five-feet-five or six inches tall. When we had pictures taken, he would usually stand on the step above me. Churchill would do the same thing. They were both shorter than I."

Truman would continue about Josef Stalin's great strength as a political leader, explaining, "He was as near like Tom Pendergast as any man I knew."

Truman's political luck was wretched after his return to Missouri. He dabbled in local and state politics, backing certain candidates and issues. His endorsement was a sure talisman of victory for the other side. Not one candidate or issue Truman backed was successful. Undaunted, Truman carried on with the same determined spirit that characterized his term as the thirty-second President.

The recent Truman craze sweeping the nation—books, movies, T-shirts—reflects a transition from the 1960's antihero worship to a new respect for a hard-working person trying to work within the system. This attitude was best expressed by Truman when he quoted his favorite epitaph from a Tombstone, Arizona, cemetery. "Here lies Jack Williams. He done his damndest."

9. THE MONEY TREE

As much as we like to think that people move to Kansas City in order to attend Philharmonic concerts, shop the Plaza, and drive home down Ward Parkway, the hard truth is that people usually move here or choose to stay here because of a job. Once here, they fall in love with the beauty of the city. But for the most part, the initial attraction is a good economic climate. This chapter's intent is to discover what the business make-up of Kansas City is, what the great success stories are, and where the future fortunes are likely to be made.

Kansas City ranks high nationally in a great many industries. The problem lies in translating those "firsts" into human terms. For instance, being a leader in per capita construction spending is too vague to mean much. But when that is translated into seeing the new convention center downtown, people can get excited.

The H. Roe Bartle Convention Center is symbolic of the recent $3.5 billion construction boom. Driving past the huge triangle-motif building, Walt Bodine reminisced about his work on the bond election in 1973. "I talked myself hoarse telling voters about the boost to the construction industry, hotels, restaurants, shops, all the services for visitors. Five thousand new jobs have been created—because that bond issue passed by a margin of fifty-four votes. Why, every time I go to a medium-sized party, I like to think that roomful of friends are the ones who literally saved the downtown area."

The convention center is also symbolic of why Kansas City is important economically. Almost every industry here, whether it be manufacturing, agribusiness or transportation, has an edge on other markets because of the central location. Kansas City is nearly equidistant from both coasts—about 1,900 miles. And because it is also within 250 miles of the center of the nation's population, Kansas City can move things for a minimal cost. It is as cheap to move things or people in or out of Kansas City as from any other major city in the U.S. In the case of the convention center, this means national conventions can be held here with a minimum transportation cost. The same is true for food and commodity distribution, which is why many national and foreign firms are looking at Kansas City as a regional center. There is a cash flow savings for those businesses able to maintain a smaller inventory because of the short distance in-transit advantage.

Historically, Kansas City has been a trading post and a distribution center. François Chouteau, one of a large family of fur traders from St. Louis, established a fur collection post here in 1821. Recently Kansas City has attracted international attention from such firms as Toyota and Datsun (Japanese autos), and Chemagro (fertilizer), for many of the same reasons which attracted business here 150 years ago. Kansas City is still centrally located—now internationally so—and a major transportation hub by truck, rail, barge, and air.

The Santa Fe Trail has been supplanted by interstate highways in all directions, twelve main railroad lines, a deeper Missouri River channel, and an international airport. Instead of the old line, "you can't get there from here," it's a case of "you can't get there without going through here." Former Mayor Ilus Davis claims that a line from Tokyo to Buenos Aires passes through Kansas City. And that straight line is what transportation of goods and the accompaniment of services are all about.

A brief rundown of the major industries in Kansas City reveals national rankings in almost every area. And the diversity of these industries is a crucial factor in what is hopefully a depression-proof economy.

CONSTRUCTION

Projects in the planning and execution stages in the mid 1970's total more than $3 billion. That's over $2,600 per person. And most of that money (75 per cent) is from private investors. This indicates a great deal of confidence in the market area, from local developers as well as newcomers from St. Louis, New Orleans, Los Angeles, Chicago, New York, Toronto, etc. Pershing Square, River Quay, Crown Center, 1100 Main, and Executive Park at I-35 and Front Street are excellent examples of large private developments. The convention center, Truman Sports Complex, Kemper Arena, and the UMKC Performing Arts Center are examples of major public constructions. In the early 1970's, Kansas City ranked first nationally in per capita construction spending.

WAREHOUSING AND DISTRIBUTION

When a Kansas City business entrepreneur makes a seemingly apologetic claim that "there is more to Kansas City than meets the eye," he or she may be stating a simple fact, because Kansas City leads the nation in underground storage space. One of the foreign trade zone sites (more on that later), the Inland Center division of Beatrice Foods Company, is a huge underground cave. Another is the Great Midwest Corporation, which was excavated with explosives and mining techniques from the Bethany Falls limestone ledge.

This ledge, while not the proverbial "gold mine," does have intrinsic value. Any limestone which is removed to make storage space is marketable at reasonable prices. This is similar to the sale of sand removed from the river to clear the river bed for barge traffic.

But back to the caves, which must be seen to be appreciated. This was exactly the thought of one enterprising "cave man," Morgan Maxfield, who threw a lavish dinner party for the opening of the Great Midwest Corporation's cave. The setting was a baroque scene from Kublai Khan—red-velvet-draped cave walls lit with hundreds of candles (no doubt from Hallmark). The guests sipped champagne and mingled on the slightly tipsy rock floors.

Another local cave is located midtown, on the west side, just north of Roanoke Park. Located at 1201 West Thirty-first, Downtown Industrial Park is halfway down the hill leading from the WDAF-TV tower to the bottoms. Several businesses are headquartered there. Just around the next stone pillar might be an executive office or ten thousand pounds of candy. The principal advantages of these underground caves are inexpensive construction and maintenance, enormous space (sixty railroad cars can be stored or unloaded at one time), and the constant temperature and humidity afforded by an underground site.

As the national leader in freezer storage space, Kansas City could probably corner the market on frozen broccoli or any other frozen food stuff with no trouble. One of the leading local firms is Beatrice Foods.

Kansas City is also a leader in farm equipment distribution. The makers of motorized equipment, Allis-Chalmers, J. I. Case, John Deere, Farmland, and Ford produce much of the Midwest's machinery for tilling the soil—right here in River City. In addition, Butler Manufacturing Company, headquartered here, produces a good deal of the silvery silos dotting the landscapes of America.

These are examples of how a related industry, agriculture, touches Kansas City in dollar terms, rather than simply numbers of people engaged in farming. Of the Kansas Citians who have made their fortunes in agribusiness, few are from the farm and most have never touched a cow except at the children's petting zoo in Swope Park.

For example, Butler Manufacturing Company's leading representatives in the community would include George and Joan Dillon. They are hardly American Gothic. George is a sheepishly straight, bow tie man, and Joan is an architectural historian. While the food on their table comes from selling silos, her days are spent saving the Folly Burlesque Theatre or shepherding the city's visual interests for the Municipal Arts Commission.

MANUFACTURING

Kansas City leads the nation in greeting card publishing, mostly through the efforts of Hallmark Cards. There are a few independent artists who publish cards, many of them former Hallmark artists. Hallmark is one of the few places on earth which has a factory-sized building full of working artists. As the fourth largest employer in Kansas City, Hallmark employs more people than Ford Motor Company locally.

In addition to being one of the nation's largest greeting card publishers, Hallmark is one of the largest private corporations in the U.S. The firm's product line has gradually expanded from the picture postcards that founder Joyce Hall used to peddle, to greeting cards, and now to candles, books, party goods, and puzzles. An immense warehouse employs one of the largest computers in Kansas City to fetch the appropriate card or book or candle when an order is ready to be filled.

A spiritual descendant of Henry Ford, who used to reward his automotive workers with dimes, Kansas City's Joyce Hall is remembered by many of his early artists for the silver dollars he gave out. Before the new building was constructed, the company's layout was much like the newsroom of the Kansas City *Star*—a vast green-gray warehouse of desks in rows, no partitions, artists crouched over their work like intent kindergarteners. At the end of the day, the artists turned in their drawings (they are still not permitted to *write*, for that is someone else's job) to Mr. Hall. In the morning, Mr. Hall would award prizes for the "best" drawings—three silver dollars for first place, two for second, one for third place.

The fact that Hallmark is privately owned masks its size. Founder Joyce Hall, and his son, Donald, the president, are able to accomplish great things like Crown Center by lots of low-key quiet negotiation. Hallmark was the major architect of the Chamber of Commerce Prime Time campaign, financial backer of the *Jaycee* magazine, and major patron of the Chamber's *Kansas City Magazine*. Unfortunately, when the time came for Hallmark to wean the beautiful magazine, other corporations came forth only with condolences for its demise instead of cash for its continuance.

The Hallmark Corporation has a healthy social conscience, as well. They produce the Hall of Fame television series which continually wins an Esquire/Business Committee for the Arts award. Here in Kansas City, Hallmark has assisted events such as the Charlie Parker Memorial Foundation's annual jazz concerts, plus the hundreds of free community events on the Crown Center Square. In keeping with the corporate motto, Hallmark cares enough to do the very best.

A natural complement to the greeting card industry is the envelope industry; again, Kansas City leads the nation in producing this everyday product. Envelopes are the sort of thing about which nobody gets very excited but a few people get very rich. The Berkley family owns Tension Envelope Company, which does all right. The steady income it produces has provided Kansas City with an excellent city councilman and a real gentleman, Mayor Pro Tem Richard Berkley.

A city council member receives only $4,800 for virtually full-time work. Thus major corporations like Tension Envelope, Armco Steel, and Hallmark actually subsidize part-time government by freeing certain executives' time to serve in public office.

Another major envelope producer is the Sosland Press and Envelope Company, headed by Louis Sosland. He dedicates much of his free time to supporting the visual arts. In addition to his own collection, Sosland provided the Nelson Gallery with acquisition search funds—travel money for art purchase visits to New York. These funds placed the Nelson Gallery in the propitious spot to buy art when the Metropolitan was selling off part of its superb collection. In addition, it was the Sosland family which donated the George Rickey sculpture to the city to be placed at Tenth and Main. This *Two Planes Vertical-Horizontal Gyratory* was so controversial that for two years it was listed as an anonymous gift; only later did the Sosland family admit it was their gift. Thus it was left to an envelope maker to create the biggest flap the Kansas City art world has ever seen.

The third area of manufacturing where Kansas City leads the nation is vending machines, the one-armed bandits of the culinary world. Vendo Company in Kansas City is the largest manufacturer of vending machines in the world.

A Kansas City native, Jerome Hagstrom, built the first vending machine during the 1930's—all for the love of an ice cold bottle of Coke. Many a thirsty historian will remember that machine, which was the mechanical predecessor to today's electrically operated vendors. The short six-ounce bottles of Coke sat upright in a tub of ice water. The quenchee (Coke being the quencher) deposited one nickel and pulled the lever which moved the rotating top until the bottle appeared in the proper hole to be lifted up and out of the ice tub.

From those simple days, the vending industry has advanced to dollar bill readers, coin changers, and identification card makers. Though not for the price of a nickel.

The fourth leg of Kansas City's manufacturing fame is in automobile and truck assembly. Kansas City is second only to Detroit in the number of motor vehicles assembled, because of the economy of distribution to such markets as Denver, Memphis, New Orleans, Chicago, and Omaha. Every Maverick in the world comes from Kansas City. Most of the cars produced here are middle-class size—Ford Mavericks and Pintos, Chevrolet Novas, plus some Buicks, Pontiacs, and Oldsmobiles.

In the case of Ford and General Motors, the leaders who can really make decisions (the big wheels) are all shipped in from Detroit. So unfortunately Kansas City has not benefited from much of the usual philanthropy or civic involvement, although several national appeals receive local automotive industry contributions. Hopefully, more dollars will be forthcoming for local projects. This branch office syndrome has been a nagging problem for Kansas City, one of the few disadvantages to being centrally located yet not populous enough to be a headquarters city.

AGRIBUSINESS

To a Kansas farmer, hard winter wheat may be a grain, but to Kansas City's market moguls, it means lots of dough. According to Morton Sosland, publisher of the trade journal *Milling and Baking News,* most of the great fortunes in Kansas City are agribusiness related. Herbert Hall was a grain man who later built the superb research library, Linda Hall Library, in honor of his wife. Another grain fortune, the Crowell's, developed many of the second-floor collections at the Nelson Gallery.

Other industries like transportation and banking have been primarily grain-fed. The railroads have long had a marriage of convenience with the wheat industry. One hundred years ago, at the completion of construction, the railroads created business by offering advantageous freight rates for the shipment of wheat. Passenger traffic on trains and barges has come and gone since then. But grain is still rolling on the rails or floating down the Missouri to the Mississippi River from Kansas City.

Morton Sosland, a thoughtful, cultured man with civic interests in private education and the visual arts, is cautious in predicting where the future fortunes will be made. He was undoubtedly one of the first to know about the Russian wheat deal in 1972. He points out that the windfall profits benefited all of Kansas and Missouri.

The role of agribusiness in world diplomacy is another area for speculation. According to Sosland, wheat played a significant role in U.S. détente of the 1970's, specifically in the settlement of the Vietnam War.

Sosland describes agribusiness in general as the focal industry of Kansas City. Kansas City is the capital of the milling and baking world. The state of Kansas produces the most flour in the U.S.—31 million hundredweights in 1974. Missouri adds another 23 million; together that is 25 per cent of the nation's annual flour production. In consumer terms, if all the wheat grown in Kansas in 1974 was baked into bread, there were 4.9 billion loaves.

On the commercial end of the wheat business, Kansas City is one of the few cities in the nation which has all four major bakers in residence. Wonder, Manor, Tastee, and Butternut Bread are all baked here. Not even Chicago or Minneapolis has this kind of competition. While Interstate Brands is the only large bakery with national headquarters still in Kansas City, the Wonder Bread Company saw its future rise here before moving to Rye, New York, as ITT-Continental Baking Company.

But the real fortunes in agribusiness rise and fall at the Kansas City Board of Trade Building before the bread is baked. The trading floor is an oblong pen about fifty by one hundred feet which holds the lean-faced brokers who scramble for the best prices for wheat, corn, milo, oats, soybeans, and barley. The visitors' balcony corrals the anxious viewers, hedgers, and speculators who are respectable versions of the gamblers of yesteryear.

The stakes are much higher than those in Main Street's old faroh card game halls. If a mill is stocking wheat to its storage capacity in one transaction, the drop of one penny in the price per bushel could mean a $10,000 loss to the seller.

The brokers in the pit strip down for the day's action to striped neckties and short-sleeved shirts with ballpoint pen holders in the pockets. Now that the new Board of Trade Building at 4800 Main is air conditioned, their straw hats have been stored in mothballs. (Long hair is definitely not in vogue, probably because a stray hand brushing one's locks off the face could mean a million-dollar sale at giveaway prices.) All of the futures trading in the Kansas City pit is done by public outcry and hand signals, creating a hybrid cross between a cockfight and a deaf man's rally.

The other major arena for viewing agribusiness is the Kansas City Stockyards in the west bottoms. Compared to the good old days, the stockyards are a lonely place. As a business executive drops in for a steak lunch at the Golden Ox Restaurant down the street, the background sounds are of cattle bellowing, but the tone is rather hollow and the tune is mournful. Individual voices are discernible, like a church choir whose best members have died or moved away.

Few people think about the Kansas City Stockyards except in October during the American Royal celebration. Livestock is less important to Kansas City today—an example of an industry which has seen better days, because it is no longer built around Kansas City's unique advantages. As Jay Dillingham, long-time president of the Kansas City Stockyards Company, says, "The cattle business doesn't depend on the railroad anymore, so now you can have feed lots anyplace you have a road. You grow that new variety of Kansas milo in a circle around the lot, harvest the milo and feed it to the cattle where they stand, slaughter them where they are fed, pack the product, and ship it out, with no wasted weight. It's called progress, but, as the hen says, 'It may be breakfast to you but it's a pain in the ass to me.'"

The Royal is a Kansas City tradition which evokes vaguely embarrassing memories for some people. It is not a skeleton in the closet, but rather the agricultural "cowtown" image which people who are stampeding toward sophistication would just as soon forget.

With all the gala, the influx of visitors, the banners on downtown street poles, the four-color spreads in the *Star*, the Royal is to Kansas City what the Iowa State Fair is to Des Moines.

Every November, Kansas City hosts the national convention of the Future Farmers of America, which winds up just in time for the American Royal livestock and horse show. To the merchant, it is Kansas City's biggest retail month of every year—bigger than Christmas. To the thousands of teen-aged boys and girls, it is the feast after the harvest, a week off from school, and the first blush of frost which brings out those royal blue corduroy jackets with proud gold letters announcing BOISE, IDAHO, or AUGUSTA, MAINE.

But to Kansas City people who are not merchants, the FFA convention is a tug on the sleeve of memories—of simpler days when everyone's work had a visible reward, a final product, which produced pride in one's labor. Whether it is true or not, the Future Farmers of America are perceived as being whole-some, clean-scrubbed, antidrug, God-fearing freckled sons and daughters of the heartland. To watch them ogle the hookers on Twelfth Street with furtive sideways glances is to see a living version of a Norman Rockwell painting.

The Future Farmers and their parents, who join them the fol-lowing week for the Royal, bring with them a raw edge of an-other culture which jars the consciences of those Babbitts in Kansas City who are hoeing a new row and trying to forget their agricultural origins.

TRANSPORTATION

The Sante Fe Railroad employs more people than the Com-merce Bank of Kansas City, but who would know it? Sadly pas-senger service is a thing of the past, because it was so trouble-some and expensive. The railroads were forced into it, to politically justify all that free land. The real profit has always been in moving freight, especially containerized (piggyback truck trail-ers) freight. The major companies include Kansas City Southern, Rock Island, Santa Fe, and Union Pacific. Kansas City's central location provides it with twelve major rail lines, homing in like spokes of a wheel.

Recent transportation studies reinforce the city planning of a hundred years ago—the Union Station is still the hub. While Kansas City grapples with the choice between bus versus fixed rail, another team is working on uses for the air rights over Union Station. Hopefully, the Link Corporation's Pershing Square development will fill the air with income-producing properties. The Union Station building itself, a granite gray elephant for all but the most creative uses, is being saved as the home of the Kansas City Museum.

One transportation-dependent industry with a major impact on Kansas City's economy is the U.S. mail. Mail is the hobo of cargo —it hops a ride with whatever is passing through. And mail passes through Kansas City every day on 320 airplanes, 14 trains, and 103 trucks. Kansas City's central location has attracted several publishers and bulk mailers. (Note: Further research shows that every day two more trains and three more trucks of mail arrive at Kansas City than depart from it. Feeling a little crowded?)

According to Postmaster Ted Bland, the mail is a $100 million annual business (nearly half the size of the budget for Kansas City government). Greater Kansas City is the fourth largest area served by one postmaster. With this large territory come the problems of 110 communities with similar street names like Main, Delaware, First Street, or Oak. At times there are ten dual addresses which would be hopeless to sort out without zip codes.

But the real money that's made in the mail business is in undelivered mail—or rather in undelivered stamps. Ted Bland notes, "Ninety per cent of all commemorative stamps never go into the postal system. If it weren't for all of the additional income generated by stamp collectors, postal rates would be much higher."

Kansas City boasts a major bulk mail center in Turner, Kansas. The location was selected for its proximity to the Santa Fe Railroad Yards. About half of today's mail goes by truck or rail, half by air. Kansas City's bulk mail industry is a result of our rail location. This is the jumping-off point for the westward mail headed northwest for San Francisco or southwest for Los Angeles.

Trucking is a major industry in Kansas City, with 169 motor freight carriers. There is a natural advantage in being able to offer second-morning delivery to two-thirds of the U.S. An excellent highway system at times makes Kansas City appear to be one big street. Even the parks are boulevards in many cases. Six interstate highways and eight federal routes pass through Kansas City.

The airport is a source of more conversation than the weather in Kansas City. Kansas City International is propitiously placed north of the river in Platte County, about twenty miles north of downtown. Eight scheduled airlines operate over three hundred daily arrivals and departures.

Hopefully, the airport's location will prove to be a successor to the Swope Syndrome. A century ago, when Thomas Swope donated Swope Park to the city, he was besieged with mental anguish over its great distance from other activity. Swope Park was "too far out." Today, it's midtown for most of the population.

There are conflicting stories about why KCI is where it is. One claims that it was mystery man Howard Hughes, the principal stockholder of TWA in the 1950's, who bought land in Platte County for TWA's overhaul facility and then struck an agreement with famed city manager L. P. Cookingham that Kansas City, Missouri, would annex great land masses north of the river for its new airport.

Another version has particular charm in that it involves the same company largely responsible for Kansas City's government and real estate problems between Kansas City and Johnson County, Kansas. This version of KCI's location states that the city's original site was to have been Richards-Gebaur Air Force Base in south Kansas City. That plan fell through for several reasons, according to Max Norman, of the Chamber of Commerce, who tells the story. Next, a salesman for the farm department of the J. C. Nichols Company was asked by the city of Kansas City, Missouri, to assemble privately a land purchase package sizable enough for a major airport to replace Municipal Airport. Municipal is downtown, crowded, and has at times unintentionally used the Missouri River as an emergency runway. Nichols was able to assemble the required land at a much cheaper price than if the farmers had known it was for city use.

SERVICE INDUSTRIES

Of course the greatest ancillary service industry in the world is government. Like it or not, the growth of government has had enormous impact on Kansas City. State and local governments are by far the largest employees in Kansas City—60,000 employees in 1975. The federal government employs another 23,000 people here. The third largest employer is Trans World Airlines, at a mere 9,500 people.

Kansas City almost lost out on the many federal government jobs. When the Office of Management and Budget originally proposed the establishment of eight federal regions, Kansas City was not on the list. The powerful congressional delegation from Missouri and Kansas successfully lobbied for two additional regions, one of which is Kansas City.

Another service industry prominent in Kansas City is banking, especially correspondent banking, which accounts for nearly 20 per cent of local banks' total deposits.

In layman's terms, correspondent banking might have as its theme song, "Loan, Loan on the Range." It deals with providing those large loans which small town banks cannot handle. These loans are crucial in modern agribusiness, where cattle and wheat are multimillion-dollar enterprises. The small banks serve as local sponsors for individuals from their community, but the loans actually initiate in Kansas City.

In June 1975, the Kansas City *Star* published a much-debated series on leadership, "Who Runs Kansas City." Thirteen civic leaders were highlighted:

1. Miller Nichols, chairman of the board of the J. C. Nichols Company, one of the largest real estate development firms in the city.

2. Ilus W. (Ike) Davis, lawyer, banker, former two-term mayor and currently president of the Kansas City Board of Police Commissioners.

3. Donald J. Hall, president of Hallmark Cards.

4. Charles E. Curry, chairman of the board of the Home Savings Association, former presiding judge of the Jackson County Court and 1975 president of the Greater Kansas City Chamber of Commerce.

5. Dutton Brookfield, president, Unitog Company, twice-defeated mayoral candidate, former chairman of the Jackson County Sports Complex Authority.

6. James M. Kemper, Jr., chairman of the board of the Commerce Bank and chairman and president of the board of Commerce Bancshares, Inc.

7. John A. Morgan, retired chairman of the board and president of Butler Manufacturing Company.

8. Dr. Charles B. Wheeler, Jr., mayor, former Jackson County coroner and former western district judge of the old Jackson County Court.

9. Dr. Charles N. Kimball, chairman of the board of trustees of the Midwest Research Institute.

10. Robert H. Gaynor, vice-president and general manager of A.T.&T. Long Lines, Midwest Division.

11. George E. Powell, Sr., honorary chairman of Yellow Freight System, Inc., and chairman of the board of Traders National Bank.

12. R. Crosby Kemper, Jr., chairman of the board of United Missouri Bank, chairman of the board and president of United Missouri Bancshares.

13. Arthur Mag, senior partner in the law firm of Stinson, Mag, Thomson, McEvers and Fizzell.

Considering the omnipresence of agribusiness in every industry in Kansas City, one of the most remarkable things about the *Star's* list was the lack of any agribusiness leaders. However, two of those thirteen, the Kemper cousins, are bankers who have certainly had agribusiness dealings in their loan policies.

Consulting is a modern service industry which maintains a firm grip on America's pulse. One example is consulting engineers, those precise people who advise whether buildings and bridges will stand or fall on their own rivets. Kansas City is fourth in the nation in the number of resident consulting engineers. One of the nation's largest firms is locally based Howard Needles Tammen and Bergendoff. Dan Watkins, the senior vice-president of HNTB, is a model example of how international engineers keep involved in local activities. Dan, the father of fifteen children, manages to assist in civic fund-raising functions in between trips to Rio de Janeiro. He represents the wave of the business future, where executives pursue their fortunes across several continents but raise their families in a liveable city like Kansas City.

Perhaps the unique service industry in Kansas City, and the one with the greatest potential for new business fortunes, is the foreign trade zone. The secretary and general counsel for the Greater Kansas City Foreign-Trade Zone, Inc., is a young attorney, Marshall V. Miller. Miller first studied the FTZ concept in law school, when it was being developed by coastal cities with deep-sea ports. Upon his return to Kansas City, Miller concentrated on adapting the concept for inland use. Since it has complex and versatile applications, the authors asked him for a background description.

Miller began, "Foreign-trade zones are descendants of the free ports which many countries have operated to assist free trade and commerce. A foreign-trade zone site encourages international business by providing imported goods duty-free entry into the United States for an unlimited period of time. Customs duty is paid only when the goods are shipped to a final destination within the U.S., thus creating a substantial cash flow savings."

What happens to the merchandise once it gets to Kansas City? Miller explained, "Goods brought into a zone may be stored, repacked, relabeled, inspected, manipulated, mixed with domestic and/or other foreign materials, used in a manufacturing process, or exhibited for sale. The zone concept offers the ability to utilize domestic labor in the U.S. instead of overseas, while still realizing a cost savings. In the case of Kansas City, this means international firms from such manufacturing nations as Japan, Germany and Finland may operate businesses from here, pumping foreign dollars into our economy as well as providing many new jobs for Kansas Citians."

Every foreign trade zone enjoys advantages, but Kansas City's has some unique aspects. Instead of one big warehouse at a seaport (the typical zone in other U.S. cities), Kansas City's foreign-trade zone is split up, including four mammoth sites—all remote from the river, two underground, one in Kansas. One of the four sites, owned by Great Midwest Corporation, is a

2,815,000-square-foot underground cave which is larger than any other zone in the U.S.

Miller pointed out the uniqueness of the multiple sites. "Kansas City has the only zone operated without tax dollars, by a not-for-profit corporation. The individual sites, however, are operated by private corporations. Therefore, site location is a function of the marketplace. Because of Kansas City's natural advantages of geography, transportation and communications, there is every reason for foreign firms to bypass expensive, overcrowded and trouble-plagued port cities in favor of a central warehousing and distribution center. What Kansas City lacks in seaport mystique is made up by the improved cash flow afforded by its center location. In other words, for coastal cities, their wealth runs alongside their ports; in Kansas City, we have a cash flow savings running in our underground caves and warehouse/ exhibition facilities."

Will international trade be the successor to the Kansas City fortunes in cattle, vending machines, and envelopes? Hedging carefully, Miller conceded, "The foreign-trade zone is only a tool, to be used or ignored by international businesses or by Kansas Citians. Obviously, I wouldn't be working on this if I didn't believe that Kansas City is a prime place for international economic development. As the world's economy becomes more interdependent, a distribution center at the crossroads of the strongest of the world's markets is crucial. Besides, Kansas City is a great place to live and work."

To sum it up, Kansas City is full of opportunities for future fortunes. For those businesses in New York, sweating out an overtaxed economy, where the only solution to most problems seems to be even more taxes, Kansas City offers a fresh alternative. Kansas City has a balanced economy and tax base, an ample, educated work force, and a lifestyle casual enough to keep people from burning out before they wear out.

10. HOME-TOWN JAZZ

In Kansas City the establishment has always operated at one level, while the people have always had something else of their own going. So, in the late 1920's and '30's, as the respectable people made money, fought off the Depression, and worried about machine politics, Kansas City became the capital city of jazz—or, as *New York* magazine recently put it, "The heavenly city of jazz tradition."

The beauty of it was that it operated on passing-of-the-word, more than any formal notice by the community at large. When reformers hit New Orleans and shut down the town, and Chicago cops started squelching the speakeasies, Kansas City's considerable native talent was reinforced by all kinds of brilliant jazz people—and great musical things began to happen.

The musical revolution down on Twelfth Street and at Eighteenth didn't get anything near the attention it rated. After all, the city was locked in great political and economic battles; the gambling industry was going full blast; gangsters were having shoot-outs and spot murders with morbid regularity; and for the hot-blooded, one of the biggest and most wide-open red-light districts ever seen in North America fanned out from the intersection of sin, Fourteenth and Cherry.

Although white music lovers turned out in large numbers, to the establishment and the media of the time the jazz phenomenon was a black phenomenon. Whereas today Count Basie, Mary Lou Williams, and others can "return home" to a full civic welcome, in the great jazz days of the thirties, they were often taken for granted, as two-dollars-a-night entertainers well might be.

Besides, the city had much more of a Southern orientation in those days than it has today. Media took notice of black people only when they were robbing someone, shooting, or being shot. In other words, blacks made crime news or they made no news. Thus did the media put blacks in their place. The same brainless bigots responsible for that also considered the jazz music of the time to be "nigger music"—thus putting it in its place. And the place of both was no place, so far as official recognition was concerned. There was very little racial trouble then because, as a local tavern owner put it, "The colored people knew what they could and couldn't do."

While today a grateful city administration names a housing development after Charlie Parker and a street after Count Basie, the civic leadership of the thirties took little visible notice of the musical geniuses in their midst. These worthies—given a good strip show or the services of a naked waitress—paid little attention to what kind of musical setting it all happened in. These were the so-called "best people" who were out slumming. Fortunately, among the common people—and, as Lincoln said, God made a lot of them—there was a healthy appreciation for jazz, and some kind of true awareness that something great was happening right here in River City, whether the papers said so or not.

In those wondrous days when the great Kansas City jazz epic was being written daily, it was a fast track for any musician. The test of musical manhood was the jam session. Musicians had jammed before in lots of places. But in Kansas City in the thirties, the jam session became a test of endurance and ingenuity. And they were longer than any jam sessions had ever been anywhere else.

Milton Morris, who has operated bars and night clubs in the city for decades, loves to reminisce about what a wild thing the jam session could be in those days.

"You'd have fourteen cats blowing up there," Morris said, "and the band would know when a cat felt like taking off. Like Hot Lips Page would be on trumpet, and he'd feel like wailin', and the rest of the band would know it. They drift off the bandstand one by one, and he's up there blowing, and he just keeps on. Then they know when he's about ready, and they move back in. Now, he's liable to go—it could be an hour. I've seen Jo Jones sit there and wail on drums, and nobody else'd be on the bandstand for three hours; and then they'd just move back in."

Milton, who operated the Novelty Club at Sixteenth and McGee in the thirties, is himself something of an institution. He paid two to three dollars a night to showcase people like Count Basie, Benny Moten, Jay McShann, Charlie Parker, Julia Lee, Jo Jones, Hot Lips Page, Walter Page, Mary Lou Williams, and Lester Young. He once paid an entertainer five dollars for a night's work and was berated for paying such an opulent salary for a twelve-hour gig.

Today, Morris is still in the bar business. You can find him standing behind the bar in his club, Milton's, at 3241 Main, ready to talk jazz with anybody. He also maintains an avid interest in state politics, and every four years, with only one recent exception, he runs for Governor of Missouri on a platform of legalized gambling. Asked about his raucous life, which included gambling, bootlegging, and drinking a quart of whiskey a day for forty-two years, Milton Morris answers, "If I had it to do over again, I'd do it twice as much."

Morris is also known for his now famous want ad in the newspapers, which says, "I Ain't Mad At Nobody," and implies that even if you've given Milton a bad check at some time, you can receive amnesty just by coming back.

But in the grueling jam sessions of the thirties, there was no amnesty and no forgiveness if you were a musician who couldn't cut it.

A jam session was a serious thing. It constituted a commitment of some kind; it was an emotional as well as a musical happening. Once they got going, they could last for hours. It was not unusual to send a cab in the middle of the night to wake up some sleeping musician because he was needed down at the session to relieve some other player who was finally giving out.

Going out into the night to search out local musicians was especially important when the jam involved players from the coast. The Kansas City cats had a reputation to uphold, and they weren't about to lose it to some fancy outsider. The call would go out, and the best of the local musicians would flock to the site of the jam. The outsiders never had a chance. They often left town with their egos bruised and battered, and from their experiences came an expression that described the local guys as "mean cats with sharp claws."

The club owners loved the jam sessions. In the Kansas City of those days, there was no such thing as a closing hour, and the longer the players jammed, the longer the customers stayed.

The late Louie Armstrong told of how he would play a hotel date downtown and then hop a streetcar out to Eighteenth and Paseo, where impromptu jam sessions were known to break out at the Old Kentucky Barbecue.

"In Kansas City when they jammed, they jammed," Satchmo said, "and everybody for miles around came to hear it. First the barbecue place would fill up, and then the sidewalk outside. Then the crowd would overflow into the street and then right across the street, and pretty soon the street cars couldn't get by at all."

Louie was asked what happened when the trams got blocked that way. He smiled that famous smile, and said, "Why man, those motormen would just come down off there and they'd be swingin' like everybody else."

Jam sessions in the clubs were also a test for the newcomers. If you could hold your own in a jam, you were accepted into the fold. But many an overeager novice was hooted off the stage if he didn't make it. Even the great Charlie Parker ran into that kind of trouble.

Parker had jazz in his blood from the start. His family moved to Kansas City, Missouri, in 1927 from Kansas City, Kansas, where Parker had been born in 1920. He made it through grade school, but at Lincoln High School, where he played clarinet and baritone horn, Charlie's night life began to interfere with his studies, and he began cutting classes.

His mother had taken an all-night job with Western Union, and as soon as she was safely departed, Charlie Parker, age thirteen, would depart for the clubs. Not that he could just walk in the front door. Things did hang loose in Kansas City in those days, but still not that loose. The determined youngster found another way in. He made friends with some of the musicians who worked the clubs, and managed to gain entry through the back door.

He must have been something to look at. In an effort to disguise his youthfulness, Parker would go forth decked out in a long black raincoat, and a wide-brimmed hat which could be pulled down rakishly to conceal his adolescent face. From midnight until five or six in the morning, the kid would hang in there, digging the jam sessions and dreaming of the day when he would actually play in one.

But in order to play anywhere in town, Parker had to be a union member. At the age of fourteen, he had four years to wait until he could get a union card. Parker was not about to wait that long. He walked into the union office, declared that he was eighteen years old, paid his ten-dollar fee, and became a bona fide member of Local 627. Now he was on his way. He walked out of the office and began looking for a job. A few days later, Charlie Parker began his career as a professional musician—at $1.25 a night.

One of his first attempts to get into a jam session, a real disaster, occurred at one of the jumpingest places of all, the Reno Club at Twelfth and Cherry. At the Reno Club, mixed drinks moved across the bar for twenty-five cents apiece, and a nickel brought a frosty beer. In the back of the clubroom, the prostitutes hung out, plying their trade in rooms above the club for two dollars a trick. Marijuana cigarettes were sold out back at three for a quarter.

The back lot of the Reno Club was also a regular stop of a lunch wagon selling dime-a-time sandwiches. One of the varieties, a "short thigh" of chicken, was Charlie Parker's favorite. Chicken was known then as "yardbird," and Parker's appetite soon gained him the nickname of Yardbird or Bird Parker.

The night Charlie Parker first tried to jam, the Count Basie band had just wound up the last set of the evening. Now a jam session was shaping up. The fifteen-year-old Parker was a high school dropout and a novice musician; but tonight he was going to jam. Longer on confidence than musical skills, he walked up and took center stage. The session was building furiously, spurred on by Jo Jones on the drums. As Parker began to play, his confidence began to erode, and the mistakes began to multiply. Finally, when all of his nerve was gone, Parker stopped dead. What came next was silence . . . a long and pregnant silence. And then came the ultimate put-down. Jo Jones picked up a cymbal and threw it across the stage, where it crashed to the floor at Parker's feet. The crowd began to laugh, and there were jeering shouts.

A humiliated Parker withdrew, but he told a friend, "Don't worry, I'll be back. I'll fix those cats. Everybody's laughing at me now, but just wait and see."

Charlie Parker was a mixed-up kid, but not a crazy-mixed-up kid. As he was an only child, the consensus was that he had been spoiled at home. But whatever the cause, Charlie Parker could seem belligerent and bullying at times. At other times, to other people, he seemed somber and morose; once in a while he appeared to be helpless.

One contemporary, Hampton Hawes, said, "Bird was like a god. I never crowded him too close. He talked to us about things I wasn't to read until years later in books by Malcolm X and Eldridge Cleaver. I hear all of that in his music. Bird was a deeply frustrated man."

But there was a genius in Charlie Parker that was to express itself. He played as few men have ever played before or since—first in Kansas City, then later in New York. In the process, he picked up the heroin habit that ultimately destroyed him.

Charlie Yardbird Parker was frustrated to the end. In his final years of life, he came to hate Kansas City and some of what had happened to him here. He once expressed a strong desire never to be buried in Kansas City. But Charlie Parker does rest here today in Lincoln Cemetery near Blue Ridge Boulevard and Truman Road.

Bird still lives in Kansas City. Besides the memorial at his burial place, a housing area in Kansas City was named in his honor. And a Charlie Parker Memorial Foundation now exists to assist with the training of young musicians.

The Charlie Parker Center offers some of the finest jazz instruction available anywhere, with the goal of expanding the horizons of a generation of young people. In addition to teaching jazz improvisation, students learn to read music, thereby eliminating a frequent barrier to getting advanced musical jobs.

But their purpose is not solely to train professional musicians, especially since the days of full-time work for many musicians are over. Rather, the Parker Center offers an exposure to the arts (including plans for visual arts, dance, theater, and media) as a means of self-expression. The Parker Center offers the urban child an opportunity to explore what he or she can do, regardless of family income or lack of opportunities in the public schools. For many children, it is the first chance to excel at something as an individual.

Eddie Baker, president of the Parker Foundation, describes the program as "changing liabilities into assets. Perhaps, if a Charlie Parker Memorial Foundation had existed when Bird was a kid growing up in the streets of Kansas City, he wouldn't have gone through the changes that took his life at age thirty-five."

Today, the city's best known living musical son is Count Basie, who likes to recall the way in which he received the title of Count.

At that time, Count Basie's band had a radio show originating from the Reno Club. On one show, an announcer suggested to Basie that his name, Bill Basie, lacked something. He noted that titles were really in—Duke Ellington, Earl "Fatha" Hines. The announcer then said, "I think I'll call you Count Basie from now on." He asked Basie if that was all right, and as Basie tells it, he just shrugged an okay. But the name Count Basie stuck from that day on.

The name for Count Basie's long-standing theme, "One O'Clock Jump," also stemmed from an announcer's suggestion. It seems the radio announcer just didn't think the theme's first title —"Blue Balls"—was really all that airworthy.

Kansas City has produced many favorite musical daughters as well as sons. Julia Lee started her career here at age fourteen in brother George E. Lee's Singing Novelty Orchestra. Harry Truman invited her to sing at the White House, accompanied by Kansas City drummer Baby Lovett. Julia sang with Kansas City musicians until her death in 1958.

Mary Lou Williams still holds forth with her moving jazz masses. She, too, has a street named in her honor in the Parker Square development.

A young and powerful performer, Marian Love, seems destined to carry on the Kansas City tradition, along with Marilyn Maye and perennial favorite Bettye Miller, the pianist/vocalist. And zippy Carol Comer ably demonstrates that white women have soul too.

From Charlie Parker's day until now, the great names in American jazz have passed through Kansas City, and many still live and work in the city. Kansas City still has a lively contingent of jazz fans who turn out for an annual Jazz Festival, and who frequent a number of places featuring a kind of rebirth of jazz. These include Putsch's Strawberry Patch, the Levee (especially Monday nights), the Musicians Foundation Building at Eighteenth and Highland, the Alameda Plaza Rooftop Lounge, plus the thousands of jazz albums to be heard in midtown Kansas City at Milton's Tap Room. Hanging over the cash register, Milton's sign reads, "No Requests Please . . . Like Man, It's Free." For all of the musicians who play in the city, there is no way that Kansas City can be just one more gig—because this is the mother earth of the jazz improvisation movement.

When the jazz buffs gather, one hears many an argument and many an interpretation about exactly how Kansas City jazz can be defined, or whether it is a thing unto itself, more than it is an outgrowth of New Orleans jazz. There are long and fond debates over who plays what instrument best, and who has the best charts. But perhaps the definitions and interpretations don't really matter. Perhaps the true meaning of jazz is not something to be defined and analyzed; maybe it can't be done.

Today there is a new item of discussion, the question of whether Kansas City really is on the verge of a new jazz age. The preservation of the old Folly Burlesque Theatre at Twelfth and Central, with its perfect acoustics, may fulfill a community dream of putting jazz back on Twelfth Street.

After twenty wistful years of dreaming about the good old days, three local jazz organizations are anxious to "get cooking" on a jazz history museum, and a revival of those hot jam sessions. The new emphasis is on less discussion and more action, which is the way musicians seem to like it best, since music is a universal language of its own. Charlie Parker expressed it this way.

When asked by a friend to define and analyze his own musical development, Parker smiled, looked at his friend, and said, "I lit my fire. I greased my skillet. And I cooked."

11. YOU GOTTA HAVE ART

It has often been said that what's good for General Motors is good for the country. Most people accept that as a universal truth which can be handily applied in judging all situations. Another truism is that every good rule has its exception. The arts in Kansas City (and this includes music, art, dance, drama, crafts, writing, architecture, and film) seem to be the exception to the General Motors rule; for unlike GM, the arts here have thrived best in situations considered bad for society as a whole.

The greatest era of jazz in Kansas City's history not only flourished under the Pendergast machine, it was dependent upon that political machine to keep the booze flowing while the band played on. You can say what you will about the evils of alcohol and gambling and prostitution, and about all the corruption in those days, of ignoring the prohibition amendment to the U. S. Constitution. According to some law-abiding Christians, Kansas Citians' souls were in great jeopardy then. But the fact is, their ears never had it so good.

Kansas City had working musicians then—more than ever before or since. And this in an era when many other professions had no work. True, the pay was terrible, only two dollars a night plus tips for Count Basie or Benny Moten, and less than that for the unknowns. But the work was steady enough to attract the finest musicians in the country. And that work provided enough hours of playing time and appreciative audiences to produce some truly creative American music for the first time. Instead of playing the tunes of Europeans, Kansas City musicians were playing Kansas City jazz.

But the classic example of turning the worst possible adversity to the advantage of the arts was in Kansas City's visual arts world. In his perpetually solemn and dignified manner, the director of the Nelson Gallery, Lawrence Sickman, will inform you, "The greatest thing that ever happened to the Nelson Gallery was the Depression."

Art lovers in Kansas City should dismiss all visions of bread lines, dust bowls, and desperate fathers committing suicide because that same stock market crash made great art what it is in Kansas City.

Like squirrels storing nuts for the winter, Kansas City had been saving the Nelson trust funds for art works while the new gallery was under construction. Lack of a gallery in the 1920's had discouraged any overextended spending, a malady which afflicted many galleries in other cities. By 1930, the accumulated income from the Nelson family estates totaled $4 million for the purchase of works of art.

That $4 million bought a collection which would easily have cost $10 million in the 1920's. The collection included works by Titian, Veronese, El Greco, Goya, Cézanne, Manet, Van Gogh, Gauguin, Breughel the younger, Rembrandt, Rubens, Turner, Gainsborough, and the famed Poussin work, *Triumph of Bacchus.*

One of the trustees who helped select the works for purchase was the Plaza developer, J. C. Nichols. He was so proud of his bargaining ability that he didn't seem to mind the title "Greatest Chiseler in Art."

Thus did Kansas City get a great art collection that has expanded to earn a reputation as one of the finest in the U.S. But more on that later, because there is one more characteristic about the arts in Kansas City which must be pointed out. In addition to a tradition of capitalizing on adversity, Kansas City's art life is peculiar in that it succeeds best when it avoids snobbery.

In the great cities of the East Coast, the rich and the educated have a virtual strangle hold on the arts. They control the organizations and they set the standards. The result is an elite clique politely eyebrowing artists "doing their thing," in a sort of master-peon two-step.

Most Kansas Citians just can't put up with that attitude. Audiences here are more "hoot 'n' holler" in showing genuine appreciation for the arts. This does not mean that the arts are not respected here, only that things are more people-oriented and spontaneous. For example, unlike Eastern audiences, Kansas Citians are never stingy with standing ovations. We're not Beacon Hill, and don't want to be.

A chief advocate of bringing the arts to all the people is Kansas City's own Thomas Hart Benton. In 1941, Benton had these remarks to make to some news reporters from New York, "If it were left up to me, I wouldn't have any museums. The typical museum is a graveyard run by a pretty boy with delicate curving wrists and a swing in his gait. Who looks at paintings in a museum? I'd rather sell mine to saloons, bawdy houses, Kiwanis and Rotary Clubs, Chambers of Commerce—even women's clubs. People go to saloons . . ."

So, if you're looking for the arts in Kansas City, don't forget to look in unusual places. One of Benton's murals is on the first floor of Harzfeld's Store on Petticoat Lane, downtown.

Now we can briefly survey the arts in Kansas City. Our purpose is to illustrate the variety rather than to catalogue every opportunity, but we apologize to those we couldn't mention in these few pages.

Kansas City is first of all an outstanding city for the visual arts. The institution which guarantees that they will continue to develop here is the Kansas City Art Institute. Degrees may be earned in sculpture, painting, and printmaking, design, photography, and cinematography, and ceramics. The emphasis is on quality, not on some nebulous distinction between professionals and amateurs. Night classes make it possible for virtually anyone to participate.

The faculty is first-rate, and former students have gone on to jobs in every phase of design imaginable. One graduate, Cyril Directo, is helping to reconstruct an ancient Hawaiian village. Walt Disney was a student here, prior to his pioneering of animated film.

In the past few years, the Art Institute has sponsored an annual autumn raft race down the Missouri River. It's actually a classroom assignment—to design a raft which will successfully support the number of people who design and construct it.

Another Art Institute project which touches the community is Art on the Boulevards. Students' sculptures are placed throughout the city by the Parks Department. These large abstract forms have turned Kansas City into one huge sculpture museum.

Admittedly, the whole world is not crazy about these sculptures. Someone once called Walt Bodine on his Sunday evening WHB radio talk show with this comment, "Some mammoth nuts and bolts have just crashed on the Paseo parkway in front of my house. Are the Martians in town?" Universally accepted or not, at least these sculptures cause people to notice and react to their surroundings.

The Art Institute's next door neighbor is the Nelson Gallery. Lawrence Sickman has been with the gallery since it opened, and was made director in 1953. Sickman's specialty is oriental art; he studied in China in the 1920's before the forty-year period when Americans were barred from entering that country. Sickman is responsible for the Nelson Gallery's superb Chinese collection, which is one of the best in the U.S.

The art market fluctuates so quickly today that it's important to snap up a bargain before the price doubles. This necessitates being in the right place to hear about those bargains. One of the latest acquisitions at "the Nelson" is Monet's *Boulevard des Capucines*. Mrs. Helen Spencer gave nearly $1 million for it, and, according to assistant director Ted Coe, "It was a real steal for that price." One of the gallery's creative patrons, Louis Sosland, had provided the travel budget which sent Coe to New York just at the time when the Metropolitan Museum decided to sell the Monet work.

This particular Monet's importance is that it supposedly hung in the very first French exhibition in 1874 where Impressionism got its name. At that time, it was considered to be a very unrealistic style of painting, almost sacrilegiously so.

According to the account of one historian, John Rewald, this painting exhibition caused one viewer to go crazy. Gazing at the "impressionistic" brush strokes, he asked, "What are all those tongue lickings?" He then proceeded to run around the room, screaming.

How times change. If that incident happened today, the typical Nelson Gallery viewer would comment that he was undoubtedly some Volker Fountain freak from across the street.

Another very significant Impressionist work, by Degas, was purchased by Mrs. Spencer for the Nelson's fortieth anniversary in 1973. The work was originally purchased by a Mrs. Havemeyer for one hundred dollars, the first Impressionist painting ever bought by an American. That purchase sparked a furious collecting trend, and America became known as the country which first recognized the genius of this style.

While many people think of painters and their patrons as exclusively male, it should be noted that it was the great painter Mary Cassatt who walked her friend, Mrs. Havemeyer, past Degas's Paris studio and recommended the purchase. And it was Helen Spencer who gave nearly a million dollars to bring that same painting to Kansas City.

Kansas City has more than its share of art fairs at shopping centers, some under covered malls, others outdoors on streets and sidewalks. The most notable of this last version is the Plaza Art Fair, which has been held annually at the end of September for over forty years. Several streets are closed from traffic, while more than three hundred artists display their work. Special foods are sold from vendors' carts, and thousands of viewers mingle to the sounds of a string quartet. Art fairs provide a direct market approach without the usual 50 per cent markup, and an opportunity for many people to view a broad spectrum of art styles in a short time. For the person newly interested in buying original art, it's a nonthreatening way to discover your tastes. And the artists are there to answer your questions, because they want to help you understand their work.

Some of the best artists in Kansas City, however, refuse to suffer the rigors of art fairs, and must be scouted out at their studios. One excellent abstract painter, Philomene Bennett, explains her problem, "Art fairs work for artists who paint miniatures; they can display and sell many pieces. But my paintings are so huge that I'd have to rent three booths just to hold one painting!"

Another outstanding artist, who has worked in such varied formats as charcoal on canvas, the bronze Charlie Parker medallion, and those funny little Hallmark card figures with three fingers, is

Lou Marak. Lou, one of the pioneer artists in the River Quay, explains why he no longer leaves his studio to drag his work to art fairs. "Sure, it's nice to sell your work quickly. But I've spent too many weekends squatting on a little stool in a crowded booth, squinting up at people. There's always some old gal who's shopping around but knows nothing about art. She's rude, and constantly steps all over you, and whines that your painting is all wrong because it doesn't match her living room drapes."

Perhaps the best way to view art fairs is to acknowledge that they serve as an appetizer, but shouldn't be confused with the main course, which is a commissioned work. And hopefully you'll understand why then, on the third day in the rain at an art fair, an artist might look a little morose.

Filmmaking is one of the fastest growing art forms today, and Kansas City offers several opportunities to learn in that field. In addition to the Art Institute department, there is a major industrial film company, Calvin Productions. Most of their clients aren't looking for dramatic interaction, but rather a clean head-on shot of a John Deere tractor on a sunny day. Still, young filmmakers learn techniques there. Robert Altman, director of many movies, including *M.A.S.H.* and *Nashville,* first worked at Calvin. And there are several independent filmmakers in Kansas City, including John Altman and Mary Nelson at Pentacle Productions (last film of Thomas Hart Benton); and Jim Merrick, (Kansas City's history film for the Jaycees).

Crown Center's Multi Media Forum offers the services of a professional film and video staff for conference holders. The highly sophisticated equipment is housed in a meeting room complex which is also used for a community film and concert series.

When you think of theater, it is generally accompanied by theater criticism. And this is where Kansas City has a love-hate relationship with the newspaper critics, because many Kansas Citians would really prefer not to hear any negative criticism. Audiences here would rather be surprised and allowed to form their own opinions.

Kansas City *Star* critic Giles Fowler reports that once he wrote a biting review of a touring theater production. He received dozens of angry letters saying, "That's no way to treat a visitor!"

Fowler attributes this to Kansas Citians' strong Western sense of fair play and neighborliness.

Professional theater opportunities here range from Starlight Theater (outdoors at Swope Park), Missouri Repertory Theatre (professional arm of University of Missouri at Kansas City), Lyric Theater (opera in English), to the half dozen Equity dinner theaters.

Among community theaters, there are the Jewish Community Center's Resident Theatre, Westport Players, Bell Road Barn Players in Parkville, Johnson County Community College Barn Players, and the Black Contemporary Players at Linwood Multi-Purpose Center.

The universities, especially UMKC and Avila College, mount excellent productions. UMKC's director, Dr. Patricia McIlrath, is the oyster who nurtured Kansas City's new cultural pearl, the UMKC Center for the Performing Arts. She has singlehandedly guided the theater department, building a professional season along with a collegiate department. Since 1948, her department has worked out of a recycled World War II temporary building from Camp Crowder. Now after twenty-five years, "Dr. Mac" will have a real theater, which will be teamed with classrooms to house the Conservatory of Music. Avila College has recently opened its new Harry Weese-designed Goppert Theatre.

The most unique community theater is Foolkiller, Etc., at 809 East Thirty-first Street. The Foolkiller is a theater and folk music haven, as well as a communiversity group stressing participation, or, as one student calls it, "arts for the hell of it."

Foolkiller began in 1967 when a few friends decided to write and produce a play, *Deadwood Dick* instead of sitting around rapping all day. They rented an old revival tent as their theater, but it blew away during the dress rehearsal. In true improvisatory style, they moved to their current building, which is a converted chicken-plucking plant.

Founder and director Don St. Clair, a philosophy professor at Longview Community College, writes most of the melodramas, or "avant garde Westerns." They incorporate elements of farce, melodrama, and Shakespeare. The name Foolkiller is derived from a Stephen Vincent Benét short story, and refers to our creative insights into the arts—the things which keep us all from being damn fools.

Foolkiller, Etc. also sponsors the finest national folk music stars in concert. (More musicians perform here than anywhere else in the U.S., even more than in Denver's Folklore Center.) The Foolkiller Academy offers a wild variety of courses, including "Journalism for the Hell of It," which teaches you to publish a monthly newspaper. Saturday nights are reserved for Folk Opry performances, which include a play, a mini-concert, and eight walk-on musicians (whoever shows up first is a star).

As we stated before, the Depression was the finest hour for Kansas City's arts. A three-month period in the fall of 1933 saw the opening of UMKC, the Kansas City Philharmonic, and the Nelson Gallery. The Conservatory of Music, once a separate institution, joined with UMKC in 1959. The conservatory is the national headquarters of the Institute for Studies in American Music. The library collection includes first editions of such greats as Scott Joplin, Emma Lou Diemer, and Euday Bowman ("Twelfth Street Rag").

Harry Truman once said, "If I'd played the piano better, I'd never have been President." He was a great fan of the Kansas City Philharmonic throughout his life. An annual fund-raising concert to benefit the orchestra and the Truman Library is held each May in his honor.

As this chapter opened, we explained that the arts suffer when they are plagued with snobbery. Since music is known by society as the highest art form, that is where the cancer usually lodges, and such is true in Kansas City.

Like all orchestras, the Kansas City Philharmonic has been beset with financial ups and downs for years. It was unique, however, when in 1963 ours was the only major orchestra outside of New York City to decline a Ford Foundation grant for lack of a match. Every other city's symphony used those funds to establish an endowment fund. Today those endowments frequently cover the typical 10 per cent deficits in their annual budgets. (No orchestras make money; it's always a matter of how much is lost per year.)

Thus, Kansas City's cultural leaders blew their big chance more than ten years ago. The solution is to begin an endowment fund now, large enough that the accrued interest will cover our orchestra's annual deficit. Some new progressive business leadership on the board of directors is beginning to make headway, and we support them heartily.

The second problem is more difficult. Most orchestra patrons are notoriously aloof—to each other and to the musicians who provide their listening pleasure. The Philharmonic here, just like every other in the U.S., attracts a large number of people who only want the social prestige of being seen, or of having one's name in the program. Concert intermissions are like visits to an aviary of preening peacocks. This makes some genuine music lovers uncomfortable.

Orchestras everywhere seem to thrive on women's organizations. Maurice Peress, Kansas City's brilliant conductor, recalls his first visit to Corpus Christi, Texas, which was his previous post. When he arrived, the orchestra there had been defunct for two years. "But, maestro," a young matron cooed, "we still have an active guild, and our annual spring ball was a great success!"

The Kansas City Philharmonic has so many guilds, each with spring elections, cheese sales, fashion show luncheons and home tours, that even the business manager doesn't have time to read all the newsletters. And that's fine, as long as no one forgets that the primary purpose is to make music happen.

The problem develops when people get so interested in the parties that they don't go to the concerts. The Kansas City Philharmonic has two problems—money and attendance. If every guild member would buy *one* season ticket (she wouldn't even have to buy one for her husband), our orchestra would operate in the black.

At this writing, the Philharmonic is once more on strike, and, like the opening notes of Beethoven's Fifth Symphony, fate is again knocking at the door. Missouri is the only state in the nation trying to support two major symphony orchestras. Many say it is an impossible task.

If new leadership emerges, perhaps Kansas City will follow the lead of St. Paul, Minnesota, which fields an outstanding chamber orchestra of twenty-two players. Their budget is much smaller than that of their neighbor in Minneapolis, the Minnesota Orchestra, and they are able to tour the many small towns of the state which cannot accommodate an eighty-piece orchestra. In this way, two excellent arts groups complement one another, instead of competing.

The other solution to the musical dilemma in Kansas City is the infusion of new ears. The business and social community needs to pull in new listeners, who can discover the entertainment value and the hearty uplift that concerts give. It's irrelevant for the media to cover what people are wearing. What counts is whether or not people are coming with open ears and eyes.

A city of this size needs to ensure a perpetual talent bank for future years, and to provide quality performing opportunities for young people, regardless of differences in school district musical programs. Kansas City has one of the nation's outstanding youth symphonies, which has traveled internationally and recorded with the BBC. And the Kansas City Youth Symphony even has a "feeder orchestra" of its own for the really junior artists, the Junior Youth Symphony.

Other young people's programs include the Charlie Parker Memorial Foundation (see jazz chapter) and the Kansas City chapter of Young Audiences, which provide ensembles for elementary schools in a highly interactive setting.

Several civic orchestras, including UMKC Civic Orchestra, Northland Symphony, Southtown Symphony, and the Medical Arts Symphony, provide playing opportunities for those who are not full-time professional musicians. The Medical Arts Symphony was started by the many doctors and health professionals at the K.U. Med Center who missed music as an avocation.

The Kansas City dance world is hard to assess because the demand is increasing so rapidly, especially for modern dance. The Kansas City Ballet is a devoted group with an annual Nutcracker Ballet as well as a spring concert. The artistic adviser is a typically dramatic Russian dancer with her hair in a chignon, Tatiana Dokoudovska.

The most unusual dance organization in Kansas City is centered around Strawberry Hill in Kansas City, Kansas. The Tamburitzans perform authentic Croatian, Yugoslavian, and Russian folk dances. The best time to see them in their native peasant costumes with their mandolin-like instruments is at a church dinner at St. John the Baptist Church, 708 North Fourth Street. It's also a great way to enjoy Croatian home cooking.

Speaking of home cooking—it's important to realize that cooking is an art too. Often we forget to give it the proper credit, perhaps because it is the only art form which deals with the senses of smell and taste. Yet, cooking is unique in that it also involves the three other senses. Visually it means creating a sculpture using only edible materials; touchwise, it means creating pleasing textures for the tongue. And the element of sound is essential too. Every good cook needs the emotional feedback of smacking lips and scraping of plates as an inspiration for creating something else. So, cooking is an art form, which might be classified as a folk art—a reflector of an ethnic culture and the artistic by-product of a day-to-day necessity.

Kansas City has many "living museums" where one can appreciate the art of cooking. Restaurants in Kansas City feature many foreign specialties, as well as American cooking. Calvin Trillin, the food freak of *The New Yorker* magazine, seems to have dedicated his life to heralding Kansas City restaurants. Following the lead of the Chamber of Commerce Prime Time campaign which dubbed us "Kansas City—one of the few liveable cities left," Trillin now describes his home town as "Kansas City—one of the few edible cities left."

But here we want to focus on a native artistic genius who created food *worthy* of serving in a restaurant. Kansas City's Beethoven of barbecue was Henry Perry. In the 1920's and '30's, he developed a recipe for hot smoked barbecue which has marked him as an artist and statesman for two reasons.

First of all, Henry Perry wasn't stingy with his genius. Unlike Stradivarius, who took his violin varnish recipe with him to his grave, Perry shared his barbecue sauce recipe with his co-workers. Without boss Perry, there would be no Arthur Bryant's, Gates and Sons, or Sherman's Better Barbecue for people to enjoy today. Perry must have sensed that his barbecue was a "now" art form, which wouldn't improve if saved for two hundred years.

But the second hallmark of Henry Perry's genius was in civil rights. His barbecue recipe, as refined further by Arthur Bryant, Ollie Gates, and Sherman Thompson, has done more to bring blacks and whites together than the 1954 Supreme Court decision in Brown vs. Topeka Board of Education.

Every day at noon, hundreds of whites pour into the black ghetto area of Kansas City to eat barbecue. Lines of white business executives queue up outside Arthur Byrant's at 1727 Brooklyn, to the point that some black people complain that the ghetto just isn't like the good old days. And that's why Henry Perry deserves to be in the hall of fame for arts for the people.

Another seldom recognized folk art form is crafts. Crafts are generally handmade items which are both utilitarian and an expression of the individual. People who work with such common materials as wood, fibers, and fabrics often cannot believe they are actually artists.

In Kansas City, crafts instruction is available at the Art Institute and through many "recreation" programs such as the Parks and Recreation Department and at the Jewish Community Center. The Johnson County Library has excellent programs. One of them, Ginny Graves' Discovery Series for preschoolers and their parents, is a national model.

Unfortunately, one particular population group, old people, is generally discriminated against in the arts. With limited incomes and transportation difficulties, they seldom benefit from ticket discounts or transportation assistance. Worse yet, they are subjected to very uncreative programming in the arts, especially regarding crafts, due to untrained staff.

More and more, people are becoming interested in making something individually with their hands, because it provides a creative way to be distinctive. This is particularly appealing to older people who have more leisure hours to invest, and who have a significant need to feel like they are still valuable human beings.

The problem is that old people are generally set to work stamping out ceramic ashtrays or stringing beads. Limited professional training for instructors and the commercial push of crafts supply companies combine to direct people into "supply gobbling" art forms. This is a problem facing not just Kansas City but all other cities with a sizable aging population. The shameful fact is that these people are being robbed of their time, money, and dignity when they are guided into making repetitive, uncreative, unmarketable knickknacks in the name of Art. It is condescending to believe old people are not capable of more creative work. It's no wonder that many of the old people who attend community centers prefer to play Bingo for four hours a day. After all, it's senseless to make ceramic ashtrays when all of your friends have given up smoking for their health.

Only when there is artistic expertise available will we be able to steer people into those art forms which utilize time and a creative use of available natural materials instead of tons of industrially produced craft supplies. For the aging population in Kansas City, this would be one small way to make Kansas City more liveable.

Since architecture is treated in another chapter, the last art form to be surveyed is creative writing. In Kansas City, some of the finest modern poetry is published in a periodical sponsored by UMKC, *New Letters*. Live poetry readings are sponsored by the Jewish Community Center, which annually sponsors the Devons Award for contemporary poetry. The Jewish Community Center has long been one of the innovators in the arts in Kansas City, and many of their programs are later adopted by other organizations here.

The Bookmark Press is a local publishing house in Johnson County for contemporary poets. They publish small twenty-page volumes which cost about the same as one large fuzzy greeting card but have infinitely better verse.

And the Mexican-American community has an excellent creative writing periodical, *Entrelíneas,* which is edited by Francisco Ruiz. Señor Ruiz, an instructor at Penn Valley Community College, explains the problem facing all writers—the difficulty of getting into print. "We publish periodically. That means whenever we have enough money to pay the printer."

Such is the plight of the arts in Kansas City, and elsewhere. Many Kansas Citians are just now discovering how the arts affect the quality of life here. Eventually it is hoped that Kansas City will have an arts tax to support a neighborhood arts program so it will be even easier for all to participate. After all, you gotta have art.

12. THE KANSAS CITY SPORTS FAN

For the sake of the immortal souls of thousands of Kansas Citians, one would pray that the Second Coming not take place back to back with a crucial football or baseball game.

There are towns that rather like their sports. There are cities that love their teams, and there are a few places where sports fever carries men and women almost to the brink of madness. Kansas City has gone beyond all that.

Many Kansas Citians are perplexed by world politics, content to let the Henry Kissingers of this world grope with foreign policy. They are happy enough if the governor and the Legislature will run the state government and not bother everyone else with it.

But when it comes to sports, that is too important a matter to be left to coaches and managers. Here all strategies must be reviewed, all personnel changes critiqued, for this is the stuff of which the ultimate joys and sorrows of a sports fan are made.

An election turnout can be seriously diminished by cold weather and snow, but not attendance at a crucial game in Arrowhead Stadium. In summer, people who would fear sunstroke in their own front yards will sit all afternoon on the sunny side of the stadium, so enraptured by the Royals that they are oblivious to solar waves. It may be difficult to get a Kansas Citian to come back downtown at night for a lecture, a play, or an opera, but thousands pour into the parking lots and go trudging toward the Kemper Arena on the nights when the Kings professional basketball team plays. No one can ever prove it, but there are probably more men who have provided for their season tickets for next year than have made their wills.

And all of this explains why Kansas City is one of only nine cities in the United States that can support four major league sports teams; the Kansas City Royals in baseball, the Chiefs in pro football, the Kings in basketball, and the Scouts in the National Hockey League.

The nonsports fan—the authors include themselves in that elite group of six or seven members—is a freak of the first rank in Kansas City. While it may be uninteresting to them to watch a game they are not playing, even nonsports fans can find considerable delight in watching the fans watching the game. Now that is a real sport.

How people come into the ball park and take their seats is certainly no indication of who the real screamers will be.

For instance, there was the nice middle-aged lady who came into Royals Stadium for virtually every home game, carefully choosing a seat in the same left-field bleachers where she always sat. Since 1969 she had been coming in, in this same unobtrusive way—and then erupting once the game began.

This lady had only one target: left-fielder Lou Pinella. For reasons no one including Pinella could guess, Pinella really ticked this lady off. Year in and year out she shouted abuse at Pinella, criticizing his every move, screaming and haranguing. Then when the game was over, she filed out like anybody else. Pinella moved to New York in 1974 to play for the Yankees, and the woman has never been seen since in Royals Stadium.

Every big league ball park has its share of leather-lunged screamers, but some of those in River City seem unique at that. There is the woman who sits directly behind home plate at almost every home game. She has a voice that would make Ethel Merman sound like whispering hope—and she uses it constantly to shout advice down onto the field. The trouble is that her advice is limited to exactly one refrain, namely "Get the lead out."

As sports-fan fans, the authors wonder where all of these screamers and abusers would be if they didn't have a baseball team to kick around.

While most of the hostilities are verbal, there have been exceptions to that rule, too. Bill Grigsby, a long-time sportscaster in Kansas City, remembers the night in 1959 when things became more overt.

"It had been a boring year for the fans," Grigsby remembers. "The team wasn't doing well. That was when the Athletics were here. And on this particular night, an umpire at home plate made a disputed call against Bud Daley of the A's, which sent the game into extra innings. It really got to one guy up in the stands, who began to ride the umpire unmercifully. You could hear his screams of protest all over the stadium.

"As the game entered the thirteenth inning, the irate fan could take no more. He made his way down through the stands and out onto the field. He walked across the field during play, tapped the umpire on the shoulder, and the umpire, apparently thinking it was one of the coaches wanting to talk with him stood up and took off his mask. Wham, this guy socked the umpire right in the teeth. The first- and third-base umpires ran to the rescue, and the guy whirled around and clobbered them, too.

"On came the police and security guards, who tried to wrestle the fan to the ground. The crowd was going wild, rooting for the fan. The management of the stadium began to fear a riot. Finally, they convinced this man to go peacefully. But he did so only after he was taken on a tour of the A's' dressing rooms.

"How did it finally turn out? Well the slugger went to court and was fined $300. As it turned out, baseball fans got together and paid his fine. Then they bought him a box seat for the rest of the season; they liked his style."

But in the love/hate relationships of the baseball fan, the home team has always received plenty of love. By any standards, the Kansas City fans proved their loyalty to the team and the game by giving strong support and healthy attendance figures even when Kansas City went for thirteen years without a baseball team that played .500 ball. The Royals have sharply upgraded that sorry showing.

As a result, the turnouts for Royals home games in 1974 totaled 1,173,292, making K.C. fifth in attendance in the American League. But even back in 1955, when the K.C. Athletics first came to town, the year's baseball crowd topped the million mark to register 1,393,054 fans attending games.

This is not too unusual when one considers that baseball fever was evident even in the early history of Kansas City. In 1866 the city's first baseball club, formed by D. S. Twitchell and named the Antelopes, met another team called the Hope Club on grounds between McGee and Oak streets, south of Fourteenth Street. The fledgling city team was soon challenged by the Frontier Club from Leavenworth. At that time there was strong competition between Kansas City and Leavenworth—and the Antelopes came through with a 47-to-27 win. The Antelopes counted as one of their most devoted fans Wild Bill Hickok.

Later, in 1886, Kansas City went major league. It had a team in the National League which played for a time in a ball park at Independence Avenue and Lydia. When major league ball returned in 1955, the city was in the American League, so it has the distinction of having been in both leagues.

The love of baseball helped to motivate the Jackson County voters who opted for the Harry S. Truman sports complex of which Royals Stadium is a part. When it opened on April 10, 1973, it was hailed locally as the best stadium in baseball, a title no one who has seen it since has seen fit to challenge.

For one thing Jackson County made deliberate choices that meant a few more bucks from the taxpayers (double the original estimates), but a great deal more comfort for the fans.

Royals Stadium has 40,613 seats—and it is so constructed as to put more than half of those seats between first and third bases. No other stadium can match that percentagewise. The cushioned seats are wider than in most stadiums, located on wider aisles, and have more leg room. There are no columns to obstruct the view. Parking is handy, circular ramps and escalators ease the fan up to a seat. These and other improvements have won high praise for the stadium, including that of American League president Lee McPhail, who said, "There is nothing like watching baseball in a park built for baseball, where you can be close to the field and the players."

In the 1973 All-Star game in Kansas City, network announcers lavished praise on Royals Stadium. And the local fans put on another show of devotion to the sport. When 15,000 reserved seats were opened up for mail requests, over 100,000 of these came in four days' time. And for the 5,000 remaining general admission seats sold at the stadium, fans lined up the night before. By morning when the ticket windows opened, 1,900 baseball lovers were in line and all the tickets were sold out in that one day.

The mere fact that a huge network audience was looking on did not deter the Kansas City fans from exercising their vindictiveness toward Charles O. Finley and the Oakland Athletics. Finley had committed the cardinal sin of moving his A's out of Kansas City. Local baseball addicts had to go a whole year without a fix because of that, until the arrival of the K.C. Royals on the big league scene. And so when player introductions were made at the All-Star game, every Oakland player was greeted with a fierce round of boos.

A few well-mannered folk wrote letters to the editor of the Kansas City *Star* deploring this. But these were considered to be folks who just didn't understand baseball.

The game's faithful also saw the hand of Divine Justice in the fact that Finley, with his winning team in 1973, still drew a third of a million fewer fans in Oakland than saw the Royals play in Kansas City.

Not only do the fans pour into Royals Stadium, but on at least one occasion a young newlywed husband went to the game quite against his will. He had just moved in with his new bride not far from the stadium. Headed for home, and being unfamiliar with the traffic pattern on a baseball night, the young husband found himself in the wrong lane of the freeway for one whose bride was waiting dinner. He was forced into the stadium turn, herded along by policemen who have no time for chitchat when the baseball hordes descend. He found himself entering a parking area, where there is no turning back, had to pay the buck-and-a-half parking fee and drive on in. When he had finally threaded his way through the parking maze, he at last made his way back to the highway and home. The Royals heard about it later and with apologies refunded his parking fee.

A real Royals fan would find it inexplicable that he didn't go ahead and stay for the game.

There are, after all, Royals fans from as far away as Windsor, Canada, who return repeatedly to watch the action when the K.C. team is in pennant contention. Or consider the lady in Wichita who comes with her thirteen-year-old son and friends to see the games. She buys four season tickets at $480 each, plus two parking stickers at $80 a piece. That makes her bill for being a Royals fan add up to $2,080.

All of that might make the Royals management swell with self-importance, but there is always someone to restore the balance. Take the fan in Taylor's Falls, Michigan, who wrote the Royals, "A church in my neighborhood has an annual carnival and I will be running one of the booths. I thought if you sent me some of your team stickers I could use them for boobie prizes."

The K.C. sports fan is no less devoted to professional football than to baseball. The magnificent Arrowhead Stadium—located just next to the Royals Stadium in the Truman Sports Complex—holds 78,000 people. And it generally is sold out. There are no less than 70,000 season ticket holders. The Chiefs have sold more season tickets than any other team in the National Football League, and they enjoy the best attendance record in the AFC Western Conference.

There is a special group of Chiefs' boosters known as the Red Coats, and to become a member one must sell a hundred or more season tickets. The Red Coats number five hundred at the present writing.

And they typify the undiluted passion for the Chiefs found in Kansas City fans. While that devotion may go over well in Kansas City—where the Chiefs rank just behind the flag, motherhood, and the Boy Scouts—it can constitute a flying pain for supporters of other teams.

On one occasion in Denver, a section of Red Coat Chiefs' rooters had been so vociferous in their support that when the Chiefs finally won the game the Denver fans got mad. They chased the Red Coats out of the stadium and onto their bus. The Kansas City group had to lock itself inside the bus for protection from the yowling, seething Denver fans outside.

Local pride gets all mixed up with football where the Chiefs are concerned. A slur upon the football team is a slur against the home town. And so the posthumous cult that has grown up around the late Green Bay coach, Vince Lombardi, will never be quite as strong in Kansas City as elsewhere. After all, when Green Bay beat the Chiefs in the first Super Bowl, Lombardi

came on network TV in the locker room afterward and as much
as said that beating the Chiefs was duck soup.

So when the Chiefs got their second shot at a Super Bowl appearance, in 1969 against the Minnesota Vikings, there was a
now-or-never quality about the whole thing. People had the feeling Kansas City was ready to close down as a city if it didn't win
that one.

The day that game was played down in New Orleans, the
whole city of Kansas City was—from the first moment of the
game—locked in a giant freeze frame. Traffic was nonexistent;
sidewalks were deserted; reality was suspended in favor of images on a picture tube. Next to sports, one of the things Kansas
Citians love most is their beautiful trees. But that day a lumber
hijacker could have stolen every tree off the parkways and no
one would have noticed.

And the Chiefs came through. Despite the adverse predictions
of oddsmakers, Kansas City trounced Minnesota 23 to 7.

When the Chiefs came home to Kansas City a day or so later,
it was January weather at its worst. Temperatures hovered
below the freezing mark and there was snow on the ground. But
despite all that inclemency, and despite the fact that the Chiefs'
plane was late getting in, 125,000 screaming fans filled the can-
yons of downtown. As the motorcade moved through the financial district along Tenth Street, ticker tape and reams of typing
paper joined and then dwarfed the snowstorm.

That day, if Coach Hank Stram had shot the mayor, the community would have found some way to excuse it with "boys will
be boys."

All of that may sound like enthusiasm beyond all proportion,
but somehow everyone sensed that the Chiefs' Super Bowl battle
that year was more than just a football game. Kansas City, after
years in the civic doldrums, was just beginning the painful process of reawakening and deciding to trade its smug comfort for a
new try at greatness. The great football victory served as a symbol—a rallying point for the pride of a city. Here was a city that
had been putting itself down for years, in every way. People who
couldn't think of anything else to say could always start a conversation by knocking Kansas City. After Super Bowl Day, 1969,

that kind of talk became less likely to start a conversation and more apt to start an argument.

So Kansas City owes something special to the Chiefs. Not that the Lamar Hunt team is exactly overlooked. Its players populate the airwaves as sportscasters on radio and TV—even though it is pretty hard sometimes for them to decide whether to cover a Chiefs story speaking in the third person, as a sportscaster normally would do, or to go into a first-person account of the game in a sort of self-interview on why "we" won or lost. In the news field, this kind of conflict of interest would be unthinkable. It would be like having the mayor cover what's going on in City Hall, in place of an objective professional reporter. But somehow in Kansas City the question about the self-reportage of Chiefs sportscasters never comes up.

Besides, the public is used to seeing Chiefs on the television tube selling everything from Standard Oil to Seitz luncheon ham. All kinds of commercial products become the Official This or That of the Kansas City Chiefs. They drink the official milk, eat the official meat. About all that has been lacking up to date is the designation of an official Kansas City Chiefs Toilet Seat.

But it is all built on the Official Kansas City Sports Fan whose love, support, and enthusiasm never die. The true sports fan will see a high degree of irrelevance in this observation, but one often wonders what great things might have been accomplished in the state of Missouri if the Legislature had a rooting section of citizens as devoted, or even just one-tenth as devoted, as the sports fans.

But sports go on as a number one interest of the Midwesterner. There might be communities in the United States that would question the priorities involved when an urban county spends its millions building separate stadiums for various sports. In addition to the Arrowhead Stadium for football and the Royals Stadium for baseball, the city of Kansas City also built a new arena in the west bottoms designed specifically for the annual American Royal Livestock and Horse Show and to house the National Hockey League franchise, and Kings basketball games.

Incidentally, even before the Scouts were to take to the ice, a year before in fact, the hockey tickets were selling nicely. It is interesting to note that 85 per cent of those holding tickets are from income brackets above the $10,000-a-year level. More than half of the ticket holders are women—and that, depending on one's philosophy, is in spite of, or because of, the violence of the sport.

If the reader is one of those who questions what kind of town it is that builds twin stadiums with public money, there is an interesting answer.

In 1967, when Jackson County decided to put a bond issue before the voters, it contained seven issues. Some were simple housekeeping projects, like new streets and sewers. Some had a primary goal of serving human needs, like construction of a new General Hospital. The feeling of the civic leaders and county officials who put the package together was that the twin stadiums would be the glamour issue which would bring out the voters and help the whole package, including General Hospital, to pass.

Interestingly enough, all seven bond issues gained the necessary two-thirds majority. But the advance psychologizing was completely backward. It was General Hospital that won the widest margin of voter approval of any of the issues. And the sports complex came in near the bottom of the bundle, with just a slight margin of victory.

By the way, the original plan for the twin stadiums, as everyone in Kansas City knows, called for the football and baseball stadiums to be served by an enormous tunnel-like roof. It would have run on a track and rolled over to cover whichever stadium needed it.

In all fiscal innocence, the county planners thought they could buy the two gigantic stadiums—plus the unheard-of rolling roof concept—for a tidy little $46 million. As it turned out the stadiums alone—with their parking lots and roads and highway network connecting—cost a great deal more. Optimists like to think the ultimate price tag ran around $60 to $70 million. Pessimists believe if you figured in everything it might total up about double the $46-million estimate.

And that is why the term "sports palaces" is sometimes used in the political rhetoric of Jackson County and probably will be for years to come. But since no one knows the price tag for the restoration of a city's pride—and Arrowhead and the Royals stadiums have made a big contribution there—Kansas Citians will never really know whether they got a bargain.

Now that Kansas City's triumvirate of new sports palaces is complete, the only chore left is to fill them with paying fans. And filled they are. While sports teams are naturally reluctant to release income figures, the Kansas City *Star* recently compiled close estimates of the total number of dollars spent for sports tickets in 1975 in Kansas City. And this is where the term "return on investment" should be engraved in gold on sweat socks, for the estimate was $12 million in one year. What price gory glory?

13. IT'S NOT NICE TO FOOL

ALLEN PEARSON

"A change in the weather," wrote Marcel Proust, "is enough to renew the world and ourselves." That is why it is so easy to feel renewed in Kansas City. The weather may be a great many things, but boring it is not.

To find another climate almost exactly like Kansas City's in a large city, one would have to travel to Suchow, China. Kansas City and Suchow have in common a very definite hot and cold season along with abundant precipitation (37 inches per year is the Kansas City average). Many other cities may have the hot and cold weather, but not the moisture, accounting for this area's nickname of "breadbasket of the world."

Kansas City's location (incidentally, the only major city within two hundred miles of both the geographic and population centers of the U.S.) assures the varied weather pattern. Its gentle hills and the absence of any natural obstructions mean a free sweep over the area by air currents from all directions. The frequent collisions over the area of warm moist air from the Gulf of Mexico with cold dry polar currents from the north produce rapid changes in weather.

Overall, it's a healthy and invigorating climate, with good measures of all four seasons. In a study of air quality in major U.S. cities, the Environmental Protection Agency ranked Kansas City in the top five big cities for clean air—sharing that distinction with Seattle, San Francisco, Dallas, and San Antonio.

The National Weather Service's official climate description

says the early spring brings frequent rapid weather fluctuations; summer features warm days and mild nights with moderate relative humidity, July being the warmest month. (The heat record for Kansas City, established in August 1936, was 113 degrees.) Fall, says the Weather Service, is normally mild, with the first cold outbreak generally followed by an "Indian summer" of sunny, dry days and cool nights. The first freeze usually hits about October 30. Winter is not severely cold, with January the chilliest month. (The all-time low was set in February 1899, 22 below zero.)

The official description also says the area has occasional periods of freezing precipitation, but these are rather infrequent. Heavy snows of more than ten inches are very rare. The measurable snows usually come from November through April.

And now for the bad news; for some reason the smallest bit of moisture on the pavement has a tendency to make Kansas City drivers go berserk. An evening traffic rush usually moves out of downtown with remarkable speed, thanks to the first-rate network of freeways. But when it rains, forget it. Something about the pitty pat of raindrops ignites a maniacal streak in a small proportion of drivers, who immediately go out and hit the nearest fender. Then everyone else jams up trying to get around the accident, and drivers count on an extra fifteen or thirty minutes in getting to their destinations.

Where the weather is changeable, it isn't always going to suit everyone. But it does offer some fine compensations. On a gusty day in dry weather when a minor dust storm occurs, nature still offers a sort of trade-out. At dusk on such a day, one can observe from any of Kansas City's many hills a sunset of screaming oranges and burning reds, sometimes mixed with a velvety lavender.

After an ice storm, a drive reveals long streets of pure silver trees and tree limbs . . . as if they had all been delicately shaped by some master glass blower. If there is sunshine, the trees will take on a diamond-like sparkle. Anyone who has ever seen this at dawn is not likely to forget it, and few cameras have ever done it justice.

The weather tends to be more on people's minds in Kansas City than in some other places. The moodiness of the climate is part of it. But it is also a city where many of the residents are only a generation or two removed from the farm.

And the farms are filled with gamblers who bet their money and their year's work against the weather, with odds so unpredictable that Jimmy the Greek would throw his hands up in despair. A beautiful field of wheat that is there tonight, standing like money waiting to go to the bank, can be obliterated totally by the following morning if hit by a powerful hailstorm. And that's just *one* of the weather-related hazards.

In addition, a substantial part of the city's economy is geared to the agricultural scene. When it has rained to the point of making everyone emotionally soggy, one can still hear one umbrella-toting business executive comment to another in a skyscraper elevator, "Well, it'll be good for the farmers." And they mean it.

Weather tends to be intensely personal in such a place. One of the authors, Walt Bodine, has been a television weatherman in Kansas City. Some people at the supermarket used to kid him when his forecasts went wrong, but there were a few folk who marched up to him with a crazy gleam in their eyes, and growled menacingly, "All right, guy, when are you gonna give us some decent weather?"

One forecaster said it bothered him that, when the weather on Sunday was poor, his minister would chide him from the pulpit. But the following Sunday, when the sunshine was golden, the minister would always express thanks to the Almighty for the beautiful day.

The time of greatest concern over weather is, of course, April and May, when tornado watches and warnings are inevitable; however, other seasons have other perils. Perhaps everyone has some fear fantasies here and there. A former Kansas City newsman, Bill Leeds, now of NBC News, used to stare moodily out of the TV station window and indulge his fantasy whenever it snowed.

Leeds mused, "What if the snow just keeps coming? There's no law saying it has to stop after one or two inches, or even one or two feet. What if it just keeps coming and covers up everything, cars, houses, buildings, right up to the roof tops and beyond. That could be the end of the world, right?" It was only a slight consolation to note that the record snowfall for Kansas

City was twenty-five inches in twenty-four hours, in March of 1912.

A second, very reassuring consolation where weather is concerned is that Kansas City is headquarters for the National Severe Storms Forecast Center. It is the only such civilian organization in the world, with the goal of giving people a few hours of advance notice of tornadoes. Before the Storm Center was established, the U.S. averaged one death for each of the approximately seven hundred tornadoes occurring every year. Now the total is only 112 deaths per year.

The chief of the Severe Storms Forecast Center is Allen Pearson, who came to Kansas City to establish this model program via Hawaii and Washington, D.C. Pearson headed the Emergency Warning Branch in the nation's capital during 1964. As Pearson tells it, 1964 was an extremely active year for hurricanes and tornadoes, and he made a good reputation quickly.

Pearson claims that the State of Kansas takes a bum rap when it comes to weather. For instance, it is the South, rather than the Midwest, which is hardest hit by tornadoes. The "Dixie tornado alley" runs from Louisiana through central Mississippi and Alabama to northern Georgia. Pearson wishes he could "repot" Dorothy, Toto, and the Tin Woodsman into Mississippi, which actually has more tornadoes than Kansas. One fearful newcomer to the Kansas City area phoned Pearson for special instructions on building her house, because she'd just seen a rerun of *The Wizard of Oz*.

Yes, there is a tornado season, but in Kansas City at least when the tornado warning sirens blow, several times every spring, there is matter-of-fact compliance by most of the population. If anything, Kansas Citians, padding down to their basement refuges, are a little like the Londoners of World War II; they don't scream and panic. Still, they do take the precaution of "going below."

The tornado-sophisticated population, in many cases, has a nice little corner of the basement furnished with comfortable old furniture, a transistor radio to keep track of what's going on, a flashlight in case of power failures—and, for the really cautious, a pickax, in the event there would be some sort of debris to be dug out of.

That's one nice thing about tornadoes. They keep the family together.

The truth is that for all the threats of twisters, the average person in a lifetime of routinely taking refuge has never seen a tornado. In fact, Allen Pearson has never seen a tornado. It's the old story all over about how a gynecologist doesn't have to have had a baby to know how to deliver one. Or, as Pearson explained, the Pope is known as the Holy Father, but he's never had any children.

Severe storm forecasting becomes a sensitive issue with those people who resent having activities delayed or missing part of a TV show. As one news director wryly put it, "Some people are very unhappy when a tornado threat blows over and they discover they haven't been killed." This attitude tends to grow as the memory of the last really bad tornado dims.

For metropolitan Kansas City it has been a long time. The last tornado touchdown of significance was April 19, 1966, when a twister smashed homes over an area of a few blocks near the Katherine Carter School in suburban Johnson County. The same year a deadly twister ripped through the heart of Topeka leaving a trail of death and destruction.

But for the Kansas City metropolitan area, the last major twister took place at dusk on May 20, 1957.

A fresh look at that disaster is in order. First, to remind people of just what they are dealing with when they are menaced by a tornado. And second, for some reassurance, because mistakes were made in the emergency systems then. Many of those errors have been corrected today, giving the public a better chance if it should happen again.

On that day Walt Bodine was preparing the evening news for WDAF-TV, when H. L. Jacobsen called. As chief forecaster for the Kansas City weather service, Jake asked the station to keep close to the teletypes the next few hours. There was a nasty-looking storm in Wichita to the southwest, headed straight for Kansas City.

It was the beginning of the end of life for fifty persons, and the harbinger of painful injury for hundreds of others.

At 6:12 P.M., all doubt vanished, as the storm became a tornado. A fourteen-year-old Kansas boy watched from the truck in which he was riding near Garnett, Kansas, as a huge greenish gray cloud churned right behind them. Darrell Haines described the "little tentacles coming down out of the cloud. They'd join two or three together, and then five or ten would come down at one time. They kept joining and a funnel was taking shape, getting bigger and bigger. When it touched down, the debris started to fly. And then you couldn't see anything because it got too dusty."

As Darrell Haines stared at the spectacle before him, radar officials watched electronically. As the phones began ringing, reporting a tornado on the ground near Ottawa, the radar scope picked up the familiar hook pattern.

At 6:58 P.M., WDAF aired a bulletin stating, "The weather bureau warns that the chance of a tornado in the metropolitan Kansas City area now exists." At the weather bureau, telephones were bringing in reports from nearby towns. At 7:37, the tornado crossed the state line, striking Martin City, Missouri.

Time had all but run out for the pretty Jackson County suburb of Ruskin Heights.

And then it hit. What it is like at the moment a tornado is striking is best told by eyewitnesses.

Bernard Ernest: "I was looking toward the storm and I saw what at first looked like pieces of cardboard in the air. But I knew they were larger than that. Because what I was seeing was about a half mile away."

Mrs. Clyde Officer: "It was about 7:45. I heard this rumbling, but I thought it was jets. But then I thought otherwise. I decided to put my two boys under a heavy bed to protect them. I was starting to go do that, but I didn't get that far. It blew the windows in, and then the frames, and then the walls. I saw everything flying around and falling on top of the boys and myself. My one concern was to try to get my children out."

Mrs. Jim Byrnes: "I was standing in the doorway. I saw this big black cloud. The man across the street ran over and got me and took me to their basement. The cloud looked like black foam. Just as we got in the basement it blew in all the windows and blew the house completely away. When we came back up, there were fires where gas had escaped and started burning. And everything was gone. I looked and all the other houses were gone too. And I didn't even care. I knew I was just lucky to be standing there."

Combing the tornado area the next day, survivors had that sentiment many times. One man said it with a sign in the yard on his property which read: "THE HOUSE IS GONE—BUT WE ARE HERE. THANK GOD."

As the tornado ripped across Ruskin Heights, smashing homes and schools and the shopping center, the weathermen who had been under such pressure during the warning period were left behind. Weather forecaster Joe Audsley said, "We didn't know for a while whether it had hit . . . or whether our warnings had gotten through . . . or if anyone was hurt. It was a strange feeling. I felt responsible. I thought, My God what have I done . . . Has it been enough?"

At the newsroom on WDAF-TV's Signal Hill, it was a scene of partially controlled pandemonium. Phones were ringing off the walls. Teletype bulletin bells were clanging. Police monitor loudspeakers were blaring; people were running back and forth to the TV and radio studios with bulletins. For almost an hour the newsroom staff was patching together reports, first from one location, then another, trying to learn the dimensions of the hit.

And there were terrible haunted voices on the telephones. Bill Leeds answered one and a man said, "Help us find our baby. She's just three months old, blond, blue eyed. She was swept out of her mother's arms as she stood on the front porch. Help us." Leeds broadcast the description, but as is often the case in a disaster, he never learned the outcome.

Willard Strauss had left his home in Ruskin Heights to go talk to a man in another part of the same development. Strauss said, "I heard this loud noise. The man I was visiting said it was a train going by. But it was too loud for that. I went to the door and looked and—there it was. The funnel was about two blocks wide and it was moving along fast. I jumped into my car and started back to my house on Bristol. As I got close I saw a house or two with a window blown out. And then I saw several with heavier damage. As I got to 108th Street, houses were scattered around on the street. I looked up toward my house on 108th Circle, and nothing was standing. I left my car and ran toward the area shouting my wife's name. In a minute I heard her voice. She cried, 'Over here.' Fortunately she was down in a basement with fifteen other people, all unhurt."

Part of the terror of the moment was the darkness. The tornado came just as night was about to fall. The dark cloud blotted out the light—and when it had passed, night came quickly. With all electrical lines down, the suburb of Ruskin Heights was not only stricken, it was blind.

For all practical purposes, it was also dumb, because phone lines had also gone down in the high winds.

A Kansas City Youth Bureau police lieutenant, Doral Dennison, was caught in the storm while at his home in Ruskin Heights. Digging out from his basement, Dennison used his car's two-way radio to contact police headquarters, which reached Police Chief Bernard C. Brannon. Had Brannon been a letter-of-the-law stickler, he could have vetoed involvement in the disaster since it was outside the city limits and outside his jurisdiction. In a heart-warming triumph of common sense over legality, Brannon sent word to his commander in the field, then Major Don Bishop. As relayed by the dispatcher, the message was, "Cruiser 5 [Bishop]? Cruiser 1 [Brannon] requests that you check with the law enforcement officials in Raytown and Ruskin Heights. If any help is needed, number 1 states we'll send in whatever is necessary."

Before the night was out, Chief Brannon had sent in almost everything he had. The story is that at the height of the rescue operation, only five patrol cars were left on duty in all of Kansas City.

At the time there was no other hospital on the south side except Menorah Medical Center. Ambulances, trucks, station wagons, and private cars poured into Menorah.

The acting administrator at the time, Leon Felson, was called down to the emergency room from a meeting in the library.

Mr. Felson told of the appalling sight that greeted him. "A little after 8 P.M., I received a call from the switchboard stating that there were some cars blocking the entrance to the emergency room. I tossed my raincoat on and went down there. But as I entered the lobby to the emergency room, there suddenly appeared . . . fifteen children lying on the floor. One, in the corner, was dead. In the emergency room itself, a child was on the floor, and one of the pediatricians was over him giving artificial resuscitation."

Felson continued, "I went into the dining room and started moving tables. Within fifteen minutes, the room was a sea of plasma bottles being held in the air. More and more patients arrived, and were carried into the dining room. Mattresses from a nearby storeroom were tossed on the floor. I was at a loss to understand how such a thing could suddenly be happening with no advance notification. After a few chaotic moments, the medical staff worked out a system similar to the clearing aid stations of the Army. They catalogued the arriving patients, trying to quickly survey their injuries and tag them, so they would be routed to proper stations. Some needed immediate emergency care, some called for X-rays, blood, some needed only minor care. The system took hold.

"Drug houses sent over supplies; blood donors poured in; an auditorium above the emergency room was pressed into service as was the dining room. In a very brief period, enough surgeons had arrived that eight operating procedures were going on in eight different operating rooms. And still more patients were arriving and we were running out of beds again," Felson said. "Then suddenly beds began to flow off the elevators. I found out later that some of the patients upstairs who were less sick had gotten out of their beds and wheeled them down to the elevator to help out."

As Felson learned later, to his amazement, the whole tide of human misery had settled on his one hospital. Others were ready to receive patients but nobody came. It is natural to go to the nearest hospital and that is what everybody did.

Today a better system exists. In an emergency, doctors and nurses would take up positions outside the emergency room of the nearest hospital, seeing that only those in most urgent need entered there, and sending others along to various designated hospitals where they could receive much quicker attention.

Ruskin Heights was an exceptionally brutal storm. It traveled an extraordinary distance, seventy-one miles on the ground. And when it came into Ruskin Heights, it took the deadliest form of all, that of a grounder. This means that the cloud from which it stemmed was a very low cloud. When the cloud is high, the tornado vortex extending from it thins as it reaches down—making a relatively small damage area at ground level. But when the cloud is low, the vortex is wide and vicious. This one could gobble up two city blocks at a time.

The other great danger with a low cloud is that a funnel can be only a block or two away and still not be visible. This means it can burst suddenly upon the scene. And that is why the practice of going outside to watch for a tornado is a dangerously silly one.

Ruskin Heights had the bad luck to be struck by one of the worst storms in twenty years. How bad? Allen Pearson says that of fifteen thousand known tornadoes in the past twenty years, Ruskin Heights would be among the top ten.

From all of his experience, Pearson claims his life ambition is to find a way to tell in advance the little storms from the big ones. But for now, people must live with the warning systems available—and they are not bad. The trick is to not be too fearful. Pearson advises that in an average year in America more persons die playing Russian roulette than are killed by tornadoes. At the other extreme, one must not be too fatalistic. There are those who say they just ignore warnings. One woman said, "If one has my name on it, I'll know it." Tornadoes don't have anyone's name on them; they are simply addressed, "To whom it may concern."

Like everything else, it comes back to common sense. And those who lived through the Ruskin Heights disaster can tell people that a few minutes spent in one's basement, now and then, is really not the worst thing that can happen.

14. MASTHEADS AND AIRWAVES

There is a faint ring of truth to the story of the Chicago *Tribune* reporter who visited Kansas City on assignment. Picking up the morning paper, the Kansas City *Times*, she flipped through it looking for the missing front section which would contain the breezy, abrasive stories of the day, the hard-hitting exposés with the gut-punching headlines. Failing to find it, she glanced more carefully, only to discover that what she thought was Section B was actually the front page. To her, this was the major distinction between the "Windy City" and "River City."

Kansas City does not have too many aggressive reporters. It has almost the complete opposite of too many. Here and there sporadic outbreaks of investigative reporting do take place. But not many. It is a city that believes things work out and that too much fuss about anything usually does as much harm as good.

This shakes up the newcomer. News in many cities is a highly competitive affair. Muckraking is not out of vogue in many places. For those accustomed to a shrill kind of journalism, the Kansas City kind seems hopelessly bland. Yet it is more subtle than bland. Very often the news is there, the social critique, the individual roasting, but it is done with a twist and often by between-the-lines inference.

One newcomer has described the manner of local aggressiveness in media as comparable to that of the rabbit and the wolf in a hot Oklahoma summer. The rabbit was trying to evade the wolf to save his life and the wolf was miserably hungry after several foodless days. So the chase was on, yet they were both walking.

The people of Kansas City have a love-hate relationship with the city's one major daily newspaper, the Kansas City *Star* (and its morning paper, the *Times*). The surest way to get into an argument would be to announce, in a room containing more than two persons, that you think the *Star* is about as nearly perfect as a newspaper can be. In fact, one doesn't have to go that far. Just say you really like the *Star* and respect its editorial opinions.

The Kansas City *Star* today works very hard to be with it. The *Star* is into prison reform, local government, campaign reform—all the things one would expect a good newspaper to be for. Yet there seems to be something almost timid about the *Star* of the seventies.

Indeed, newspapers in general have been sensitized. They bear no trace of their past arrogances, of which the *Star* had many, especially during the Colonel Nelson era. Today, newspapers are aware of the McLuhan concept which implies the printed page is washed up. The authors would certainly hope not. With all respect to today's TV and radio news, they are still pretty superficial reports compared with the detail available and the interpretive service provided by any good newspaper.

But the *Star* does seem to lurch about a bit in quest of its modern day soul. For example, all of a sudden, the paper seemed to come upon the women's movement. For a time a second-page box began to appear which local wags came to call "bright sayings of women." There seemed to be a standing order to deliver women's angle stories on that page every day.

Or again, one had the feeling that someone somewhere got the idea that one can identify with the reader through a common interest, the weather. So the *Star* and *Times* are long on photos of pretty girls with umbrellas up in the rain, the glowering dark clouds hovering over the west side skyline, or women struggling against the wind gusts on Petticoat Lane to keep their skirts from blowing up into their faces. Another familiar shot shows cars askew at crazy angles on a snowy or icy hill—a picture seemingly taken afresh each winter when one could assume that a stock photograph would pass muster. But that would be shabby journalism, and the *Star* is not shabby. Gung-ho about this, cautious about that, yes, but never shabby.

There are those who lament the present state of the *Star*, claiming it is no match for its former glory days. These critics usually say the *Star* has not been the same since the editing days of Roy Roberts, the charismatic reporter and White House king-maker.

A first day cub reporter at the *Star* once asked the city editor, "Who was that fat man with a cigar who offered me a lick on his ice cream cone?"

"My dear," the editor replied, "that was Roy Roberts!"

Mr. Roberts was a remarkable man, all right, and it fooled no one when he tried to tell *Time* magazine in a cover story about him that he was "just a big fat country boy." He was a big man, fat was the word, and he could be an impressive sight when angry. His face would flush a deep red and his cigar would jut upward from the pressure of clamped teeth.

So powerful was Roberts that naturally a whole legion of lackeys grew up around him. One of the comic relief items in any hard day's newspapering was when Roy stood up and prepared to leave work. A clutch of underlings rushed for the coat rack, fighting to hold the great man's coat for him. One likes to think Roberts never noticed who the daily winners were, but, lordly person that he was, took it for granted that someone would always be there.

His political intuitions were great. He was a middle road Republican who early on sensed the potential of Dwight Eisenhower as a Presidential candidate. Over the years the *Star*, while declaring itself an independent paper, virtually always endorsed a Republican for President. But Barry Goldwater was too much for Roy Roberts. In one of the last conversations Walt Bodine had with him, Roberts asserted, "Well I'll tell you something that will surprise you. The *Star* is about to endorse Lyndon Johnson in the Presidential race. Lyndon is all right. I've known him for years. I don't suppose there's a man in the Congress who knows Washington better, all the way around."

Then Roberts leaned forward and in a more confidential manner said, "The only thing about Lyndon is his ego. He's got to watch that. He can be mighty stubborn when he thinks his word is on the line. But if he doesn't let that get in his way, he ought to be a damned good President for the next four years."

Mr. Roberts said something else that day. He began to reflect on the man he had urged to run for the Presidency, and who is the last President to have served two complete terms, Dwight Eisenhower. "Ike was a good President," Roy Roberts said, "but he was awfully damned dumb about politics. I thought maybe he would catch on after a while, but he never did."

Before the advent of computers, an election night in any newspaper office was a fairly busy and exciting occasion. But at the *Star* the air almost bristled as couriers hastened from the tabulating tables and teletypes to bring results to the editors. When significant items came in, there was a competition to see who could get the news over to Roberts the fastest. That is, until the returns would start to go sour. If a race Roy Roberts wanted very much to win was being lost, the eagerness to carry the news over to the big desk by the south wall diminished to the vanishing point. Fearing the adage of "kill the messenger," lowly copyboys were dispatched to deliver the bad tidings.

But for all the Roberts years at the *Star*, having a seat in the city room was to have a front row seat to the political spectacles of the times. No candidate for high office came to town without stopping by Eighteenth and Grand to talk politics with Roy Roberts, and thus, left-handedly seek his approval. If a Lyndon Johnson or a Harry Truman dropped in to visit, it was all out in plain sight. The *Star* very democratically has never believed in private offices in the newsroom, and Roy's desk was just one in a hundred on the cavernous second floor. A lip reader could have had a heyday.

On occasions when privacy was called for, or when Roy and the other editors wanted to interrogate some pol at length, they had to step into the board of directors' room just behind Roy's chair. That room and the restrooms were the only private places on the unpartitioned newsroom floor.

It is true that the *Star* of today sometimes seems a little pale compared to the Roberts era. But that was also a time when the newspaper hit a high water mark of insensitivity. In its power, it could afford a police reporter who had a finger in the numbers racket. It could abide a man on the city desk running a horse book on the side. (This operation terminated abruptly just before Senator Kefauver's crime investigating committee moved into town.) It was also a time when *Star* reporters were so badly paid that virtually every one of them had to moonlight in one way or another on the side—many making a second and sometimes larger income doing public relations work or writing. The more ethically minded journalists tried to do it some other way, as stringers for *Life, Time, Newsweek*, or even *True Detective*.

These are things that do not happen today; the professional standards are much higher. And reporters are given their heads as they never were in the old days, to really call their stories as they see them. The *Star* today is also a great deal more liberal. It was so imbued with racism during that so called "great era" that a murder in a black neighborhood was considered no news at all; rather, it was dismissed as "just another nigger shooting." No young black woman, however distinguished her family, had her picture in the society section when her engagement was announced, and obituaries were strictly for the white and dead.

Yet today the *Star* still takes the rap for days gone by, especially from the liberals. If nothing else, they can charge that the *Star*'s coverage of a story in Uganda was not as detailed as that in the New York *Times*. Recently a *Star* reporter challenged a very vocal critic, inquiring, "Is it true you said this town needs more than one good newspaper?" "That's not exactly what I said," the critic replied. "I'll settle for just one good one. Do you know of any?" At the same time, criticism of the *Star* is leveled by the conservatives in Kansas City, the old line Republican stalwarts, who are equally certain that the *Star* has become pinko or at least loco.

Over the years the daily newspaper story in Kansas City has been a familiar one. It has been enacted according to the same script played in many another city. There was a gradual thinning out of competitive papers until, by the 1930's, there were only two. Even then it wasn't much of a slugging match. The *Journal Post* was more like a punching bag receiving the thrusts of the Kansas City *Star*.

Like all Americans, the people of Kansas City have never quite known for sure what they wanted from their politicians or their newspapers. Given that condition, it is a little less disquieting to observe how the people of that period voted Democratic, adored Roosevelt, and at the same time put their real journalistic faith in a paper they said they hated, the rock-ribbed Republican *Star*, while the *Journal* slowly dwindled and finally died of malnutrition.

It is an article of faith with some old line *Star* haters that the *Journal* was done in, first and foremost, by highhanded and unethical advertising practices of the *Star*. But the truth remains that if *Star* business executives of another day could coerce advertisers by threatening not to sell them ads in the *Star* if they bought ads in the *Journal*, the *Journal* had to be already in decline for this to happen. It had to be a measurably weaker medium of reaching people, or some business executives would have told the *Star* where to head in. And the reason the *Star* had such clout is that Mr. and Mrs. Kansas City cussed the *Star*, and its morning version, the *Times*, daily—and carefully resubscribed to be sure they never missed an issue. The *Star* may once have had a certain arrogance, all right—something that was to cost it dearly in later years, when the federal government stepped in with an antitrust suit that cost the paper its radio and TV stations. But the *Star*'s power ultimately derived from the loyalty of its readers.

As the battle went into its closing stages, the *Star* became more and more sensitive about who was advertising in the *Journal* and who was not. One large department store hung on till the end with the *Journal*, Peck's Department Store. When the *Journal* folded, Peck's was punished severely by the *Star* for its independence. It made up some of its penance by buying enormous numbers of radio spots on the *Star*'s radio station. The slogan "It's Peck's for lamps, it's Peck's for lampshades" became a household phrase. It attested to the power of radio, but to those who knew more about the situation it was ultimately a testimonial to the tremendous power of the Kansas City *Star*.

There is, of course, more than one daily paper in the metropolitan area. It is true there is but one general daily newspaper in Kansas City, Missouri—but Independence sports a lively daily of its own, the *Examiner*. Considering the complaints sometimes voiced about the *Star* as the "only daily paper in a city this size," it is remarkable—or maybe it isn't—that so few of the Kansas City complainants bother to round out their local reading diet with a subscription to the *Examiner*. According to managing editor Frank Haight, "The *Examiner* talks to every segment of the population: businessmen, housewives and kids." Its influence reaches beyond Independence to Oak Grove, Grain Valley, Lee's Summit and Raytown. Jack Anderson's column is carried in the *Examiner*, but the most read column is "Dear Abby," followed by "Letters to the Editor."

Still another daily exists in Kansas City, Kansas, called the *Kansan*. It is a bland publication which keeps its business skirts nice and clean and takes some pains not to make waves in its coverage and comment. In fact, the *Kansan* is so cautious that it remained for the *Star* to investigate alleged corruption in Kansas City, Kansas, by tavern and massage parlors in the early seventies.

It is a little-known scientific fact that twice a week thirteen *Suns* appear in Johnson County, Kansas. The thirteen *Sun* newspapers—twelve in Johnson County plus the South Kansas City *Sun*—are published by Stan and Shirley Rose and their son Steve from the modern press facilities at I-435 and Metcalf in Overland Park.

Associate publisher Steve Rose describes the readership as white, affluent, aged thirty to fifty, with two or three kids. The couple is highly educated with youngish taste and a strong interest in local government and the Shawnee Mission School District.

The *Sun* newspapers' combined circulation of 75,000 copies makes it second only to the Kansas City *Star/Times* in the greater Kansas City area. Within Johnson County, more people read the *Sun* than the *Star*, according to the *Sun*'s surveys.

Rose thinks of his papers as "more than a bulletin board. These are not just folksy little newspapers, but the main reading diet for much of Overland Park—the fourth largest city in Kansas."

The format of the editorial page is like a home-grown tear sheet of a "CBS Sixty Minutes" script—salty reflections, serious editorials, Art Buchwald humor, and public opinions winding up with a mailbag of quotes.

Better financed than most small independent presses, Sun Publications boasts ten full-time reporters. Much of their time is spent covering the small "good news" items of civic achievements and school events which get squeezed out of the city-wide newspapers.

Squire Publications is headed by an outspoken individualist, Tom Leathers. In addition to the neighborhood weekly newspapers, which are known as the *Village Squire*, the *Country Squire*, etc., Leathers publishes a monthly magazine, the *Town Squire*. The *Squire* magazine includes several local columnists including Walt Bodine. The *Squire* is also noted for its articles ranking any group or chain of competing people or items—from restaurants to volunteers to doughnuts to radio stations. As a local athletic booster, Leathers has a penchant for picking number one in any field. A great number of his in-depth interviews involve local sports personalities.

In addition to dailies, there are perhaps fifty local periodical magazines and newspapers; a small sampling is described herein. The best-looking one, the recently defunct *Kansas City Magazine*, was published by the Chamber of Commerce and modeled after the publications of cities like San Francisco, Washington, D.C., and Atlanta. Filling the void of a slick collectible account of Kansas City stories are the *City Window* and the aforementioned *Town Squire*. The *City Window* uniquely doubles as a theater bill for two dinner theaters—Tiffany's Attic and Waldo Astoria. The sharp entrepreneurs who direct this operation are Dennis Hennessy and Dick Carrothers. It is to their credit to have acknowledged that any article worth reading after dessert is worth reading by nontheatergoers after breakfast the next day.

One of the largest weekly newspaper chains is Townsend Communications, north of the river, whose new 24,000-square-foot building houses one of the most modern suburban newspaper plants in the U.S., complete with a computerized bookkeeping department. Townsend's editor, Marvin Tomme, puts out a string of papers: the *Press-Dispatch, Platte-Dispatch, Gladstone-Dispatch,* the *Liberty Tribune,* and others. Tomme describes his north of the river readership as forty-two years of age making $14,000 per year. His reader tends to be a Democrat, but hung loose enough in 1972 to vote for Republican Governor Christopher Bond and ex-President Nixon. One of Marvin

Tomme's most notable achievements is the long-term improvement in relations between people north and south of the river. In this sense, Tomme has built more bridges than the Missouri Highway Commission.

One of the best old-style newspaper offices is at the *East Side News,* located for the most part in two rooms with old wooden floors supporting two huge old bookcases, which contain every issue since the 1930's. It's a friendly and casual place, where the coffeepot is always on. Editor Helen Mullen thinks of her readership as predominantly white with strong components of Italian and Mexican-American families and some blacks. Social and economic background is diverse, obviously, but Mrs. Mullen adds, "They are down to earth, intensely loyal to their own people, and I love their attitude which rejects charity and says 'We take care of our own.'" The *East Side News* relishes bulletin board items which "fill people's needs—to stimulate human understanding and compassion." Homey columns include "Happy Birthday" and "Mr. Quizzer," which answers questions on health, history, even spelling. It is designed to help the reader who didn't finish high school. Helen Mullen typifies the spirit of the "other papers'" journalists when she spots an injustice and writes about it. "Sometimes I get cussed out, and sometimes I get complimented. Either way, I don't care as long as I've said what I want to say."

Perhaps the staunchest individual editor locally is Jim Wolfe, formerly of the Raytown *News,* now part of Townsend Communications. He also publishes a monthly political critique, *Wolfe's Version.* Wolfe is host to an annual black-eyed pea party on New Year's Day at his suburban Jackson County home which sports the Confederate flag. Wolfe describes his readership as "middle to upper middle class people who are more interested in local news of their area—their taxes and kids' education—than in the city, which is just something to complain about." Politically, Wolfe believes his paper should not tell people who to vote for in local elections, although the Raytown *News* makes endorsements in state elections. Wolfe terms himself a Jeffersonian who believes the news should stay close to the people so they can make sensible political decisions.

The K.C. *Call,* the old established paper in the black community, has its greatest impact with middle-aged black readers, though it is trying to strengthen its position with youth. Editor Lucille Bluford notes an increase also in white readership, and also comments that her black readership is much more spread out today—as far south as 103rd Street. The most individual quirk about the *Call* is the combined obituary/classified section, "In Memoriam." In it, readers pay tribute to deceased relatives with display type ads, often including a rhyming verse of grief. The front page used to feature "Murder Box," giving the box score on homicides so far this year compared to last year. Recently it has been replaced with expanded FBI statistics reflecting numbers of crimes against persons and crimes against property. A black history column receives prominent attention. Lucille Bluford describes the paper's goal, "to depict the achievements of the black community, eliminate prejudice, and inspire and encourage young people."

Virtually the antithesis in readership is reached by the society magazine the *Independent*, which is best described as name dropping in Gothic script. The *Independent* chronicles upper-middle-class club and cultural events. Its sports section eschews football and baseball for tennis and golf tournaments. A typical "news" item begins "I wonder . . ." and hints at some bit of local gossip such as "Who was that blonde with the young Harvard lawyer?" The single similarity to the K.C. *Call* is the special attention given to obituaries, believing that their treatment is more personal than that of the *Star's*. One regular feature, "After Hours," was described by staffer Pat Patzer as an informal interview with an executive about what he does in his leisure time. When asked about interviewing career women, Ms. Patzer explained, "There aren't many women with interesting positions who our readers want to read about." The *Independent* is basically the *Star's* society section, replete with photos, printed on slick paper.

The *Northeast News* stresses a working-class audience. Editor Tom Patton likes to focus on children's activities because "they just love to see their name in the paper." Virtually all the small papers carry community bulletin board notices for women's groups and civic clubs. *Northeast News* relies heavily on what readers mail in. It has no reporters in the field. However, it car-

ries columns by noted residents which reflect the very independent kind of Democratic political faith which prevails in that
neighborhood. Editor Patton was particularly pleased with Magis-
trate Judge Harry Davis's column which was a blistering attack
on the establishment of a gay church congregation. "That," said
Judge Davis, "was sacrilege." To satisfy the area's strong political interest, the *Northeast News* features a column by the area's
county legislator, Virgil Troutwine. There is also an E.S.P. column by Carol Dawn. Tom Patton sees his paper as an institution
of special benefit to older retired people. He tends to look with
doubt on such "new" types as environmentalists and, in his
words, "I still like the people who get a lump in their throat
when the flag goes by."

For electronic news in Kansas City, the rule of thumb is that
the best and most complete local and world news in the morning
is found on the radio; the television is devoted to cartoons and
national news/entertainment shows with only brief local reports
if any. In the evening, the reverse is true. Radio newsrooms send
their heavyweights home by noon and it's strictly second team in
the afternoon. Some stations give up entirely at night, or revert
only to network news. At midday, the noon reports tend to be
thin on both TV and radio, with only one television station
spending any time on local affairs; radio stations, for the most
part, settle for five-minute quickies. Only recently has an all-
news station, KUDL, appeared in the market.

Eight A.M. is the big news time in the morning on radio. On
TV in the P.M. the reports begin as early as 5:00. The three big
network newscasts go back to back at 5:30, and the major early
evening local newscasts come at 6:00 P.M. Time zones force Kansas City into this very early coverage of the national news at
5:30. Perhaps one reason why many Midwesterners are little
concerned with national news is they seldom see any. Even with
speedy freeways the average 9:00 to 5:00 or 5:30 worker has to
really hustle in order to catch Walter Cronkite. A great portion
of Kansas City's business community gets home in time to hear
"And that's the way it is . . ." and then on to the local 6:00 P.M.
news.

At night, the big news hour is 10:00 P.M., again an hour earlier
than the East Coast. In this case, the advantage seems to be the

Midwest's. As one Kansas Citian-moved-east describes it, "If I wait up until 11:15 P.M. to hear the weather report, it's so nearly the next day that the forecast is virtually a live broadcast." Kansas Citians view their weather forecast as wishful thinking. The weather is so unpredictable that predictions are basically a humor forum for "good old boys" making jokes about cold fronts.

The *Star* has one thing going for it that is missing in the electronic media—home ownership. Of the AM radio stations, only two or three are home owned. One of those is KBEA, a news and good music station, owned by Robert Ingram. All three of the TV majors are owned out of the city. The UHF channels do have community roots, KBMA-Channel 41, is owned by BMA Insurance Company. And KCPT-Channel 19, the public television station, has general public support from memberships and a yearly auction, plus some school and foundation money.

The radio stations number some old-timers in their midst. Nationally, radio stations have call letters beginning with "W" east of the Mississippi River and with "K" west of it. A "W" call letter in the west indicates an old station that went on the air before that K and W dividing line began, decades ago. Kansas City has two such stations; WHB and WDAF.

WHB in recent years has been owned by Storz Broadcasting Company, and was one of the very first "top forty" music stations in the U.S. It is still one of the great success stories in local radio both in audience and revenues.

The radio stations are interesting for their ownership and also for their emphasis on music with talk and news programming a distant second. A few stations make a reasonable effort at news, concentrating, as mentioned, on the morning reports. No one is doing a great job in news at present. Kansas City is a ripe market for a talk radio station, programming eighteen to twenty-four hours of talk and news daily.

A quick survey of the radio picture would include WDAF (610), which is owned by Taft Broadcasting, and plays middle rock to rock news format; then WHB (710) with contemporary and rock, plus a heavy Sunday talk schedule of six to seven hours, including Walt Bodine's Town Hall show, 8 P.M. to midnight; KCMO (810) is owned by Meredith Publishing and plays

mod country music. KCMO has one of the better news operations. KPRS (103.3 FM) has the major share of the black audience. KPRS broadcasts the National Black Network News and
plays "soul" music. Finally, there is KMBZ (980), which is
known best for its "fun and games" from 6:00 A.M. to 10:00 A.M.
with the resident crazy disc jockey, Mike Murphy. KMBZ plays
middle-of-the-road music, is conservative editorially, has above
average news in the morning largely because of excellent helicopter traffic reports, and airs Royals baseball games and Kings
basketball games. KMBZ is owned by Bonneville, Inc., the business arm of the Mormon Church of Salt Lake City.

The three major television channels are NBC (WDAF-TV4),
CBS (KCMO-TV5), and ABC (KMBC-TV9). In addition, the
local viewer has access in many areas to the output of KQTV-
TV2 in St. Joseph, Missouri (great movies on this channel). On
the UHF, there are KBMA-TV41 and KCPT-Channel 19. Johnson County cablevision is available for those whose houses are
specially wired. This station does a small amount of local
programming.

As mentioned, Channel 41 is owned by BMA Insurance, which
provided it with the $4 million in working capital necessary to
make a television station eventually self-sustaining. This was the
crucial difference between Channel 41, run by station manager
Bob Wormington, and the now defunct Channel 50, which was a
short-lived venture in the late sixties run by Bob's twin brother,
Bill.

The Kansas City area is the largest market in the country
(soon to be in the top twenty) with only one independent
noneducational television station. The brothers Wormington,
now modishly fifty years old, both work for Channel 41.

Their boss, BMA Insurance chairman of the board Bill Grant,
is a Kansas Citian with a sheep ranch in Australia. In a unique
version of the delayed boomerang effect, Grant once sold KBMA
to his Aussie next door neighbor rancher, Benno Schmidt. Two
years later, when finances were better, Grant bought it back.

According to Peter Brake, a talented young sales executive at
KBMA, the FCC permits greater flexibility of programming for
non-network stations. Therefore, Channel 41 is able to strongly
reflect local viewing interests. "And that," says Brake, "is what

makes television the last great market on earth." For instance, KBMA programs a great deal of local sports, including Royals baseball and Scouts hockey games. And when the networks were heavily programming several violent crime series, KBMA instead appealed to the Kansas City audience which was more interested in good old family entertainment. Kansas Citians preferred reruns of "Leave It to Beaver," "Star Trek," and the "Andy Griffith Show."

The big three network stations all have their moments of daring to say what ought to be said in their judgment. Almost always their reward for this sort of virtuous risk-taking is a thorough tongue lashing from those who object, and a resounding silence from what the novice might assume would be a grateful community.

WDAF-TV had the temerity to suggest to sports-crazed Kansas City that the Kansas City Chiefs' organization was not perfect, and in fact profited quite handsomely from the interest and generosity of local fans. The station's news director at that time, Don Keough, as well as the station manager and the sponsor caught large quantities of hell, not only from some spokesmen for the Chiefs, but also from many of the very same fans the TV special had referred to. The city does owe something to Lamar Hunt for bringing his team to Kansas City when he could have moved it to Indianapolis, Toledo, or, if he had wished it, Slippery Rock. At the same time, the local fans lived up fully to expected ticket purchase support. The media turned out and did handsprings, almost entirely for free, so there is some question whether Mr. Hunt, a likable enough fellow, should be enshrined as untouchable for all time to come.

If anyone was going to do a critique on the role of the Chiefs in Kansas City, it had to be Channel 4, WDAF. KCMO-TV5's sister radio station carried the Chiefs' games, while KMBC-TV9 had as its sportscaster no less than Chiefs' quarterback Len Dawson.

But every station takes its turn in the critics' circle. KCMO-TV5 had the courage to leap hard on a miserably operated home for retarded children—despite the fact that the home's board of directors contained many society and blue chip business names. The simple fact was that the board members had goofed it. They had failed to keep track of what was going on. TV5 cameraman Charles Campbell—in one area of the home while on a feature story—ventured into other parts. He found and filmed unbelievable squalor from faulty plumbing to inadequate heating of the home, complicated by poor or nonexistent supervision. The pressure began when word got out that the story would be told on Channel 5. It mounted to a fury when the film was aired. Very Important People called to express their indignation, not at the dreadful mistreatment of children but at Channel 5's audacity in bringing embarrassment to the home and its board.

Finally, Channel 9 (KMBC-TV) and its news chief, Claude Dorsey, take on some local sacred cows with a regular feature known as "TV-9 Probe." There has been, at times, substantial backlash. One series which criticized probation and parole decisions made by local circuit court judges brought down the combined wrath of the Lawyers' Association and the Bar Association.

Local news organizations have produced their share of big names. Walter Cronkite, Hughes Rudd, John Cameron Swayze all worked in Kansas City, and the most distinguished of all— Ernest Hemingway—was once the *Star*'s General Hospital reporter. Hemingway credited the late managing editor C. G. Wellington with teaching him how to write.

To sum it up, Kansas City is not a red hot town journalistically, with massive grudge fights between rival media dynasties. Competition is at a level that seems almost leisurely. But the media does keep in perspective what news people in more sensational environments do not. It recognizes that there are more days when the news comes in ripples than in tidal waves.

Get used to that, master the art of reading between the lines, give some encouragement to the broadcasters and writers who provide good news, talk shows and specials, and a viewer or reader will get along all right. And for those who find they just have to feel a tidal wave, they can always hop down to the neighborhood market and swoop up the *National Enquirer*.

15. CITY OF SCIENCE AND MEDICINE

It is a fortunate city that has one first-rate university medical
center. Kansas City has two.

When the University of Kansas City emerged into the Missouri state system, the Kansas City campus was selected to high-
light two areas, the health sciences and the arts, as two examples
of "the programs unique to a metropolitan campus." Regarding
the health sciences, greater Kansas City has been twice blessed,
for it is the home of two outstanding medical schools.

Kansas City, Kansas (Wyandotte County), is the location of
the Kansas University Medical Center. Eleven of the twelve
"colleges or schools" of K.U. are located thirty miles to the west,
in the quaint burg of Lawrence, but the prestigious medical
school remains in Kansas City. The obvious reason, of course, is
that metropolitan Kansas City has more sick people with a
greater variety of ailments than Lawrence can produce in a decade. Such are the advantages of urban living!

"K.U. Med Center" is principally a teaching hospital, to train
medical professionals. In that effort, patient care, research, and
community service are also essential.

The Med Center has special facilities for children's rehabil-
itation, mental retardation, toxicology, and disease control. The
History of Medicine collection is one of the finest in the country.
In fact, when it was determined that Linda Hall Library in Kansas City, Missouri, would specialize in science and technology,
medicine was one area of exception. The Clendening Library at

the K.U. Med Center participates in a co-operative program with Linda Hall Library to avoid costly duplication of efforts.

During the late 1970's, the size of the K.U. Med Center will double, providing for an eight-hundred bed clinical capacity and teaching facilities for classes of two hundred students per year.

Across the state line in Missouri, the medical school is a very recent development—the first class started in 1971. Here the medical school may be understood as a solution to other problems and a shining excuse to do things in a first-class manner.

For seventy years, old Kansas City General Hospital has been the receiving room for the indigent and eventual harbor of many people who have gone broke staying at the expensive local private hospitals. It is no one's first choice, and everyone's last resort.

The change in name from University of Kansas City to the University of Missouri at Kansas City was the catalyst to tackle several problems with one solution, that of developing Hospital Hill. The second-class charity hospital will now become a first-class university teaching hospital, under the moniker of Kansas City's greatest statesman.

Hospital Hill, a five-square-block area just east of Crown Center, will contain the Truman Medical Center (which replaces General Hospital); UMKC Medical and Dental Schools; Children's Mercy Hospital; Western Missouri Mental Health Center; Health Resources Institute, and the Public Health Department clinics.

Teamwork is in evidence in both the hospital and the medical school. In the hospital, visiting outpatients get an appointment instead of a four-hour wait in line. Each patient is assigned to a small, decentralized clinic staffed by a health care docent team. On repeat visits, the patient has an appointment with the same team. This continuity of care is very rare in public hospitals, and it aims at returning to the "family physician" tradition. While medicine will probably never get back to house calls, at least now it's possible to see the same doctor more than once.

Inpatients at the new Truman Medical Center will no longer be quartered in large open wards, but in very spacious semiprivate rooms. These large rooms will permit visits by an entire health care team: physician, nurse, clinical pharmacist, unit manager, medical record technician, medical social worker, and dietician plus students from the adjoining UMKC Medical School who are training with the team leader, or docent.

This docent program is an outstanding feature of the new medical school, which incorporates several novel approaches to medical education.

Beginning in 1971, the Kansas City Medical School was the first to introduce clinical work so early in the student's experience. The six-year program is designed for the high school graduate and combines a baccalaureate with a medical degree.

One can imagine the thrill of seeing real patients on the first day of medical school, at age eighteen. Of course, students are not attending patients then, but they do make rounds with a docent team.

The first two years are crammed full of liberal arts studies; from there, the final four years are strictly medical. Year Three brings a permanent assignment to a docent who is a physician-clinician-adviser for twelve students per year, three from each medical school class. These twelve students meet daily with their docent to discuss what they have learned from their rounds with the health care team. Instead of traditional medical school departments, the students learn from their on-site experience treating real patients and working with the team of health professionals.

Some will surely criticize the six-year program for its diminution of the humanities and the lack of emphasis on the basic sciences. But for those of us who, due to the tremendous physician shortage, are tired of waiting six to twelve months for a routine appointment, this program offers a realistic, practical solution.

One of the more remarkable aspects of the entire Hospital Hill dream is the co-operation which made it possible. What other major urban area can claim that county money is building a hospital on city property; that state money is building the school which will work with the hospital; and that federal money is matching all of it?

Just as health care in Kansas City is a success through co-operation, the same is true for the research industry. As mentioned earlier, Linda Hall Library of science and technology works with the Clendening Library; additionally, they maintain the needs of UMKC, Midwest Research Institute, and such firms as Chemagro and Spencer Laboratory. In fact, Chemagro attributes its move to Kansas City to the presence of Linda Hall Library.

Oddly enough, those who use the collection the most never enter its doors, but send for information for all fifty states and twenty-six foreign countries. The collection contains over thirty thousand journals in thirty-five languages. Only 27 per cent are in English; 24 per cent are in Russian. Japanese is also very popular. In fact, the journals account for 70 per cent of all the library's holdings, because in the sciences current research is generally published in this form rather than in books.

Fortunately, the language barrier is not quite as bad as it could be, since the greater part of most texts is in the universal language of numbers. A Kansas City scientist can get the gist of a Japanese study, although a few nuances might be missed.

An interesting dilemma regarding building expansion faces the trustees of Linda Hall Library, the second largest scientific library in the U.S. While the collection is constantly multiplying, so too is the technology of storing and retrieving all that information. Should new storage space be built, or will we soon have everything so miniaturized that a little closet will do?

Whatever the answer, the Kansas City research industry people agree that Kansas City needs to maintain and expand the collection at Linda Hall.

The cornerstone of this industry is the Midwest Research Institute, Kansas City's version of the Rand Corporation . . . a think tank for scientific, technological, and economic problems. MRI's work product is studies—on environment, impact, solid waste, leisure and recreation, air, water, metal, urban and regional studies. MRI is the Dear Abby of industry.

Some of MRI's projects have included analyzing anticancer drugs before human use, analyzing why new products fail, and evaluating the Kansas City Police Department's patrol operations. One study of crime and the aging victim went so far as to interview parolees who had earlier victimized older people. The result was "professional" criminal advice on countermeasures.

Some of the smaller fishes in the research pond have focused on problem-solving social research.

The Institute for Community Studies reviews public institutions, evaluating many projects supported by tax dollars. These include Model Cities, General Hospital, schools, and the federal government's Administration on Aging. Sometimes ICS studies the success of a program, as with Model Cities projects. In other cases, they study things before they happen, such as the potential success of communal living for the aging.

A second small research organization unique in the U.S. is ERDF—Environmental Research and Development Foundation. They study how people react to the architecture around them.

Did you ever stop to think that the color of your walls might be making you antsy? ERDF did a study on just that, to find out how people look at paintings. ERDF president, Dr. Robert Bechtel, invented the world's first hodometer, and hid it under the rug in an art gallery. The hodometer counted the number of people stopping in front of each painting, and how long each one stayed in each spot. When the walls of the gallery were painted a different color, it affected the traffic pattern; with the new shade, people moved around much more frequently and spent less time in the room. Little did those people know that their feet were being wiretapped.

The final arena of research depends ironically on chance, the phenomenon of Presidential births, and the accompaniment of historic libraries in their honor.

Just when it seemed like the thirteen colonies had a strange hold on U. S. Presidents, the Midwest appeared as the new cradle of leadership. Kansas City is within two hundred miles of three Presidential libraries, with a presumable fourth in the planning. And all four Presidents are from different states ringing Kansas City.

Herbert Hoover's birthplace was West Branch, Iowa; Harry Truman came from Lamar, Missouri; and Dwight Eisenhower was raised in Abilene, Kansas. The next anticipated library might be in Omaha, Nebraska, birthplace of Gerald Ford.

16. FROM KEYSTONE TO CORNERSTONE

Kansas City's police force has come a long way, to the point where it has now produced the cornerstone of American justice, the director of the FBI. Such was not always the case. If there is one thing the long-time citizen of Kansas City has had from the police department, it is variety. "The worst cops since Keystone," was one description. "America's best police department," was another of the more recent ones.

During the days of machine rule in Kansas City, the quality of law enforcement and the morale of what few honest cops there were declined in tandem. It was during that period that *Time* magazine termed the K.C. force "the worst cops since Keystone."

The description was not without a strong basis in fact. In those days the police force and even the cars they drove in their official rounds were motley affairs. At one time seventy-five ex-cons were on the police force. Here and there the occupants of a patrol car made two livings at once, one as policeman, the other as bootlegger—with the illegal goodies being dispensed from the trunk of the prowl car to the thirsty man with a few bucks to spend. Later in the evening, the same cops might bust their former patron for drunkenness.

It was a day very short on scientific crime detection. A rubber hose used on a hapless suspect in an investigation room at head-quarters usually produced a solution to most crimes where a solution was necessary. It was a time of payoffs, when the houses of prostitution outnumbered hamburger stands, and when illegal gambling and liquor operations of all kinds were going on everywhere. People assumed that every cop either knew all this was happening right under his nose or was so incompetent as to be committing a fraud by accepting a salary for doing police work. And when a cop knows that a law is being broken openly and he does not effect an arrest, one has to assume that something has come between him and his duty, something green that folds and fits in the pocket.

The worst police abuses occurred in Kansas City during so-called home rule, meaning during a time when the local city hall government had total jurisdiction over the police. Understandably enough, it has given home rule a bad name. And in Missouri the alternative—which finally came to pass in Kansas City—is a state-rule setup in which the police department functions under a nonpartisan board of police commissioners, the commissioners being appointed by the governor. That system prevails today. Occasional suggestions are made about a return to home rule, but old fears die slowly and the return is not likely to come quickly. The state operation of the police department is jurisdictionally awkward. For example, the Board of Police Commissioners, acting for the state, requests an appropriate amount from the city's budget to operate the police department. State statute requires the city to budget a minimum of 20 per cent to the police department, though the current police budget is nearly 25 per cent of the city's funds.

Personalities have always been prominent in the Kansas City police force, ever since the days when Wyatt Earp instructed the police in shooting techniques. Little is known about Kansas City's first city marshal, Tillman Crabtree, except that he initiated the first community relations program. While he was on duty on rainy days, his job responsibilities included carrying young belles across muddy streets. Today, Tillman Crabtree is buried in Union Cemetery, probably with mud on his boots.

Tillman Crabtree's fellow companion in Union Cemetery is George Caleb Bingham, artist during the Civil War, and a sworn foe of "vice and dissipation." Bingham was the first president of the Board of Police Commissioners, in 1874. At his death in 1879, he startled everyone by leaving instructions that he be buried facing south. The common custom was to bury the dead facing

who must put up with the real problems and with more frequ
exposure to danger too, goes along unsung. He watches the F.
on television and he shifts in his chair and thinks the G-men are
overrated and underworked.

And so Clarence Kelley's coming to the post of Kansas City
police chief was not welcomed with cheers from the lads in the
brown uniforms and gold badges. Kelley had to prove himself,
and there were plenty who thought that would be impossible for
him to do.

Worse yet, he even looked like an FBI man. There is some
special zing in the crease of a G-man's pants. Every man shaves,
but somehow the FBI men always look closer shaved and
cleaner. And Kelley had all of that, along with something else.
He looked for all the world, when viewed in profile, like an improved Dick Tracy.

Clarence Kelley joined the Kansas City police force as its chief
in 1961, when he retired as a special agent of the Federal Bureau
of Investigation after twenty years of service.

The FBI is an interesting agency. Together with the Central
Intelligence Agency, it is one of the few areas of governmental
employment where one need not be a United States citizen.
Even more amazing, in a society which constantly practices discrimination against the aging, is that eleven years after his retirement from the FBI, Clarence Kelley was rehired as its director.
Who ever would have guessed that J. Edgar Hoover was a social
reformer?

Kathy Tretbar, a free-lance writer, interviewed Chief Kelley in
1974 about his Kansas City experiences. "How do you train to
become head of the FBI?" she asked.

Kelley burst out laughing as he contemplated the variety of
possible answers. He offered good-naturedly, "Well, I'll tell you:
I suppose the better response would be that you live a good
clean life! Actually, while I was in the FBI before, I did go
through administrative training and various offices. But the finest
thing that prepared me for this post was the twelve years in
Kansas City as chief of police. The problems encountered there
are very similar to those here, only multiplied. But that administrative training has already proven most helpful."

Kathy then asked, "Does Clarence Kelley, the director, think

east, with the belief that they wouldn't see God if their back
were turned. Bingham believed the Lord would find him no mat
ter which way he was facing.

Policemen aren't normally the most popular folks in town.
And that goes for police chiefs, too. Now and then a police chief
emerges with some political appeal as with Rizzo of Philadelphia, who was able to ride a law-and-order tide right into the
mayor's chair, but with no special honor to Philadelphia.

In Kansas City, a chief named Clarence M. Kelley—without a
moment's pandering to anyone's racism, and without appealing
directly for anyone's support—could have been elected to just
about any office he chose.

Who was Clarence Kelley? He was about the coolest and most
solid operator many in the local media have ever seen behind a
badge of any kind.

People get used to the shortcomings of cops, even top officers,
after a while. Some of them murder the king's English, others
have only a lip service relationship with the Bill of Rights and in
practice consider it an insane bother foisted on them by the
ACLU and other such groups.

Kansas City has seen police chiefs who played politics to a
dangerous degree, or who seemed to close their eyes to all kinds
of Mafia misdeeds. Kansas City has even seen one who would
get up to give his chair to an underworld lord.

But all in all people tend to overlook it. And for several
reasons. One is that there has never been a top cop who didn't
have some defect, and as long as he holds it down to only one
glaring feature he can be considered run of the mill. For another
thing, police chiefs—like the cop on the beat—catch a lot of hell
and only a fraction of it deservedly. In short, the reporter recognizes that the chief and his co-workers have rotten jobs, thank-
less jobs, often politically sensitive and racially insensitive jobs.
And that is just the way it is.

And then along came Kelley. Before his official installation he
was subject to the usual round of police rumors and o
prejustified bitching. Kelley was coming out of the FBI and it i
no secret that many city cops all over the country view the FB
with very mixed feelings. They are considered to have garnere
for themselves all the good press, while the poor cop on the bea

much the same as Clarence Kelley the agent or the chief? Do you find yourself changing along the way?"

Kelley replied, "I think my philosophy regarding law enforcement is very much the same. People in the United States are entitled to honest law enforcement. That shouldn't ever change. What I hope to bring, in a very visible manner, is our determination to be responsive to public needs."

During Kelley's tenure as police chief, the Kansas City Police Department advanced on two seemingly divergent fronts—the use of machines and the importance of human relations.

The computer was introduced to crime in 1968 in Kansas City. Today it's hard to imagine *not* having access to one. But prior to 1939, clerks were still writing down every offender's name on long yellow sheets of paper; in that year, the department progressed to giving each offender a page of his or her own. So 1968 was quite a stride.

The Kansas City police computer operation has been described as the best in the United States. While the computer here was first used in organizing data on individual criminal records, its use has now expanded to assist in police management. Kelley's successor in Kansas City, Joseph McNamara, explains, "If a computer can predict a national election with less than one per cent of the vote in, and determine the almost infinite number of calculations needed for space flight, it's time we used it to deploy our limited police resources to fight crime."

A visiting ABC news team at one point had access to the police computer through the city prosecutor's office. It was possible to look up any city resident's police record by typing that person's name on the computer keyboard. Punching out the name of Mayor Charles B. Wheeler, Jr., they learned that his dog, McDermott Wheeler, had been arrested once for running loose in the neighborhood. As an ex officio member of the Board of Police Commissioners, the mayor was quick to acknowledge his criminal record to the television cameras. Soon afterward, the police department tightened the security measures to limit public access to criminal records only to personnel with special clearance.

A second innovation during Kelley's tenure here was the development of a helicopter patrol program in 1969. There are now six whirlybirds hovering over Kansas City; these, too, are sometimes dispatched through computers.

Kansas City has been described as being in the midst of a forest. The use of helicopters has helped considerably in providing surveillance of those areas of the city with lots of trees and fences and other barriers to the patrol car. It is both spooky and reassuring to be strolling late at night through a park, and suddenly be bathed in a yellow spotlight amid the chugging whir of a propeller.

The other great advancements made during Kelley's reign dealt with people. A regional officer training center was established, and a strong community relations program was begun. The focus began to shift back to the neighborhoods; several beat patrolmen were assigned in special neighborhoods to become more familiar with the citizens.

This has been good for the neighborhoods, where people have developed a first-name relationship with one or two individual officers. People learn not to jump whenever they see an officer, that perhaps it's just a friendly call. Too often the traffic ticket mentality of "What have I done now?" makes us fear the police, whether it be fear for our pocketbook due to a fine or guilt feelings about all those times we didn't get caught.

Just as important, the "neighborhood beat" concept has been a way for the police officer to deal more frequently with normal, law-abiding folks. Too often, the police only participate in volatile situations where they are in contact with criminals. If this isn't balanced occasionally, pretty soon everyone seems to be bad.

It is important for anyone serving the public to feel that his or her efforts are welcome and appreciated; thank you is not a frequent response to an arrest. It all gets back to that admonition we heard as children, "The police are your friends." Finally the public can believe it.

In another chapter, the authors mentioned the use of the Metro Squad, a regional pool of investigators assigned to any participating community requesting assistance with a particular vicious or unsolved crime. Clarence Kelley formed the first Metro Squad in the mid-1960's, and the program has since expanded to other areas in the U.S.

The complete lab facilities of the Regional Center for Criminal Justice are available to the several hundred volunteer Metro Squad members. Special areas of expertise include scuba divers and pilots—talents not every small police force would have.

A classic Metro Squad case illustrates the potential. A Kelley protégé, Norman A. Caron, who is now a lieutenant colonel with the Kansas City Police Department, worked on that case in the spring of 1964, just after the formation of the Metro Squad.

As Colonel Caron tells it, a mother and daughter had been murdered in Platte County. The daughter was found on a lover's lane which was a dead-end dirt road. At the time, Platte County had but one sheriff and three deputies. The sheriff called in the Metro Squad. Sixty-one investigators worked ten days, logging interviews with three thousand people.

Metro Squad members, on their hands and knees, crawled the entire length of the lover's lane and the fields on either side. They picked up every piece of foreign matter, labeled it, and sent it to the lab.

Norman Caron recalls an officer picking up a beer can that had dew on it from the night before. The officer thought it didn't have any prints on it, but Caron told him to send it anyway. The lab discovered four good latent prints on that can.

Five months later, a suspect was linked to the area. He admitted he had been "possum huntin'" in that vicinity, but denied being near the lover's lane. However, his prints matched those on the beer can, and the case was solved.

In 1972, J. Edgar Hoover died at the age of seventy-seven. Clarence Kelley was called out of retirement from the FBI to assume the directorship. The Kansas City Board of Police Commissioners faced a real dilemma in selecting Kelley's successor.

They chose a tough little Irish cop with ten years' experience in Harlem and a Ph.D. from the John F. Kennedy School of Government. He is believed to be the only police chief in the country with a doctoral degree from Harvard.

In his first month in Kansas City, Chief Joseph D. McNamara was faced with a community-police crisis involving the shooting by an officer of an unarmed black youth caught stealing watches from a vacant house. McNamara was forced to deal with revised gun policy immediately, and a subsequent poor police morale.

Rather than enjoying a slow transition into his new position, Mc-Namara weathered a real baptism by fire.

In a demonstration of compassion for the youth's family, McNamara attended the funeral. In a city rocked by riots after Martin Luther King's assassination in 1968, McNamara's presence was an assurance to the black community that people needn't choose up sides, for we are all living in this community together.

17. COMICS, CHARACTERS,

AND OTHER FRIENDS

Years ago the stand-up comics all worked Kansas City, in the great days of the vaudeville circuits. Today the comedy outlets for a straight comedian are pretty well limited to Mother's Place south of the Plaza and during the summer Starlight Theatre.

But once upon a time, the stages included the RKO Missouri at Fourteenth and Main (now a multicinema house) and the Pantages, later the Tower Theater on Twelfth Street. Red Skelton, Burns and Allen, Olson and Johnson, and all the rest paraded across these stages—as they did in every city.

Walt Bodine always wondered how, in the first show of their first day in town, comedians knew what the kiddable things were in any given city. But somehow they knew. They could localize a joke and tie in the names of the fat cats of the town, the business institutions, and the local scapegoats.

"I ate in Wolferman's cafeteria today. They had a sign to watch my hat and coat so while I was watching my hat and coat somebody stole my lunch." That was a typical line. Or, "I was talking to a guy in front of the Muehlebach Hotel today. That's where I stay, in front of the Muehlebach Hotel."

But most of all they liked to zero in on the scapegoat. Olathe always caught it.

"Olathe is a Coke machine with a mayor," the late Jack Carson quipped. "I was over in Kansas City, Kansas, today," Ben Bernie commented with a flick of his cigar. "I like the way that town is laid out; I wonder how long it's been dead." It was an automatic laugh like a joke about Brooklyn delivered at the Old Palace in New York. Walt remembers another line George Burns used. "Kansas City, Kansas, is the only town in the world that has streetcars that don't know where the hell they are going."

The local sense of humor would respond to anybody who was really funny. Red Skelton was a runaway favorite with local audiences.

But it didn't always work. Not for the show biz slickie who decided that he didn't have to use his best stuff because this was the sticks. After he hurled a few retreaded zingers over the footlights the audience would fix him with a glassy stare. Kansas City audiences always thought it was dishonest to laugh if something wasn't funny, so they didn't. Some monumental egos melted away completely in five minutes time on the stage of the Tower Theater. And when the sharpie came out for his next turn, he'd be using every good line in his repertoire.

It was at the old Playboy Club on the top of the Hotel Continental where black comedian Flip Wilson formally introduced his Geraldine routine. That is, after a run-out audition in Kansas City business places to see if "she" was believable. Flip was working at the time (1967) at the Playboy Club with vocalist-comedian Nick Noble. One afternoon, Flip dressed in drag and asked Nick to escort him around town for a trial shopping trip. They posed as a married couple and drove to a Johnson County real estate firm in search of housing. If it's possible, Johnson County was even more conservative than it is today; a mixed-marriage couple, especially a crazy one like Nick and "Geraldine," was met with less than open arms by the real estate agents. Later, Flip and Nick clowned their way through Macy's downtown store. They were convinced by the sideward glances and mutterings of customers that the routine was believable. That night, Geraldine formally flounced onto the Kansas City Playboy Club stage.

But professional comics are not the only ones in Kansas City. Most of the truly humorous people here make a living doing something else, and happen to be incidentally funny folks. One great sideline for comics is street engineer. And those comics who don't qualify for that often become drivers on Kansas City streets.

The Kansas City sense of humor takes many forms. For example, there is the company that does typesetting and has printed on the sides of all its trucks GNITTESEPYT NRETSEW. Or there is the venetian shade firm that for years printed on the sides of its trucks, "A blind man drives this truck."

Transportation has always been a problem for Kansas Citians. At one time there were only two cars owned by individuals in Kansas City. And sure enough, at Third and Grand avenues, they collided.

The same automotive sense of humor carries over to the designing of freeways. There are little jokes every now and then. There is the high speed Sixth Street expressway whose exits go right across entrance ramps. If getting up your adrenalin regularly is healthy, the people who use the Sixth Street often should be a hardy lot.

Or there is the famous vanishing fast inside lane on the Southeast Freeway. Whirling along at fifty-five, the newcomer is incredulous to see a sign that announces that the lane ends in a few hundred feet. It does, all right. A thrilling experience for the survivors, and let's not discuss the others in a happy chapter like this.

The other funny thing about local drivers is what happens to them when two or more drops of rain hit the pavement. For some the sight of moisture on the pavement is the sign in Kansas City that we are all ready to play the traffic jam game.

Traffic is exciting enough that radio stations employ one helicopter and several airplanes to broadcast reports on it during rush hours each day. When a really good jam gets going on some interchange down below, there is the making of an aerial traffic jam overhead as they all move in to cover it. One trusts that they have worked out a system.

But whatever happens in Kansas City, Missouri, in the way of snarls and tie-ups, there is nothing to match a good rousing snowstorm. That would be anything from about two inches up. The fender benders are so numerous that the police attend only those where injuries have occurred. Any decent snowstorm will make weeks of work for insurance adjusters and body repair people.

When a major snowstorm occurs, say six inches or more, the

game plan is switched. Then the game is let's-all-sit-in-long lines-and-just-give-up. We have had bumper-to-bumper stoppages that lasted for hours. On occasion entire busloads of passengers have gotten off A.T.A. busses to visit some nearby tavern, rejoining the bus an hour later at the other end of the block. Walt Bodine once observed two drivers, one headed north and one south and stalled in traffic side by side, playing a quick game of gin. Local disc jockeys keep husbands out of the doghouse by announcing the tie-up frequently and advising the women at home to keep the dinner simmering. The smarter downtown types grab up hotel rooms and let it all go by. And a spirit of revelry takes over.

Except for weather, anything else that happens to tie up traffic is easily explained in Kansas City, Missouri. It is simple. Some Kansan up there has messed things up again. It is an article of deepest faith with most Missourians that most Kansans become incompetent the moment they slip behind the wheel of a car. Of all who hold this belief none cherish it more warmly than cab-drivers. If a cabbie comes through a jam and finds that the car that caused it has a Missouri license, the cabbie doesn't waver for a minute. It simply means that some Kansan has stolen a Missouri car.

Kansas Citians have a practical Midwestern sense of invention regarding problem-solving. In the days of the horse and buggy, a horse once collapsed and died in the middle of Bellefontaine Street. In those days, not every street corner had a sign naming the intersection. As the investigating police officer began to file his report, he was stymied at the spelling of Bellefontaine, especially because in Kansas City the pronunciation is Anglicized in a perverse way. Seeing no street sign, the officer decided not to puzzle over the mysteries of the French language; instead he hitched the dead horse's carcass to his wagon, dragged it one block west to Agnes Street, and completed his report.

Another avenue for Kansas City humor is politics. Politics in Kansas City has always been sufficiently active to produce volumes of stories. In fact, someone once labeled Jackson County politics as "one big joke." While that is debatable, one does occasionally pause to wonder at the need for elevator operators on the automatic elevators in the Jackson County Courthouse.

The courthouse has been the stomping ground of countless characters, but none less creative than the old man who operated his "business" out of the courthouse lobby. Always ready to "put the fix in" for an anxious offender, his offer was hoarsely whispered to all interested parties. For five hundred dollars, he would have a chat with the judge, encouraging him to return a verdict of not guilty. Success was never guaranteed, but if you were found guilty, your five hundred dollars was "cheerfully refunded." Years later, people discovered that the old man never did have private chats, but only walked around the corner awaiting the verdict. He simply played the odds, raking in five hundred dollars whenever a "client" was acquitted.

Across Twelfth Street, in City Hall, things are just as wild. In the 1950's, after the Pendergast machine's power had disintegrated, fourteen successors to city manager Carleton Sharpe filed through City Hall in rapid succession. As one department head left on his lunch hour, he directed his secretary, "If the city manager calls, be sure to get his name."

Faction leaders continue to snipe at one another, even on personality matters. Henry McKissick used to accuse his political rival, Ben Nordberg, of being "so rude that he wouldn't give you the time of day if he had two watches."

One of the few professional politicians in Kansas City today, Jerry Jette, has sharpened his verbal jabs to some classic one-liners, including these comments:

"Political science is to politics what botany is to neurosurgery."

"It's impossible to be a young Republican."

"The River Club is so exclusive that no one belongs."

"The Kansas City Club is a perfumed gin rummy palace for exiled Citizens Association members."

"If you stretched a canvas over Prairie Village, you'd have the world's largest outdoor insane asylum; the city council there is even thinking of starting daily bus service to Menninger's."

"When the Democratic Party has a firing squad, everyone gets in a circle."

"In order to save time, the next meeting of the Democratic Central Committee should be held in the grand jury chambers."

Jerry Jette also relates this incident of the classic free-enterprise attitude of the American businessman. When he was administrative assistant to Mayor Charles Wheeler, Jette once welcomed a national convention of morticians who were meeting in Kansas City. After the program, he chatted with the morticians, who exchanged positive statements about the need to improve their business by working closer with government, and other noncontroversial ideas. Finally, a senior gentleman, obviously respected by the group, cleared his throat and offered his suggestion. "You can say what you will, gentlemen. What we really need is an epidemic."

Jette also remembers a political club leader, long deceased, who was by trade a mortician with a sharp business acumen. The club leader carried a small black notebook, and inquired of everyone he met what size clothes and shoes they wore. Reportedly, many a wardrobe was sold after the family had its final viewing of the body.

One widow was distraught at discovering her late husband dressed for his funeral in a brown suit. "But he only wore blue!" she protested. As a busy mortician, he was not anxious to laboriously change the man's suit. Retiring to the back room, he soon reappeared, the deceased husband now agreeably clad in blue. It was a simple matter of surveying the color of clothing of the other clientele in the back room, and switching heads.

Kansas City has been home to a variety of town characters, though none was more well known twenty years ago than Kirby McRill.

Kirby McRill looked like a young Moses. His face was weathered and ruddy, and his long red hair flowed over his shoulders like a mantle of heavenly knowledge. McRill was a junkman by vocation, and an acquaintance by avocation. He pushed his cart up every street in Kansas City, picking up odds and ends, occasionally selling whatever anyone would buy. Virtually everyone knew his name, and he always waved to passersby and stopped to tell wild stories to the neighborhood children.

Nobody knew where Kirby McRill lived; many claimed he lived a hobo's life outdoors. Regardless of the temperature, he always wore a red flannel lumberjack shirt.

His cart was hand-propelled, and therefore Kirby tended to ignore stoplights when he had gotten some speed up. But everyone in Kansas City seemed to know this; the drivers obliged him and let him pass, regardless of red lights.

Great legends grew, of how he had been a mountaineer, or a sailor, or a war hero. Kirby McRill was Kansas City's mysterious friend, until one day a driver from out of town didn't yield his green light to the heavy-laden junk cart rolling through a downtown intersection. In Kansas City, even a town character is not safe from the invasion of visitors.

The late Speed Mahon was another town character. Speed was devoted to operating the only bar in Kansas City which would put your picture—anyone's picture—on the wall. No matter what a nothing you were to the rest of the world, at least at Speed's, you were a star. The only place which comes close to duplicating that great public service is Nardi's on the Plaza, which showcases hand-prints in white paint on the walls.

But Speed's, on McGee between Eighteenth and Nineteenth, had other highlights, as well. One of the stools in the women's restroom was wired to a seat-activated tape recorder which played the message, "Would you mind using the other stool, madam? I'm down here working on the plumbing."

Just up the street from Speed's place is a back-up slot of railroad track, used to dock private railroad cars. The mysterious and elusive Howard Hughes used to park his railroad car there for a month at a time while he was in Kansas City. He lived in the railroad car and, after attending to business, would stroll into Speed's for a drink, looking disheveled and wearing dirty sneakers. The crowd at Speed's knew him only as "Howie." One day, some TWA executives walked in, and recognized Howie as the chief stockholder of their firm. Hughes never visited Speed's again.

Speed Mahon was also the owner of a small cheap walk-up hotel on Truman Road. He named it the Hilton, placing the appropriate sign atop the dumpy establishment. Hilton International had to sue Speed to force him to remove the sign and change the hotel's name.

Kansas City's modern day town clown, however, is undoubtedly radio announcer Mike Murphy. And he almost had the trophy to prove it. One day, in a fit of curiosity and boastfulness, Murphy decided to nominate himself for the Nobel Peace Prize. Posing as a chemist, Murphy phoned Sweden and told a doctor in the Academy of Literature that he wanted to nominate himself for the prize. The insulted Swedish professor protested that it is impossible to nominate oneself. Murphy never could discover how one does get nominated; he claims nobody really knows. Murphy's local radio fans learned of his audacious prank and countered by writing letters of endorsement to the academy favoring his nomination for his humanitarian radio work.

Several years ago when disc jockeys and payola were synonymous, Murphy discovered a town near Kansas City named Paola. Armed with the incredulity of it all, he visited the town and collected taped statements from residents stating that they were only living there because they were "trapped." Murphy implied to Kansas Citians that these people were being held by nefarious forces, and organized the "Invasion of Paola—the Great Liberation." A twenty-mile caravan of five thousand cars, tanks, a battleship on wheels, and citizens armed with marshmallows and slingshots marched heroically into Paola to rescue those who had been trapped.

Murphy has also made the "Search for the Holy Stone," a loose analogy to the crusade for the Holy Grail. Murphy assured his radio audiences that there was a real "glad stone," and that believers should look for it. Soon after this announcement, Murphy journeyed to Ireland. He returned with some Kilkenny marble and proclaimed it was the real "glad stone." The piece of marble now sits on a pedestal in the Gladstone, Missouri, City Hall.

Despite Mike Murphy's charismatic qualities, or perhaps because of them, he is sometimes caught short on organizational talents. Several years ago, Murphy proposed a new Kansas City tradition similar to that of other great cities—a St. Patrick's Day Parade.

So every year beginning March 1, Murphy harps on the radio to recruit people for the big event. On the appointed day, generally but not always March 17, the local Irish, as well as other fun-loving citizens, dress up in the hall-closet variety of costumes, hats, flowers, and noisemakers. A few stray animals are rounded up, and all gather at Eleventh Street just west of Baltimore. As one yearly parade participant commented, "It's all downhill from there."

Murphy's homage to Ireland always turns into the world's shortest and tackiest St. Patrick's Day Parade. Hampered from the start by the absence of a parade marshal (Murphy is mingling wildly with the crowd), the two-block-long procession lurches around the corner and then disintegrates completely a block and a half later, as the paraders all head into Hogarty's tavern.

One lone police officer is assigned to Mike Murphy's St. Patrick's Day Parade—and some debate whether he is sent to direct automobile traffic or to shepherd the celebrants. He described the parade to police headquarters as a "loosely formed, benign, mobile riot."

In 1971, Mike Murphy unofficially ran for Mayor of Kansas City, Missouri. In order to find time to campaign door to door with the people, Murphy had to find someone to fill in on his 6:00 to 10:00 A.M. radio show. Mike recruited former Mayor H. Roe Bartle, who ably played records and bellowed about what a fine city Kansas City is, while Murphy was out campaigning. Bartle closed the show with a rousing endorsement for Murphy.

Naturally, political candidates are ripe for such public relations gimmicks. For instance, Mayor Wheeler has ridden a jackass, wrestled a bear, and appeared in television ads for a radio station and a car dealer. He also does a weekly Monday morning KMBZ radio appearance with his alter ego of antics, Mike Murphy. On the fifteen-minute program, Wheeler plugs upcoming civic events but has also been prompted to sing old drinking songs, reminisce about his childhood, and snort like an old racing horse. Wheeler's notorious monotone speaking voice is so unusual on the radio that the contrast from a typical deep-throated voice attracts attention to his messages.

If Kansas City has ever had a sage, it was the late LeRoy "Satchel" Paige, the first black baseball pitcher in the American League. Though he was a native Alabaman, Paige adopted Kansas City as his home town. He was very loyal to the Kansas City

Royals because the managers of its predecessor team, the Monarchs, gave him his big chance. During a spell when his pitching arm was nearly lame, they brought him to Kansas City.

While here, Paige bought a house on Twelfth Street near downtown. In the back yard, he raised two hundred chickens and a cow, until the city inspector chanced to spot the cow ambling into the front yard.

Satchel's pitching career lasted into his late fifties, incredible for any athlete. And at times, fame had a hefty clutch on his personality. Flying one night into old Municipal Airport, Satchel peeked out his airplane window and spotted fire trucks ringing the runway. Turning to his manager, he said, "Man, look at all them fire trucks and ambulances blowing those sirens just to honor Ol' Satch." Years later, his manager revealed that the plane's wheels would not descend, necessitating calling out the fire trucks. The wheels dropped prior to the landing, so the pilot never bothered to alarm his passenger because it would have discouraged Paige from any more flying.

Satchel Paige was too busy pitching to do much writing; instead he let sports writers chronicle his incredible verbal rambles. Paige eventually distilled his thoughts into six rules for staying young. The authors of this book include them as reflective of the easygoing Kansas City life style, and suitable for all lovers of the liveable life.

"Avoid fried meats which angry up the blood.

If your stomach disputes you, lie down and pacify it with cool thoughts.

Keep the juices flowing by jangling around gently as you move.

Go very light on the vices, such as carrying on in society— the social ramble ain't restful.

Avoid running at all times.

And don't look back. Something might be gaining on you."

18. 77 THINGS TO DO IN RIVER CITY—
MANY OF THEM FREE

It used to be said that Kansas City was a great place to live but one wouldn't want to visit there. But the snotty humbug who said that went off to New York and soon died of smog inhalation. Little did he know that after he left people discovered lots of reasons to visit Kansas City. In fact, for those who live here, it's possible to take an extended vacation—spending a few hours every weekend—discovering all kinds of new and interesting sights and spots and people.

The authors have selected some of these experiences, based on the criterion of the six senses—sight, sound, taste, touch, smell, and that sixth sense, entertainment, which belongs not only to booking agents and travel guides but to all people who have some spare time and an urge to experience different things. Except for the first five, which are five-star Kansas City musts, the remainder on this list are in no order whatsoever.

Abject apologies are offered to all those places, things, and people events which are not listed. This chapter is not intended as a complete menu of what there is to do in Kansas City. Rather, it is an appetizer to whet people's appetites for self-discovery of the new, the exciting, the pleasing, the weird, the cosmopolitan, the homey, the funky, the solitary, the groupish, the thoughtful, the beautiful, and, most of all, the fun things to do here. The other criterion was the cost, and the authors have tried to identify places and events which are free or have only a small admission charge.

Of course, it is exceedingly dangerous to single out any five best events or places. One of life's great pastimes is disagreeing with anyone else's list of the five best anything. Armed with this knowledge, the authors have proceeded, because readers cannot argue with or debate what writers fear to write.

One thing is almost certain, however. Kansas Citians will agree on the best way to get to these five places—via the boulevard system. Kansas City has a network of streets just like most cities. But its network of boulevards is something else. Long, green winding avenues with trees, flowers, grass, sculpture, and fountains connect major portions of the city. They are maintained by the Parks Department because they are considered linear parks. Several of these boulevards, including J. C. Nichols Parkway, Gillham Road, and the Paseo, can be used in getting from one five-star place to another, as well as traveling to the other places listed in this chapter. The boulevards are such an integral part of Kansas City that it would have been demeaning to place them in a ranking with anything else; thus they get top billing.

1. Kelly's (tavern and deli), 500 Westport Road. Cherished not for its ample historical stature, but for the wild hodgepodge of people who drop in for a beer. Well before 1850 this building was an outfitting post . . . the last stop before setting out for the new frontier to the West. One hundred years later, Kelly's was a drinking outpost, a neighborhood bar, the last stop for the weary working person before setting out for home in nearby Broadway-Westport. Twenty-five years hence, Kelly's is almost too popular. It is a neighborhood bar to the whole city. Many of the artists and writers who used to hang around, hands plunged into the pockets of their tan trench coats, have moved on to quieter spots. Today's Kelly's is a must stop for a younger, less serious crowd, as well as the occasional working person stopping off for old times' sake. The jukebox no longer plays Irish folk songs; instead, there is pop music. One old-timer has begged Randall Kelly, the bar owner, to put in one recording of silence, so he could have three minutes of reminiscing about the good old days for a quarter. The universal appeal of Kelly's was recently confirmed when a group of old people from a "congregate eating site" spent their one free afternoon on a field trip to Kelly's. One

eighty-year-old glanced over her shoulder as she sat at the bar and remarked, "Well, Randall, I see you haven't changed one bit of the lousy décor since I was here thirty years ago." And that, of course, is Kelly's appeal.

2. Weekends should always have time reserved for the City Market, Fifth and Main. Ringing the farmers' market stalls are the wholesalers who are there all week, too. Several of the wholesalers are old Italian families like Mazuch and Sons Produce Company, DeFeo Fruit Company, and Vito Gulotta Produce Company; they have ruled the City Market area, now being modernized as Market Square, for a hundred years. The farmers' market is best visited about 9:00 A.M. on a Saturday morning, before the crush of noonday heat and twenty-seven thousand other shoppers overtake the peripatetic bargain-hunter. Listen to the Spanish and Belgian accents. Look for the two eighty-plus-year-old sisters. One wears her wig perpetually askew. These hardy women sell vegetables from their farm; by midsummer they will offer peonies from their front yard. Also look for fresh horseradish, chickens, dead or alive, rabbits at Easter, fresh squid, shrimp, oysters, fish, barbecued beef, country eggs, honey, home-grown houseplants, puppies, kittens, Western cut blue jeans, eight-track tapes, kitsch gold-sprayed yard statues of Venus de Milo or a frog, antique furniture, and, of course, the freshest produce in town.

On Sunday afternoons, the City Market or Market Square becomes an artists' market. Artists create works on location, as well as displaying works for sale. They are accompanied by musicians, dancers, and sometimes street theater. It's all somewhat like having the Plaza Art Fair every weekend. And it's free, sponsored by the Kansas City Parks and Recreation Department.

3. Scimeca's Super Market, 1447 Independence Avenue in the Northeast, is a great people-watching neighborhood grocery. Originally a bakery, the store was opened in 1918 by the late Phillip Scimeca. His sons, Louis and Frank, have expanded it to include groceries, a butcher counter, liquor, and wine. Louis Scimeca makes mild and hot Italian sausages, *pepperoni*, Genoa salami, *capocollo*, and *prosciutto*. "We have veal every day. We're never out, because we buy sides of it," he explains. Mediterranean cooking requires olive oil. Scimeca's has an entire aisle

of it, including several brands in gallon cans. At the back of the store, behind glass cases, assorted pasta shapes are available in bulk. Nearby are crocks of olives—big green Sicilian ones, Greek ones, and the withered black oil-cured Moroccan olives. Other goodies include several brands of *jardiniera* marinated vegetables, *caponata* eggplant mixture, and assorted imported cheeses. Noon on the third of the month, when the welfare and social security checks arrive, is an enlightening lesson in what it's like to struggle to make ends meet. For years, Italian women from the North End have fed their families exquisite food on minuscule budgets. Scimeca's has been their shopping cupboard.

4. The Nelson Gallery on a Saturday or Sunday afternoon is to Kansas City what Central Park is to New York. Most everyone is there. The gallery swells with a pleasant humanity, offering a warm shelter on snowy winter days and a cool haven on sweltering summer ones. These are the only two days of the week that the Nelson is open for free, and half of Kansas City seems to spend its weekends there. It is a time when the weekday art students generally sketch the visitors instead of the paintings and sculptures. It is a place for fathers who see their kids on weekends; for couples who need an experience of solace and greatness; and for young people who don't want to dress up. The Nelson offers free chamber music concerts and films every month as well. The best part is the great ambience, a feeling of crowded anonymity, where one can ignore the crowd and stare at the walls if one doesn't feel like talking. Instead of loud pop music, the sounds are of hush puppies sliding on marble floors, and low murmurs about how great Monet's technique was, and how even their daughter could paint better than Willem De Kooning.

5. The final five-star must place to visit is the Truman Library in Independence. For some reason, monumental places of historic significance are seldom visited by local people. In New York, only visitors see the Statue of Liberty; in Paris, one hears many English accents at the Louvre; and in Kansas City, the Truman Library's parking lot is filled with cars with out-of-state license plates. Yet, the authors highly recommend it as a place to visit because it reveals much about the spirit of Kansas City. The Truman Library is perhaps the finest Presidential library in the U.S. in terms of size and quality of exhibits. The Oval Office has

been entirely recreated with all the furnishings, and the tape describing those furnishings was made especially for public consumption by Harry Truman himself. The Presidential car is on display, as well as hundreds of historical artifacts. The importance of these objects lies in their ability to evoke a feeling of the majestic forces of history. The Truman Library reveals the mystery of a plain man from Independence, a haberdasher in downtown Kansas City. It is the story of a person who completed the story of Lincoln, in that Truman was a plain man who rose to greatness when called by his country; then just as quickly, he returned home and resumed a quiet life in middle America.

6. Swope Park Zoo is notable for the African Veldt; the Feline Exhibit, known as the cat house; the Tropical Habitat; and the train rides throughout the zoo. Children are admitted for a quarter any time when accompanied by an adult.

7. Former "real live Indians" are buried in downtown Kansas City, Kansas, in Huron Cemetery. A pleasant park and rose garden area overlooks a very unusual sculptural mall which stretches from Sixth to Ninth streets on Minnesota Avenue. A great picnic spot. If that's not enough for an hour's visit, the local library is next door, with monthly art exhibits on the third floor.

8. From April 15 to November 1, the River Queen river boat, led by Captain Richard Lynn, sails for short voyages from the old Westport Landing at First and Grand. There is a modest fee.

9. Additionally, the Hannibal Bridge is a great picnic spot, regardless of river-boat rides. Takeout sandwiches are abundantly available from River Quay delicatessens, and the view of the river provides a relaxing way to turn off the noises of downtown city life for an hour.

10. The roof tops of downtown buildings serve several puposes besides keeping out the rain. Commerce Bank Building has tennis and a full heath club membership which uses it. While men from the Commerce Tower Building stand at noon at street level, girl-watching, women who office in the adjoining Commerce Bank Building are guy-watching from their windows overlooking the tennis courts. At last count, it was luv all.

11. Other downtown roof tops serve as sunbathing decks. Vista Del Valle apartments at Ninth and Holmes have a sun deck, exercise machines, and a swimming pool with a movable roof.

Nearby is the laundry room. The people who live in this building are known for their tan skin and clean clothes.

12. The roof top of City Hall is an observation deck which is entered off the Twenty-ninth floor, near the mayor's office during office hours. A guard answers questions and keeps the despondent from jumping off.

13. The Mayor's Office is known for its open-door policy and the collection of over five hundred hats. Each hat was given to Mayor Wheeler to mark a visit or a dedication or an event in which he participated. It's much more creative and interesting than a plaque collection. The hats range from sombreros to hard hats, Indian headdresses to hand-crafted hats fashioned by the children of Nelson School. (That hat looks like Nelson School, with little people running about on a playground, which is the hat's crown.)

14. During the week, the public is invited to observe livestock auctions in the stockyard area. Auctions are in the large round building west of the Livestock Exchange Building, at 9:00 A.M. on Tuesdays and Wednesdays, 10:00 A.M. on Thursdays. With the advent of so much synthetic food, beef may soon be a thing of the past. The authors recommend a visit before the stockyards become a chapter in a history book.

15. For people-watching and sandwiches, Putsch's Sidewalk Cafe offers a great view of people on the Plaza. For some reason, foreign students love to gather there, and the atmosphere is definitely cosmopolitan.

16. Other people-watching spots abound in the River Quay, at Dinkledorf's Deli (free music on Friday and Saturday nights) and at Papa Nick's, beneath the Cinzano umbrellas. Colorful street vendors and occasional street bands may be seen and heard on weekend nights.

17. The Christmas lights on the Country Club Plaza are lit on Thanksgiving evening and stay on throughout the holidays. The lighting ceremony offers carols, short speeches, and the old-fashioned sense of community which reminds people that even the largest city can be like a family during times of celebration.

18. The Plaza also celebrates other seasons, including Easter, when huge rabbits with glowing eyes, maxi-coats, and baskets of

eggs are perched about the area. Each rabbit has a name and a store which it annually patronizes.

19. The Plaza Art Fair, oldest in Kansas City (forty years), takes place the last weekend in September, offering visual art for exhibit and sale, chamber music accompaniment, and vendor carts featuring such varied foods as artichokes, cotton candy, and tacos.

20. Liberty Memorial is another "Statue of Liberty" place visited most frequently by out-of-town visitors. But it deserves regular attention because of its remarkable view of Crown Center and downtown. There is a modest fee for taking the elevator to the top of the 216-foot shaft. Free carillon concerts are presented throughout the week, usually at 12:30 and 5:30 P.M. Also, there is a fine collection of World War I posters (a good study in the evolution of graphics) and a mammoth mural in the Hall of Memories which deserves a viewing and an explanation of the cast of characters portrayed. Entitled *Pantheon de la Guerre* by the artist Daniel MacMorris, a few of the characters weren't even alive when the scene was to have taken place.

21. There's no need to travel to New Orleans to hear excellent Dixieland music. Just head for the Levee, 16 West Forty-third Street, between Main and Nichols Parkway, on Monday nights. The six-person band has one of the oldest books around, sticking strictly to time-honored rags with a classic lineup of banjo, trumpet, clarinet, tuba, piano, and drums. The Monday band doesn't clutter up the music with sing-along, and is strictly for fun, attentive listening.

22. Only two or three theaters offer film fare which is not generally available. The Bijou, the Festival, and occasionally the Fine Arts show film classics ranging from Marx Brothers, Buck Rogers, Bogart, and Superman to French and Italian dubbed or subtitled flicks, like Truffaut, Buñuel, and Fellini. It's nostalgia or a trip to Europe for a small admission charge.

23. Communiversity of UMKC offers free courses, noncredit, for the self-motivated lover of learning. Any interested person may convene a course on any subject, and meet anyplace. A sample of courses from the various "departments" follows:

24. *Women:* Women and Anger: Auto Mechanics Workshop.

25. *You and Me:* How to Fight Fairly and Effectively in Marriage; On Being a Parent—How to Understand Children.

26. *Crafts and Skills:* Oneology (winemaking); Dowsing, Water Witching, Radiesthetics, or Biophysical Effects; Chess for Blood; Corn Husk Angels.

27. *Inner Paths:* The Bible as Literature; Creating an Alternative Church; Kundalini Yoga.

28. *People's Law School:* What to Do with a Drunken Sailor; Tenant Rights and Landlord Responsibilities; Trial Procedures in the Courts.

29. *Social Scene:* Chardin and Further Explorations of Omega; United Farm Workers—Sal Si Puede; "Free to Be" Collective Day Care.

30. *Foolkiller Academy:* Theater for the Hell of It; Victim to "Purposiveful" Person; Ya Hoo, Who Do, Foolkiller Canoe Trip; Dulcimer Pick-In.

31. *Body:* Smoker's Clinic; Early Pregnancy Series; Westport Free Health Clinic Shop Manual for Homo Sapiens; Astrological Birth Control.

32. *The Arts:* The Not So Magical Art of Color Photography (one of the best courses available in Kansas City); Poetry Writing Seminar; German Drama Workshop; Dialogue on Film.

33. Johnson County Park and Recreation District offers superior programming in many subjects. Fees vary. Courses include: Musical Comedy Workshop, Ballet and Mime, Jazz Exercise, Batik, Karate, Satisfied Seniors Club, Family Vegetable Gardening, Kayaking, Coed Innertube Water Polo, Scuba and Skin Diving, Kitemaking, Scout Arts Project Workshops, Preschool Creative Dramatics, and the very popular Preschool Discovery series for children and parents in co-operation with the Johnson County Library.

34. The Jaycees annually sponsor the Kansas City Rodeo in the summer near the Fourth of July at Benjamin Stables.

35. Johnson County Parks and Recreation Department offers free outdoor theater in June and July. Bring a blanket or a lawn chair to Shawnee Mission Park, 7900 Renner Road, for light and entertaining drama and musicals.

36. The American Institute of Architects and the Convention and Visitors Bureau have published a walking tour of downtown

buildings with architectural merit. The tour features landmarks as well as new buildings. Guides can be arranged for large groups.

37. Another area worth touring is near Gladstone Boulevard in the Northeast, including the Kansas City Museum. Jim Ryan, curator of the museum, conducts occasional walking tours. His great love for the area and vast knowledge of architecture are evident as he points out each unique home. A favorite is at 512 Benton, where the corner "pillar" of the porch is an exact copy of a temple guard from an Assyrian tomb.

38. While touring the Northeast, one can stop in at Kelly's Bakery for a cup of coffee and a peanut cookie or two, while seated at an eyelet-covered tea table in front of the red-canopied window on St. John Boulevard. The bakery has operated for nearly thirty years, and is a common visiting point for the entire amply fed neighborhood.

39. There is only one place in Kansas City where the Musicians Union permits jam sessions like they swung in the thirties— the Mutual Musicians Foundation, 1823 Highland. This little building housed the black musicians' union before it merged with the white union in the sixties. The foundation was started to save the building and maintain a clubhouse for the old black musicians. Special memberships can be arranged for visitors. The greatest action is after the clubs close at 1:00 A.M., when the working musicians drop in after their gigs for a little jamming.

40. During warm weather, avid bicycle riders gather at Loose Park tennis courts on Sundays at 2:00 P.M. for an extended trip about the city.

41. The Midland Theatre (Loew's Midland for Kansas City old-timers), at 1228 Main, offers popular films and rock concerts (the ones which used to play at Cowtown) in the most baroque luxury imaginable. The ceiling is a fresco of roses, the soaring drapes are really red velvet. It's quite a change from the typical plastic kitsch décor of most theaters.

42. People with sensitive noses will enjoy several smells in Kansas City. Downtown, sniff about for roasting Folger's coffee, wafting from 330 West Eighth Street. At first, it may smell like chocolate chip cookies just before they start to overbrown in the oven.

43. Another great sniffing spot is at the corner of Broadway and Westport Road. Nearby, at 4050 Pennsylvania, fresh bread is being baked at Manor Bakery. The best smelling hours are from 5:00 P.M. to 4:00 A.M.

44. While there are antique shops and flea markets scattered throughout the city, there is one antique district which offers quality and variety without a lot of legwork. The shops are clustered on Forty-fifth Street from State Line to Bell; a visit to any of the twenty shops will yield a brochure listing the other shops' addresses and specialties. The goods range from grandfather clocks to old circus sideshow canvas paintings of freaks to downright dilapidated nostalgia pieces.

45. Some of the most fun people events are sponsored throughout the year by the Kansas City Art Institute, including monthly show openings and the student sale in early December, which offers original art work perfect for holiday gift-giving. A call to the Art Institute will put your name on the mailing list. Any trip to the Art Institute should include enough free time to stroll the grounds. Students have erected monumental modern sculptures surrounding old Vanderslice Hall, and the juxtaposition is startling.

46. The Jewish Community Center offers so many excellent programs in so many fields that it seems almost a university. The public forum speakers are always involved in the most up-to-date fields. There is a full range of arts activities, including poetry and community theater, historical and religious studies, a health club, and lots of early childhood education. It's truly a family center, with a family membership rate or a low individual event ticket rate.

47. Many Kansas City natives are not aware of their good fortune in having free tennis courts provided by the city. Well over half of Kansas City, Missouri's, parks and playgrounds offer tennis courts. Municipal swimming pools are at a minimum, but tennis, baseball, and basketball facilities number well over one hundred.

48. Swimming pools have an interesting history in Kansas City. In Kansas City, Missouri, there are only three full-sized public pools, at Swope Park, Parade Park, and at Grove Pool, Fifteenth and Paseo. The Swope Park Pool, integrated in 1952, is open to

anyone who has seventy-five cents. On the other side of the state line, Johnson County has a dozen swimming pools which limit permits and memberships to Johnson County residents. Tennis courts are also restricted there.

49. Andre's (tearoom) at 5018 Main is probably the only place in the U.S. where one can drop in to pick up croissants, petits fours, and the latest in travel tips from the ambassadorial consul to Switzerland. Andre and Elsbeth Bollier have created the finest candies and pastries available in Kansas City for twenty years, as well as representing their native country. Andre's offers dainty luncheons year-round, and hearty fondue or raclette on Friday nights in the winter. The pastries and candies present a great view of food as an art form.

50. While there are many little plant shops in Kansas City, there is nothing like the Missouri Botanical Gardens in St. Louis. However, one place comes close to that, on a smaller scale. Bill's Tropical Greenhouse in the southern part of Kansas City, Kansas (call for directions first), has a real jungle of plants, winding paths, and a rippling brook, all stashed in a tin warehouse. It's incredible to see mammoth versions of one's puny little houseplants.

51. One of the founders of Kansas City, Kansas, lived in a fine home in western Wyandotte County. Moses Grinter's home is now open to the public as Grinter Place Museum, 1420 South Seventy-eighth Street. There is also a room available for catered luncheons, a nice change from renting a hotel ballroom for a club meeting.

52. For those who like to hear the soothing sounds of water rushing by, the site of the old Watts Mill is a good spot (103rd just east of State Line). Originally known as Fitzhugh's Mill or Fitzhugh's Grove, it served as a campsite for hundreds of wagon trains before they headed west toward Santa Fe. The Watts family bought it in 1850 and operated it until their deaths. The mill was razed in the 1940's. Today, it's a pleasant thinking spot. The rock ledge creates a waterfall, and there is lots of busily rushing water swirling through Indian Creek on its way to join Tomahawk Creek.

53. The Shawnee Mission Historical Museum, at 3403 West Fifty-third, preserves the grim realities of white civilization

"helping" the Indians of this territory. There are two buildings open free to the public—the Shawnee Methodist Mission and the Indian Manual Labor School.

54. Lake Jacomo is a man-made thousand-acre lake in southeastern Jackson County. Power boats and sailboats are permitted, and picnic shelters, fishing, horseback riding, hayrides, free guided hikes, and nature films are available.

55. On the east shore of Lake Jacomo is Missouri Town, 1855, a restoration of early buildings which have been clustered together in a village setting. Missouri Town served as the filming site of a movie. The site includes homesteads, a church, blacksmith shop, livery stable, law office, tavern, barns, and outbuildings. There are exhibits of household furnishings, livestock, and seasonal gardens, and a self-guided nature trail. It's open every day free to the public.

56. Crown Center Square at Pershing Road and Grand Avenue programs a wide variety of free, family-oriented activities especially on weekends, such as food fairs, book fairs, farm fairs, children's fairs, art fairs, ethnic displays, jazz concerts, etc. In addition, there is an outdoor ice-skating rink, the *Shiva* sculpture by Alexander Calder, a forty-nine-jet fountain, grass, trees, bright yellow and white umbrellas, and a band shell. At least one of the authors has always wanted to dash through the fountain on a steamy summer night.

57. Inside Crown Center Hotel, there is a jungle-waterfall with a five-story walkway through it. A mammoth modern painting by Philomene Bennett hangs at the end of the second-floor ballroom hallway, right before the window offering a spectacular view of the people on the square from the climate-controlled nest of the hotel. A spectacular wall hanging spans nearly three stories of the space near the elevators, which, by the way, run up the outside of the building, offering another great view of downtown.

58. Speaking of wall hangings, the Alameda Plaza has a very gutsy one executed by Janet Kuemmerlein which is visible from the lobby stair well. The sculpture and paintings in the lobby, the lower levels, even the restrooms and hotel hallways at the Alameda Plaza, form one of the finest collections in Kansas City. (The art was selected by Paul Robinson, the eclectic wizard of Gilbert-Robinson restaurants, who also designed Houlihan's,

Plaza III, Annie's Santa Fe, and Sam Wilson's Meat Market.) It is worth a visit there just to tour the hallways and stop for an excellent hot chocolate in the coffee shop. The roof-top restaurant there serves weird cracker-like flat bread, and the lounge features the finest in Kansas City sophisticated jazz. One of the busiest nights is Thanksgiving, to view the 7:30 P.M. lighting of the Plaza Christmas lights.

59. The Agricultural Hall of Fame, just north of Bonner Springs in Wyandotte County, features old farm implements, steam traction engines, and rural living memorabilia which one's homesteading grandparents might have used. It is the only major museum of its type in the U.S., and there are plans for greatly expanding it.

60. Kansas City is a hamburger heaven, as witnessed by Calvin Trillin's rave reviews of his home town's cooking written for the *New Yorker* magazine. Picking up on the prime-time motto, "One of the few liveable cities left," Trillin terms Kansas City "one of the few edible cities left." It is important for every Kansas Citian at some time to sample several home-grown varieties of hamburgers, including Winstead's, Sanderson's (the Elmer), a Yu'all (like a Maid-rite, if you are from out of town), and a Town Topic (with fried onions). Another famous Kansas City food is Plaza III steak soup, which is simply unparalleled, available with warm monster oyster crackers which resemble collapsed Southern biscuits.

61. Barbecue—meaning really smoked ribs, though also including brisket or ham with the same hot sauce—is treated in greater depth in another chapter, but let this record show that one has not been to Kansas City if one has not been to Arthur Bryant's, if only for the God-awful mess of it all. The French fries are lard-fried, the sauce is slopped on the meat with a two-inch paintbrush, and the soft drinks are out of the machine. It is a rich experience which adds to the meat's superb flavor, causing the hours on the clock, which reads A-R-T-H-U-R-B-R-Y-A-N-T instead of 1 through 12, to fly by.

62. North of the river at Waukomis Drive, north of 71 highway, lies Line Creek Park. In addition to standard recreational facilities, it contains an archaeological preserve of the Hopewell

Indian civilization. As a reminder, there is a herd of buffalo and elk roaming the park.

63. One of the most potent and inexpensive ways to recapture a sense of one's history and roots is to wander through a cemetery. Union Cemetery, 227 East Twenty-eighth Terrace near Gillham Road, is the final resting place of many early Kansas City pioneers. A quiet walk through Union Cemetery is a good refresher course in Kansas City leadership. The Sexton's Cottage, vintage 1883, has been renovated and is open to the public on weekends from 1:00 to 4:00 P.M.

64. Old Independence Courthouse at Liberty and Kansas avenues (yes, Kansas) in Harry Truman's home town is one of the oldest standing courthouses west of the Mississippi. Nearby, at Main and Maple streets, are the restored office and courtroom where Truman began his political career as a judge of the Jackson County Court.

65. Louise Sandstrom is the old-fashioned kind of restaurant operator who personally greets guests at the door and gives them the royal tour, and in this case the tour is of a pioneer home built in 1849. The home is in Clay County, 5410 North East Oak Ridge Road, now known as Sandy's Oak Ridge Manor. In case Louise doesn't tell you everything, the complete history is on the place mat. The restaurant-museum is brimming with antiques including a church organ. Homey waitresses serve family style sauerbraten and fried chicken. Of course there are biscuits and honey, and salad dressing in a squirt bottle. There are more antiques to view in the attic. The yard contains a small chapel for weddings, a white plaster sculpture which is a modified version of the Statue of Liberty (overlooking Interstate 35), and live peacocks that wave as visitors drive by.

66. Nearby is the Clay County Historical Museum, on the west side of the square in Liberty, Missouri. It features a pioneer drugstore with stained-glass partition and walnut woodwork. The two floors of historical exhibits include eight dioramas by the miniatures artist Paul McNeely. It is free, open in the afternoons except Mondays.

67. Another country restaurant north of the river is Dolce's Highland View Farm at 1333 North East Barry Road. A finely restored parlor serves as a waiting and cocktail room before one

is seated in a chandeliered dining room. The frozen fruit salad and cream-baked chicken are reminders of old Southern cooking. The rolling green yard and lake are right from the days of the old plantations.

68. Nearby Fort Leavenworth, Kansas, is a good stop for a Sunday drive. The Fort Leavenworth Museum includes the Von Schritz collection of military miniatures, "Regiments of the World 1880–1914," plus a fine transportation collection including a Conestoga wagon, a stagecoach, and the carriage Lincoln used during his Kansas visit in 1859. This museum is free to the public, open until 4:00 P.M. daily.

69. The family home of Miss Ella Carroll serves as the Leavenworth County Museum, which features Victorian period rooms and costume exhibits. It is a marvel what vitamins have done for our physical size today. The Victorian clothes indicate how shrimp-sized people used to be.

70. Milton's Tap Room, 3241 Main, is billed as the home of a hundred stars. Actually there are five thousand, but they're all on recordings now. Milton Morris is the bar owner and resident philosopher, historian, and jazz aficionado. Milton's superb record collection is exceeded only by his personal knowledge of jazz. Nearby Penn Valley Community College has sponsored classes at Milton's, where he lectures from behind the bar, which bears the gold-glittered sign, "No Requests—Like Man It's Free."

71. One of the most true-to-life views of Kansas City can be seen while riding in a police squad car. The Linwood Police Station (Linwood and Troost in a converted drive-in bank building) sponsors the Ride-Along program. It's geared for those who live in the area, though any city resident may participate by calling for an appointment at 931-7396.

72. A tour and demonstration of the police helicopter unit is available for those who visit 4700 Eastern by the Municipal Farm. Arrangements may be made by first calling the Public Information Office at 842-6525.

73. See Spot chase the man. See Spot apprehend the man. See Spot keep him in his place. The Police Department of Kansas City, Missouri, offers canine demonstrations using officers to pose as felons. It keeps both the dogs and the officers in shape. Group demonstrations can be scheduled by calling the PIO office.

74. The Police Department also has programs which bring crime prevention techniques to public areas. Speakers are available to meet with groups and clubs on the subjects of self-defense, rape prevention, drugs, home protection, traffic safety, drunk driving. A crime prevention van demonstrates locks and safety devices, and the crime-alert trailer illustrates other safety measures.

75. One of the more interesting and serious study groups which meet regularly is the Psychical Research Society. They study all forms of psychic phenomena, leaning toward believability more than a typical occult group. *Wednesday* magazine and the Sunday listing of events in the *Star* carry announcements of the monthly speakers.

76. A forty-five-minute drive from Kansas City ends at Weston, Missouri, where the drugstore offers coffee for a nickel. In the fall, the Historical Museum (Spring and Main streets) sponsors a tour of the ante-bellum homes of Weston. The tobacco market on Main Street features tobacco auctions just like the old Lucky Strike ads. Weston is also the home of McCormick Distillery. During May and November, free samples of whiskey are offered to Sunday visitors. Always the unequaled fresh spring water is available to quench a more subtle taste.

77. "Take Me Out to the Ball Game" is still the theme song of thousands of amateurs who aspire to one day play for the Kansas City Royals. These young men and women spend each spring and summer at Little League diamonds in Kansas City, which are among the most elaborate in the country. With the growth of kids' baseball leagues in the past twenty years, many parents are demanding finer quarters in which to spend their summers. Gone are the splintered spectators' seats, replaced with bright orange plastic ones. Even the food and restrooms have improved. Only the quality of baseball, generally a comedy of errors, remains the same. A Sunday afternoon from May through July at one of the diamonds, Three and Two Baseball Club, Ninety-sixth and Blue River Road in southern Kansas City, is a visit to middle America. The authors note that it is still the mothers who yell with the greatest verve.

19. THE EMOTIONAL TERRAIN

PART I

Going into any city and purchasing a street guide will give a newcomer, strictly speaking, the ability to find his or her way around.

But getting to really know a city consists of developing some understanding of the nature of each of its major parts. That is why the authors are attempting to draw an emotional map of Kansas City—tracing the topography of attitudes and traditions in various parts of the city. Part I talks about the communities surrounding the core city; areas where 800,000 of the metropolitan area's people live.

This is no exact science; it is done by trying to experience the feeling of each of the places being written about. It is in the last analysis a matter of opinion; and all the authors can offer to give weight to these opinions is a lifetime spent in Kansas City and its environs, and a tendency to wander about the city and contemplate what is seen and heard.

INDEPENDENCE

Independence has always felt a certain independence from, if not resentment toward, Kansas City. Its most famous inhabitant, former President Harry S. Truman, used to manifest this attitude when he encountered news reporters or visitors who spoke to him of Kansas City as his home town. "Kansas City," Mr.

Truman would say, "is just a suburb of Independence." And if the person speaking to him took that too lightly the President would set him straight in a hurry. Harry Truman—as any newsperson who ever covered him could tell you—was a quick man to give you a history lesson. And Mr. Truman would inform anybody he thought was too dumb to know it already that Independence, after all, was around before there ever was a Kansas City.

That, of course, was true. Independence was there first. It was the jumping-off place for the Santa Fe Trail. And it was a place where steamboats could come, bringing the westward-bound pioneers as far into the wilderness as one could go in comfort. It probably didn't seem possible, once this vital traffic had started to arrive and flow through Independence, that the upstart town of Kansas and its Westport landing, fourteen more miles to the west, could be any great threat to its eminence. When the California and Oregon trails began to attract settlers, Independence was ready to serve as a jumping-off place for them too. But it didn't stay that way. Fourteen miles was fourteen miles. And the infant Kansas City was aggressive in attracting river traffic. In time, the bulk of that traffic left Independence for the newer city to the west.

To this day, there is a spirit in Independence which reflects that city's feeling that it is important in its own right, and not just because it is nestled up to the big Kansas City metropolitan complex. The feeling of independence, if not of resentment, is very much alive.

Independence is the biggest of the several communities in the eastern part of Jackson County, Missouri, the most populous county in the metropolitan complex. "Eastern Jack," as some downtown politicians refer to it, is about as easy to understand politically as the inner power apparatus in Peking. The liberals in western Jackson County, or, in other words, Kansas City, like to speak of Eastern Jack as "Archie Bunker country." And in some ways it is. It is not exactly the most inviting terrain that an upward-bound black family might select to move into. Only a few have tried it so far, and with the exception of Independence, their experiences, while not too violent, could not be described as painless. The attitude of Independence residents brings to mind their pioneer heritage: as long as a person does a full day's work and supports his family and his town, it's nobody's business what color he is!

Depending on one's frame of mind, a visitor may find Independence a sleepy sort of place, a little dusty about the square, where a pickup truck is a lot more at home than a Cadillac limousine.

There are distinct Southern influences in the town of Independence. It has the old-fashioned town square with the courthouse in the center. The new courthouse replaced one that might have changed places with any of those in the towns immortalized by William Faulkner down in Mississippi. Even with a more modern courthouse structure centered there, the remaining square does suggest a town down South. Today it also suggests urban blight. Independence, with its population swollen to almost 120,000, is suffering the same flight from the center city as is found in other and larger communities. Shopping centers open and grow, and downtown ages and diminishes.

But if the emotional make-up of Independence contains these elements of self-assertiveness and traces of the old South, it also embraces a continuing subterranean conflict. Down below the surface most of the time, occasionally coming out into public debate, is the feeling of townspeople about "the church."

"The church," in this case, is the Reorganized Church of Jesus Christ of Latter Day Saints. To this denomination, springing from the teachings of Joseph Smith, the prophet, Independence is what Salt Lake City is to the Mormons. Serving as the world headquarters for the 207,000 members of the RLDS, Independence was designated as Zion—the center place for the kingdom of God—by Joseph Smith in 1831.

Here, as in Salt Lake City, there is a feeling that the denomination is extremely powerful. Spirited involvement in community affairs is actually a teaching of the religion, and the political activity of its members is encouraged by the church. For those within the religious fold in such a community, there is a chance to form a city of God; there is the warmth of a community which seems to reaffirm in so many ways the things the believer holds dear.

But to those who are not of the dominant faith, a feeling—yes, it can be called a prejudice—begins to grow. It is easy to speak of "them" as controlling the city, its politics and its wealth. It is human nature to view "them" as people who are, first of all, not "us," and to talk about "how they stick together." Independence does, of course, have other Christian churches, Protestant and Catholic, but no synagogues and no mosques or churches of the Eastern Rites. But in the mind-set of the town, that is somewhat beside the point. For time and again in the history of Independence, the dividing lines have been only those between the RLDS on the one hand and all the rest of God's faithful and unfaithful on the other. Where such feelings once blazed into passionate reaction and violence, today they only simmer along. And that gap is easily bridged by putting forth one proposition to which all, on whatever side of the great divide, can agree: that Independence is a good place to live, and would be a good place even if there were no Kansas City at all.

RAYTOWN

The other large community in the eastern portion of Jackson County is Raytown. Unlike Independence, Raytown, while boasting some attitudes and political styles all its own, still has the manner and the feel of a place that knows it is a suburb and a bedroom town for another place. Raytown is much more "with it" than a typical American suburb. It has people from the lower-middle to middle-middle (mostly) plus a few people in the upper-middle economic bracket.

The emotional tone of Raytown is built around a life style in which frequently the man and the woman work. It is a Chevrolet kind of place. It has a no-nonsense chief of police named Marion Beeler, who assumes correctly that Raytown is the kind of place that takes law and order seriously. Mr. Average may not take as kindly to the radar trap that ensnares him as he does to witnessing the apprehension of some juvenile vandals who've been shooting out street lights; but basically he wants his cops to keep things safe. He has seen enough on TV and on newspaper front pages to convince him of that.

The people of Raytown are basically Democratic politically, but the loyalty to the party comes to a screeching halt at about the same point where the liberality of the modern party begins.

Depressing as it may seem to many "liberals," it is just possible that Raytown is more typical of Basic America in the first half of the 1970's than any other part of the metropolitan area, with the possible exception of Kansas City North.

Materialism is there, and people slave for it. Religion is there, mostly comfortable and unchallenging. The love of children which makes people pay some attention to their schools is there. And the generation gap, when those children grow old enough for a little self-assertion, is also there. In short, Raytown is a family of four eating out at McDonald's—a summer evening at a drive-in theater, complete with shock that the children see too much female breast in the preview for next week's more adult attraction. It is a community docile enough to put up with two-lane highways in areas where a four-lane freeway should be a commuter's right. And some say that Raytown, as much as anyplace in the Kansas City area, might look just as natural if it were shoved up against St. Louis as it does hugging the eastern rim of Kansas City. It could even pass for a part of Denver or Joplin.

For Raytown is a little bit of everywhere. It is about as near to the good life as most people get in this country. What people think of Raytown may very well be what they think of America in the 1970's.

"SOUTHTOWN"

To the south of Raytown, in the far southern part of the metropolitan area and to the east, with U.S. Highway 71 serving as its spine, is a section of the city where the Air Force has been the status symbol.

The large Richards-Gebaur Air Force Base is located there, and around this impressive installation—this open manifestation of the military-industrial era—live thousands of persons who have a vested interest in the Air Force. Civilian employees are employed there in substantial numbers, though reduced greatly in the post-Vietnam cutback. Air Force personnel live in the ranch houses and apartment compounds of the area, mixed with a fair number of retired Air Force personnel who liked the life style in the Kansas City area and chose it as a permanent abode.

Near the air base is the splashy Truman Corners Shopping

Center. If one wanted a very "shopping center" kind of a shopping center as a movie location, there's no better spot. It's all there. The huge Milgram supermarket; the shoe store featuring shoes for all the family; the HFC loan office with "money when you need it."

Truman Corners Shopping Center is not the most beautiful, nor the ulgiest, manifestation of commercialism in our time. But it does have one distinction that sets it apart from all the thousands of other shopping centers which look very much like it in this nation. It was on this spot that Harry Truman and his brother Vivian once worked as farm boys. One old-timer in the area once commented, upon seeing Harry and Lyndon Johnson campaigning during the 1960 presidential race at Truman Corners, "Hell, what's all the fuss about? I knew Harry when he looked a mule in the ass all day." This then—is where he did it.

The emotional map of Kansas City must chart other sections too. In the residential areas south of the main section of the city, lying beyond Eighty-fifth Street, there is a basic mood of affluence. Out on the hills southeast of the Bendix plant at Bannister Road (Ninety-fifth) and Troost are some of the most beautiful and liveable-looking homes in all of Kansas City, situated in wonderful wooded hills on winding roads. This is upper-middle class in suburbia. Some attractive country clubs are in this sector, including the Hillcrest Club and one named Oakwood Country Club.

Oakwood was the Jewish community's answer to exclusionism. And it was the scene of an important moment in U.S. political history. For it was here that President Truman received help he could hardly do without during his famous uphill election battle against Thomas E. Dewey. At Oakwood Country Club in the summer of 1948, an earnest group of Jewish leaders came up with enough money to bail out the plucky Missourian and get his stalled campaign train rolling again. Rolling, as it turned out, toward victory.

There are some who say that this incident and Mr. Truman's long-time friendship with Eddie Jacobson were the reasons behind his historic decision to recognize the state of Israel. That was a difficult step to take, but Harry Truman, in later years, gave the impression that it was a decision in which he took particular pride.

But to return to the emotional topography of southtown Kansas City, the area directly south of the Country Club district carries on the tradition of a life style both well heeled and relaxed. Homes into the six-figure bracket are found in the western sectors of southtown.

It is also a good location for viewing the life of affluent Catholicism. This is reflected by the fact that old-line Roman Catholic schools operated by the French Sisters of Notre Dame, another by the Sisters of St. Joseph (Avila College), and still a third by the Sisters of Loretto (though Loretto Academy is now nonsectarian) have all moved from close-in areas to locate in this section. Just a little bit north of the area, the Jesuits caught the idea too. They moved their large Rockhurst High School from the midtown campus on Troost Avenue in the city to a more spacious southtown location on State Line Road.

A mile or so east of the large homes and fashionable schools is a section of beautiful new homes known as Red Bridge, served by a tasteful shopping center.

Here is the good life of Raytown with a little more icing on the cake and a little more chrome on the car. And here is a slightly greater derring-do in the realm of ideas—a tendency to have a moderate openness to ideas other than one's own. It is a world built around the automobile. The ATA, Area Transportation Authority, has been breaking its heart and its bank account for years on attempts to win over Red Bridgers to various kinds of commuter bus services. Now the bus serves Red Bridge once in the morning and once in the evening, and the riders seem to have a common denominator: the basic complexion is dark and the occupation is maid and cleaning lady. And to that, and for places like this, what else is new?

The business tycoon and the government executive from southtown can be seen each morning in long streaming lines of traffic that form and move with reasonable dispatch along Wornall Road and along Holmes Street, headed for downtown or the Plaza. With luck, most of these men and women can be in their buildings within thirty to forty-five minutes at most. Without luck—that is, when one or more inches of snow or ice has fallen, or even a rousing good rainstorm—they have been known to be an hour late. And every few years, Kansas City treats itself to one royal, massive, dead stand-still city-wide tie-up. And when that happens all bets are all the way off.

In southtown there is a sprinkling of black families—analogous economically to the white neighbors. One young Red Bridge attorney could kid that he was thinking of moving out, because the neighborhood had been made unliveable by his new black neighbor. That neighbor, in the attorney's words, "is making the rest of us look bad. He's out there every Saturday pruning those shrubs and manicuring that lawn, and every wife for two blocks around is holding up that blankety-blank as a good example."

That is southtown. To sum it up in a few words, the southtown life style is a lively school board election; finding a wonderful new place to get oriental food; and comparing the relative costs of orthodontists. And if southtown had to be moved somewhere else, it would be a little bit out of place. It seems very naturally rooted in its environment. But if that move had to be, its easiest point of connection would be with Johnson County, Kansas.

JOHNSON COUNTY

So let us move across the state line to the remarkable Johnson County. This can be done in most of Kansas City from about Forty-seventh Street southward by the simple expedient of walking across the street—State Line Road—whose white center lane is one of the few state lines actually painted on the surface for all to see.

It is worth digressing to note that State Line has had its moments. In past times, when police were vying to hold down adverse traffic statistics, there had been, according to police pressroom legend, some minor grisly moments. They tell of a man killed in a head-on crash of his convertible with another car. It happened apparently in dead center of State Line. Was he a Missouri fatality or a Kansas one? Did he indeed perish at the moment of impact—which would put him in Missouri—or did he depart this world because he flew out of the car and hit the pavement head first, which would be in Kansas. Indeed, whose coroner shall certify that he is dead? And whose lucky mortician shall be called to spirit away the remains? Maybe it never happened and maybe it did. One thing is sure—it could happen.

That said, the next stop on the emotional map is beautiful Johnson County, Kansas, which ranks in the top five counties nationally in per family income. It is possible to be poor and even to be black and live in Johnson County. But it is so rare that if people in either status seek help, they will have to face sheer disbelief when they announce they are from Johnson County.

Here, to the fullest possible degree, is the typical big city well-off bedroom community. And that's with all that the accompanying state of mind embraces: encounter groups; great books; kids who quite easily go their own way; police who have so little on their minds people get busted for just littering with a candy bar wrapper; yoga classes; quotes from one's new non-Freudian shrink; and the outdoor barbecue and steak-broiling, raised on weekends to the level of a frenzy. When Walt Bodine lived in Prairie Village (one of dozens of bedroom cities in northeast Johnson County), he used to come home from the TV station on a Saturday evening and encounter a haze of blue smoke (produced by hundreds of outdoor chefs), which would have done credit to an artillery duel on a battlefield.

Johnson Countians are aware of social problems, and may even let the preacher talk about them. Johnson Countians can often be at pains to assure people, especially if they've moved to Johnson County from Kansas City, Missouri, that it really isn't copping out on the city. It's just that they have kids, and Johnson County has these really fantastic schools. And it does. It is probably as school conscious an area as one will ever find. And today more and more school battles seem to revolve around a confrontation between parents who say they are tired of experimentation with their children, and those supporting up-to-date and progressive modes of teaching. There is also, in what has always been a Republican stronghold, a growing tendency to jump the political fence to teach someone a lesson, or even possibly because of the old best-person-for-the-job gambit.

Johnson County seems to spread out forever physically. Fortunes have been made there, obviously from selling houses, but also from installing shrubs or keeping up the air-conditioning or a variety of other goods and services that thrive on the house-centered society. Impressive new publications grow there, like the Squire papers, rated one of the top examples in the nation of the nonthrow-away and well-read suburban press; and the thriving Sun Publications which look more and more like potential daily newspaper ventures, soon to blossom.

And so Johnson County is the life that offers most of what money can buy and, at its most wholesome, a great deal of what money cannot buy. But for all its lovely schools, its landscaping and winding streets and homes planned by the building genius from another decade, J. C. Nichols, there are some serious deficiencies in Johnson County for some people.

For those who feel that part of an education is exposure to all kinds of people, the kids in Johnson County see too much of too many other kids very like themselves, with little difference in annual family incomes. They will not, most likely, rub shoulders with real poverty, other than the occasional encounter with the emotionally impoverished child neglected by a career daddy and a career mommy. If it is important for a kid to know that there is more than one race in this country, or that a black person can be seen in something other than a maid's white dress or a handyman's overalls, Johnson County misses the mark. Likewise, if it is important for children to know what being around old people is like, one can spend long days in Johnson County and see very few of the elderly. And with the absence of the elderly, death is absent as a sort of natural force, a proper end to life. Death there is the cruel interruption of a young life; the stunning loss of a friend's mother; the suicide down the street that neighbors and even police whisper about and hasten to forget. When it is in evidence death almost always involves some person taken out of season; the untimely passing; someone who "had everything in the world"; or "had so much to live for." However, when death does come, the cemetery parks in Johnson County are like the rest of the place—neat and well landscaped—and seem more an affirmation of the comfortable life than of the inevitability or finality of death. This comment is not meant to deny the existence of heaven. But a person is set to wondering just what kind of heaven one might fly to from a quarter-million-dollar mansion in Mission Hills or a block-long ranch house in Leawood.

The basic Johnson County state of mind then is, for the most, wholesome. Who wouldn't rather have green grass than dusty concrete? And who wouldn't rather send their kids to a school immune from what the media call "a racial disturbance." Who wouldn't rather get away from it all after a hard day at the office?

And so Johnson County is a woman in a station wagon filled with three kids and one dog; it is a Bruce Smith drugstore, one that somehow seems nicer than a plain old drugstore; it is men in casual sweaters down at the hardware store in the shopping center trying to tell the man what size nails they want; it is a desperate mixture of contempt and need directed at tradespeople and repairpersons of all kinds; it is kids running confidently across everybody's lawns and shouting happy shouts. And it is Mr. Jones from Twenty-ninth and Forest in the inner city sitting (outside) in his battered '64 Chevy waiting for Mrs. Jones to come on out so they can go home—riding through the rich streets and saying inside that car whatever they say to each other and thinking what they and God alone will know.

One footnote to Johnson County should be added, concerning Mission Hills, which is relatively close in to the Plaza (in midtown Kansas City), and only a stone's throw from the Missouri line. Mission Hills puts every Los Angeleno automatically in mind of Beverly Hills, except that some say it looks a little richer. There are homes that cover all of a long city block. While driving past the magnificent home of the late Mrs. Russell Stover, co-founder with her husband of the Stover Candy empire, a visitor asked, "My God, what is it; it can't be a house, can it? Isn't it some fancy school or institution?"

But there it is, the house that candy built, and maybe part of it built by the Eskimo pie which was invented by Russell Stover. But it sits among the other houses; the house that chemicals built, the house that vitamins built, the house that banking built, the one that an exceptional medical practice built, and so on and so on and so on. Like Beverly Hills, there's even a mansion or two that motion pictures built.

In its leanest years, here was a neighborhood the Republican party could depend on; and it still holds true. In the 1972 presidential election, for example, Mission Hills went for Richard Nixon over George McGovern by a margin of six to one.

Here then are people who can look rich even on a field of rich people. And yet this must be said too. At this highest economic level, as in the much more humble bungalows in old northeast Kansas City, the Kansas City person who makes it, a little or a lot, tends to put it into a house more than anything else. And of the Mission Hills state of mind, people should note that in general the rich of Kansas City are not given to flashing it. The rolling stock, in Mission Hills, for example, looks not too different from that of other Johnson County neighborhoods. Buicks and Oldsmobiles seem every bit as "in" as Continentals and Mercedeses. And the chauffeured limousine is a genuine rarity. When observed, it generally contains an elderly rich person, or someone who might hasten to explain to you that his eyes aren't what they used to be. But the native rich of Kansas City are at pains not to lay it on, and to apologize or rationalize a little if they do.

The only notable exception that comes to mind is the man who led Marion Laboratories to the financial big leagues, and who owns the city's major league baseball club, the Royals. Ewing Kauffman may be observed moving about the city in a chauffeured Cadillac that was built to be nothing but a limousine. It borders on the obvious with its color scheme of bright blue under snow white, the colors of the Kansas City Royals. And on its top are one, two, three shortwave radio aerials.

Some might put Mr. Kauffman down a bit for this un-Kansas City-like show of pizazz. But some people like to see somebody enjoy money now and then, and Mr. Kauffman seems to be such a man. More than that, Ewing Kauffman, unlike many a more staid member of the millionaires' club (K.C. has four hundred of them), has freely plowed back huge chunks of money into the fortunes of the city where he himself waxed fortunate. On him, a touch of pizazz looks good, and after all, a little pizazz never hurt anybody. Besides, it does make life a little more interesting for those people who live well down the road from Mission Hills.

KANSAS CITY, KANSAS

And so to Kansas City, Kansas—the suffering municipal also-ran right across the Kaw, still striving to achieve an identity of its own; and still in many ways entitled to a pride it doesn't really claim in the field of human relations.

Kansas City, Kansas, has a state of mind best described as simply the state of mind of second cities everywhere. St. Paul looking at Minneapolis; Fort Worth looking at Dallas; the plain twin looking at the beautiful twin. Why, even Chicago is said to harbor a second city inferiority complex toward New York.

The question is: do second cities try harder, and if they do, will it do any good? Judging from Kansas City, Kansas, they do try, and it doesn't do much good in competition with the big sister across the river, but it has seemed to help in giving the city a somewhat improved self-image.

Kansas City, Kansas, makes no great point of it, but as a city it seems to have done a better job overall than Kansas City, Missouri, or most places for that matter, in achieving a kind of peace among its large variety of ethnic and racial groups.

KCK, as it is often called, comes nearer to resembling an Eastern city in its ethnic mix. It has large areas of Eastern European nationalities; there are lively Polish dancers in action up on Strawberry Hill, a place where Catholic churches recur every few blocks. Kansas City, Missouri, tends to have well-defined ethnic groups only among Italians, Mexican-Americans, blacks, and—if the term ethnic may be stretched—Jews.

In Kansas City, Kansas, one finds Poles, Hungarians, Romanians, Croatians, Russians, plenty of Irish, lots of Mexicans, a smattering of Indians, and a significant black community.

Furthermore, the contrast in the ability to handle social explosiveness was manifest in those tense hours and days following the assassination of Dr. Martin Luther King. In both Kansas Cities, students from mostly black high schools began to march toward their respective central business districts. In Kansas City, Missouri, despite personal efforts to intervene on the scene by a courageous mayor, Ilus W. Davis, the situation was already out of hand. Aroused blacks and edgy police were squared off and the inevitable came to pass—a riot that lasted several days, the burning of numerous buildings, the ultimate loss of eight lives, and intervention by a Southern-minded governor who brought in the National Guard and extra highway patrolmen.

Missouri Governor Warren Hearnes was as insensitive as he

was ineffective. He went on the radio to reassure the citizenry, but to many, it seemed to be a white-on-white speech. One young black mother recalls, "There I am in a house at 30th and Wabash, huddled under the dining room table with my kids. And I can see that orange light flickering on the wall that tells me something nearby is burning. And I can hear the pop pop of gun fire. And I have this transistor radio there and do you know what I hear? I hear the governor making this speech which sounds like, 'Don't worry Whitey, out there in Overland Park [Johnson County], I'm here to protect you.' And I'm there wondering if I'm going to be able to stay alive and keep my kids alive, and I think, 'Hell, don't I have a governor too? Who's going to protect me?'"

That was Kansas City, Missouri. But in Kansas City, Kansas, where the same kind of scene had begun to unfold, the students were met by Boston Daniels, that city's first black police chief. He offered to go with the marchers and urged them to make it a peaceful and sober event that would be a fitting statement to the world about the Reverend Martin Luther King. They were joined by Mayor Joseph McDowell, the former mayor of KCK who enjoyed strong public support for years—and incidentally was the first mayor of a city that size or larger to publicly proclaim a moratorium when the Vietnam War protest movement surfaced in earnest. That day, there was an orderly march, with very little damage and admirable control all around. And the result, furthermore, was that Kansas City, Kansas, went through that tormented period without a riot.

So live-and-let-live has to be a part of the Kansas City, Kansas, psyche. And otherwise, well, some people think of it as a gossipy city; one can always hear a good rumor in Kansas City, Kansas, and people really enjoy them. For a city that never had a riot, it was a town that rumored a new one every two and a half minutes.

It is a very political city. For those who like the strong mayor concept, Kansas City, Kansas, is capable of producing it—the only Republican mayor ever elected lasted only one term, in 1971. In Kansas City, Kansas, municipal government at the top is blessedly simple. There is no big complicated city council; three people do all the deciding, the mayor and two other commissioners of finance and streets.

Former Mayor McDowell once said, "I feel sorry for the mayor over there in Kansas City, Missouri, having to wrangle with that big council and a city manager everytime he wants a new box of paper clips. Now, over here, I just walk down the hall going to the men's room, and I can see one of the commissioners and say, 'Hey, I want to talk to you.' We can go into the men's room and stand at adjoining urinals while I tell him something we need to take care of, and if he agrees, we pass the measure and it's settled right then and there for all practical purposes—before we even zip up and walk away. Now you can't beat that for speedy and efficient government."

One other note about Kansas City, Kansas, should be added. In recent years, the suburban attitude has grown to dilute some of the second-city feeling in Kansas City, Kansas. Western suburbs of the city have picked up enough population to have real political punch; indeed, the former mayor, Republican Richard Walsh, was a product of such a political base himself. And so the tug of war goes on between Center City, the attempt to beautify, modernize, and mall-ize the downtown area along Minnesota Avenue, and the new outlying shopping centers of which the Indian Springs Shopping Center is the largest. Indian Springs would be considered large in any national competition for size and diversity in a shopping center.

So there it is: Kansas City, Kansas; doomed to see and hear the mass media emanating from the Missouri side speaking of "Kansas City," and "City Hall" as if they were the only ones around—and carefully adding the state name in any reference to Kansas City, Kansas.

There is language to go with the state of mind too. In Missouri, reference is made to things which happen "on the Kansas side," or "over there in Kansas." In KCK, little old ladies, to the despair of local boosters, still speak of going "over town" (to KC, Mo.) to shop at Macy's or the Jones Store.

There is at once something a little bit run down when one conjures up the image of Kansas City, Kansas. And yet there is also something folksy and wholesome about that place which seems so much like the places where so many people grew up, even "on the Missouri side."

In recent times, there has crept in a small note of defiance when a Kansas City Kansan refers jokingly to the town as "Sin City." This is the reaction to a Kansas City *Star* series exposing certain vice, gambling and liquor law violations there—most of which have been going on almost as long as memory in KCK. And perhaps characteristically as his townspeople's representative, former Mayor Walsh only smiled a boyish smile when he excused himself early from a governmental gathering at the Plaza in Kansas City, Missouri, only to have some waggish reporter ask, "How come you've got to rush back home, Mayor; are you dedicating a new massage parlor or something?"

But that's it—feeling a little sheepish about Kansas morality, on the one hand, and the human urge to live it up a little on the other; that's all part of the Kansas City, Kansas, way of thinking.

But that is how it is. And there may be some truth to the statement of one old KC hand who said, "If the Second Coming should happen to occur in Kansas City, Kansas, it will be some little time before they get the word out to Kansas City, Missouri. And they still won't be as impressed as if it'd happened somewhere else."

To carry on the transplant analogy once more, if Kansas City, Kansas, had to be moved, it would probably fit reasonably well next to Columbus, Ohio, or perhaps Oklahoma City. But never *in* those cities; always across the way—a little bit envious, but also somewhat self-possessed.

KANSAS CITY NORTH

And so the emotional terrain tour comes around full circle to look at Kansas City North. Kansas City North did not embrace Kansas City like a convert, it was dragged in. By annexation, shrewdly perpetrated by ex-city manager Perry Cookingham, Kansas City suddenly threw the lasso of annexation around a squealing Clay County area of impressive size. Much of it was undeveloped at the time. One annexed farmer asked what city services the municipality could offer his cows. There was a mighty hue and cry, a rebellion led by—as one KC establishment man put it—"blue eyed reformers." A leader in this was Randall

S. Jessee, who was a commentator for a station then owned by the Kansas City *Star*, even while the *Star* was vigorously supporting Mr. Cookingham's action.

But when the last court battle had been lost, when the last plea on a talk show had decried annexation by a council vote when those to be annexed hadn't elected the council (taxation without representation), the resistance finally died down. Police cars began to patrol the streets in Kansas City North; fire department drivers were out studying maps and locations (it would be humiliating for a fire truck to have to go into a filling station and ask directions), and the annexation became an established fact. Later, a portion of Platte County, also north of the river and the site of the city's new super airport, was similarly annexed.

For years, the Clay County state of mind was one of sullen resistance to almost anything City Hall might say or do. There was widespread hostility toward the nonpartisan "reform" party, the Citizens Association, which Clay Countians felt had afflicted the world with Mr. Cookingham. It didn't matter that L. P. Cookingham had become the dean of city managers and was held in high regard by great numbers of people at every level of society. He was the devil's instrument, if not the old boy himself in Clay County.

The Clay County state of mind is much like that of Raytown. It has the same mixture of white collar workers, business people, skilled and upper level blue collar workers, and a large number of persons concerned with the auto industry and employed at Ford's big Claycomo plant; and with this, a strong representation of TWA employees, since the airline's great international overhaul base is located in Platte County.

These are the upward mobile families who have put a lot into a house, in many cases, and above everything else don't want to hear themselves saying someday, "Well, there goes the neighborhood." So Clay County—the part of it in Kansas City—comes very close to being truly lily white.

There is a noticeable lack of folderol in Clay County, and families tend to spend a lot of time at home. One wag chided, "There are even houses for sale which come complete with a car up on blocks."

There is an interesting legend about Clay County, which the

mind of the community knows about and seems to take in stride, and even approves of. According to this legend, certain purported leaders of the Mafia had sought to move to Clay County and in doing so arrive at a bargain with the reigning lawmen there. The deal, roughly, was: if you don't bother and harass us, we will see that you have a nice crime-free county. And the legend says that is just what happened.

There is a further legend that certain of these leaders have enormous homes in Clay County which are said to be connected by underground tunnels. Years ago when Walt Bodine was news director of WDAF-TV4, the NBC station here, David Brinkley called up about a piece he was doing which took the unusual attitude that maybe crime does pay. He wondered if WDAF couldn't get him some film of those fabulous houses in Kansas City North that he had heard about.

The alleged Mafiosi, by the way, are men who have never had a serious enough conviction to earn a day in prison. Yet it says something about their reputation, despite all their protestations, that the roughest and toughest cameramen on WDAF's staff did not care to earn a hundred or so by cruising up north to bring back the brief footage requested.

Supposedly, the network finally accomplished its goal by hiring a private detective who shot through a two-way mirror in the back of what appeared to be a telephone company truck.

Clay County is another place where people pay some attention to schools. But the wrangling over far-out progressive methods doesn't emerge there, as it does sometimes in Johnson County. This suggests that a more conservative kind of educator has been ensconced there from the start. Clay County, Missouri, like Johnson County, Kansas, abounds in large and impressive new high school buildings.

Clay also has a fine network of freeways to speed the locals along. But at the same time, the outlying and thinly populated areas have some of the most neglected streets and roads in the metro area.

The basic Clay County emotions are geared to that home in the suburb, that car in the garage, the kid in the school, and maybe—in dreaming time—a boat to take on fishing get-aways to the Lake of the Ozarks or to one of the many other good fishing lakes in Missouri and Kansas.

And with all of that goes an abiding distrust of politicians from Kansas City south of the river. The underlying feeling is that if they've done Northlanders in once they may do it again.

An earlier chapter mentioned the way a river can be a much bigger barrier than its physical depth or width would suggest. Nowhere is this more evident than in the division between Kansas City and Kansas City North. Not only have the Northlanders become a people who only trust their own, but in their discontent they have also been an enigma to the southside politician. Even former Mayor Ilus Davis, a thoughtful and sensitive man ordinarily, was once heard to complain, "What on earth do *those people* want anyway?" The truth is that in much thinking in Kansas City proper, the Northlanders are "those people." And whenever a group is known as "those people" they are likely to feel some justifiable alienation.

20. THE EMOTIONAL TERRAIN

PART II

Having taken a "feeling" tour of the suburbs and outskirts of Kansas City, Missouri, the authors turn here to the emotional topography of the central city itself. That would be from the Kansas state line on the west to Independence on the east—and from the Missouri River on the north to Eighty-fifth Street on the south.

While Kansas City has some seventy-five neighborhoods and ten thousand city blocks within it, it has been broken up into some larger pieces for the purpose of analysis.

An apt place to begin is a portion of the far north side that is called Little Italy. Little Italy is only a shadow of its former self. It has been shrunk physically by the incursions of freeways. And a great many of the descendants of old Italian families have moved to other parts of town—choosing assimilation over devotion to motherland culture.

The essential flavor of Little Italy is still there, however, including Passantino's funeral parlor—scene of Catholic wakes beyond the counting and, in days long past, the site of several gangster funerals complete with all the trimmings befitting the departure of a gangland lord.

Holy Rosary Catholic Church is still there at 911 East Missouri. And the present pastor probably shakes his head as did one a few years ago, who lamented that in this neighborhood the

women and children come to church, and the men only for
Easter, weddings, funerals, or in their own old age; "cramming
for their finals" as the pastor put it.

Little Italy is still a symbol of the sizable Italian population in
Kansas City. Visitors will find there some of what is best in Italian life; some places to eat that are as sensationally good as their
exteriors are unpromising. One also sees some of the physical
beauty of many Italians, men and women—and the inevitable
motherliness of the Italian woman who in later middle age seems
to gain both weight and empathy.

In general, there is a tendency toward defensiveness—a kind of
mass self-pity. This relates to the feeling that there is still much
prejudice in Kansas City against Italians.

"If your name ends with a vowel," says lawyer and businessman E. L. Polsinelli, member of a well-respected family,
"you are always on trial. When you meet a stranger and he hears
your name, he looks at you more closely as if to see if you are
some kind of hoodlum. And that gets very, very old."

It is true that some of the infamous names in crime or
machine-style politics ended with vowels; Johnny Lazia, Charles
Binnagio, Charles Gargotta, all three of whom were eventually
rubbed out in gangland-style slayings.

Studies of prejudice in Kansas City by the Jewish Community
Relations Bureau have verified a fairly strong strain of anti-
Italian feeling. But the studies were made some years ago. And
to those who don't feel the direct brunt of such prejudice it
seems that this kind of feeling is dying down.

Emotions do run high among Italians when there is any effort
in politics or media to rekindle this form of discrimination.
Significantly the Kansas City Italian community made the most
vocal protest that was registered nationally to the motion picture
The Godfather.

Local Italian leaders bought out *The Godfather* at the big
Missouri theater downtown. A ceremony was held in the lobby
just before the performance, denouncing the film before TV
cameras—including the national CBS Evening News. When the
projectionist rolled the film they walked out en masse, leaving
The Godfather to be played out before a completely empty
theater.

That is Little Italy. The rest of the north end—"the river wards," as politicians know them—is absorbed by the River Quay development.

Downtown is another story. It is going through the change of life so familiar to many American cities.

While many large stores have closed up, surrendering to the shopping center trend, the new downtown is taking shape. The $30-million H. Roe Bartle Convention Center should trigger many other new facilities for housing, feeding, and entertaining convention delegates.

The skyline reflects the city's resurgence. For years after World War II the skyline stood unchanged, with seven basic skyscrapers. Visitors quoted in the press often like to say something nice about the city they are in. One English visitor turned the poverty of tall buildings into a virtue by saying he liked the Kansas City skyline because it had left space between the tall buildings for sunshine and blue skies. Today, started by the Trader's Bank skyscraper, new towers have gone up all over downtown and more are abuilding.

The basic emotions of downtown then are those of the older observer who feels all is lost for downtown—and those of the new planners who foresee a different kind of downtown.

But there are specific areas of downtown which have a different mood about them. The area just west of the Muehlebach Hotel on Twelfth Street is one example. Here is a section of honky-tonks, burlesque theaters, third-rate hotels, and porno peep shows which provides a look of visible sin.

Hookers and vice squad cops play hide and seek; bartenders, bellhops and go-go girls watch the passing parade with the imperturbability that goes with having seen it all with no big surprises left.

Yet even there, one finds some of the spirit of moderation that characterizes Kansas City. For this is not an open red light district by a long way—although the dentist from Omaha can look hard enough and figure how to connect with the fun and games. The strippers don't quite strip—pasties and G-strings are used to conciliate civic sensitivities. The expected gambling games in the backrooms are not there. In other words, there is about as much sin as River City will tolerate—and no more.

Even so, in the executive suites where the architects of the new Kansas City labor, there is an avowed determination to tear down honky-tonk row and put up something more seemly next to the convention center.

Around downtown there are sections of high-rise apartment buildings constructed to accommodate those who like heart-of-the-city living. But those people are such a diverse group, and so briefly visible as they fade into their buildings each evening, that it is difficult to detect their state of mind.

Civic Center, however, has a vitality and a feeling of being a big part of what's happening. It is on Twelfth Street just east of the business area. A skyscraper city hall faces a skyscraper county courthouse. On the sides of this pairing of giants is located a modern public library and school administration building, a municipal courts building, police headquarters and a beautiful block-long, eighteen-story federal office building housing many federal regional offices and a daytime working population of six thousand.

Standing on the sidewalks near Twelfth and Oak, a people-watcher will eventually see everyone who is anyone in the governmental and legal professions. At noon when courts recess, one can walk along and eavesdrop little snatches of various court cases, as the lawyers, court employees, and others head out for lunch. Now and then the viewer will see what looks like a moving huddle; after getting closer it turns out to be some handcuffed bad guys being led from police headquarters to the prosecutor's office and jail in the courthouse.

To the north of Twelfth Street is one of the more melancholy areas of downtown, Ninth Street and several nearby cross streets. These blocks, with their tacky-looking small businesses, third-rate hotels, and restaurants that don't wash their windows often enough, serve a mostly elderly clientele. Old men and women living on Social Security or other modest income inhabit the ancient hotels. It is a rare stroll down the block in this area when one does not encounter the old man who has had a stroke, walking with a cane, one arm dangling at his side, or an alcoholic, totally discouraged about life.

In a smaller city, these older people would sit around the courthouse square. But here they "put in the time" staying in lonely rooms, talking with each other in lobbies in a kind of despair too painful to acknowledge, or venturing out for a cup of coffee and a seat at the drugstore fountain for as long as they will be allowed to stay.

If the accent is on age on Ninth Street, there is a distinctly youthful look about Crown Center, at the south end of downtown. Since they are described in other chapters, the authors will pass over Crown Center and the nearby Hospital Hill section for now.

The next point of interest in an emotional topography is the Westport area in midtown. Around Thirty-ninth and Main the vestiges of the youth culture of the sixties and early seventies remain; head shops, cheap clothing stores, quick lunch places, and empty storerooms. This area is some kind of magnet that attracts the teen-age runaway.

Swinging away from all this is Westport Road, which runs southwest from Fortieth and Main toward better times on Broadway. Along this street with its record stores, boutiques, Italian delicatessens, health food havens, and other attractions move young people from all parts of the city.

In this section of Westport there is an interesting mixture of old and young. This is where the young couples, married and otherwise, find inexpensive living quarters.

It is also where many old settlers hang on in their one- and two-story houses. That same kind of mixing of the new and old is embodied in Kelly's tavern and deli at Westport Road and Pennsylvania. Kelly's occupies one of the oldest buildings in Kansas City. While other hangouts come and go, Kelly's is the one "in" place that stays "in" with the college intellectual crowd.

Westport sprawls out from this area in several directions. To the north and west of Westport Road is the Broadway Valentine neighborhood, where residents and developers with big ideas slug it out in public relations political and legal battles to see who will inherit the earth.

To the west, in the Westport Roanoke area, a wonderful collection of big rambling houses speaks of past affluence and of present-day residents who respect their beauty and comfort. The Roanoke section in particular has an artistic cast to it. Architects, sculptors, and painters are sprinkled liberally through the population here. Foremost among them were the late artist and his business associate/wife, Thomas Hart Benton and Rita Benton. After their deaths three months apart in 1975, the home of "The Duke and Duchess of Roanoke" was purchased by the State of Missouri as a gallery and community meeting place.

Through much of Westport one finds the young professionals fixing up big old homes and remnants of the older wealthy families still hanging on. In some sections houses are split into apartments for student living. Taken altogether, the human spectrum is as wide in Westport as in any part of Kansas City. It is a melting pot of economic and occupational groups. It is a cheering thought that, with all its diversity, Westport is an urban environment that works.

Before leaving the northwest quadrant of Kansas City we should speak also of the merging West Side—situated along the hilly areas of near downtown and midtown. The West Side, heart of the Mexican community, has a great deal of the closeness characteristic of immigrant communities. One reason is that a sizable number of the inhabitants are first-generation U.S. citizens. Neighborhood dances may have gone by the boards almost everywhere else, but on the West Side they are major events, attracting throngs of people. The politically passive nature of the West Side is now beginning to change. The West Side's Mexican population of the seventies is at the same stage of awakening and development of leadership as the black community experienced a decade or so before.

Turning to the Country Club Plaza, one encounters not only a life style in the area around it, but the Plaza is bound up with the consciousness of the whole community. In San Francisco the cable car and the Golden Gate Bridge are the symbols of what that place is all about. In San Antonio the heart place would be the Alamo, in Boston, Beacon Hill and the Commons. And in Kansas City, that place is the Plaza, with its Spanish architecture. Some sneer that it is camp—a rich form of Spanish kitsch, or the art of the grotesque. But all will agree that it is cohesive . . . one of the few cases where a developer maintained complete control, down to the last painted tile.

Designed in the 1920's by J. C. Nichols, as the world's first shopping center, the buildings bordering the shops of the Plaza

have tried to repeat the themes of sandy brown brick and graceful lines.

We live in an age of self-serving egotism, when most people
who have buildings built for them completely ignore the site's
surroundings, concentrating solely on pleasing their own sense of
taste, making their building a real "I-full." The Plaza is exceptional in that it evokes an emotional loyalty from people all over
the city who care about keeping it the way it is. In the Plaza
area, a business person planning a building will take great pains
with the architect, and with great flourish and waving of hands
admonish that the design must blend in.

To some people, it is a mystery why people would take such
pains to preserve Spanish architecture in a city so devoid of
Spanish heritage that someone once rumored the last real Span-
iard in Kansas City was an exotic dancer at the Folly Burlesque
Theatre. Perhaps it is because the grand style of the Plaza is
more imaginary and dreamlike than plain old Midwestern func-
tionalism. The Plaza is a fun place because it feels like
someplace. It is not a polyglot of architectural competition, but a
whole area that feels like one cohesive place. And today that is
very rare, and much to be appreciated, Spanish or not.

To most people, the Plaza embodies both the good life and
good taste. In a materialistic sense, it extols what the good things
are. But it does it in a physical setting that everyone can share.
Anyone can come to the Plaza, rich or poor, and it will be soft to
their eyes. The flower baskets hanging from the light posts cheer
the pathway for the lady from the limousine and also for the
busboy coming from the Alameda Plaza kitchens.

Every city has a center place where boy meets girl, where the
residents take their out-of-town visitors, where women meet for
lunch and shopping. In Kansas City that once was downtown.
But in the sense that the Plaza is really where these things happen now, the Plaza *is* the new downtown.

The human side of the Plaza is varied by the points of the
compass.

On the north side of the Plaza, with one or two exceptions, are
older apartment buildings and some individual homes. Working
young women, bachelors, young marrieds are found here in large
numbers. Many are in that economic bracket which lets them

live better than in a rented room but not as well as those in the new "singles' town houses," some of which cluster near the west end of the Plaza.

East of the Plaza along Forty-seventh are rows of older apartment buildings and a mixture of age groups, still with a good share of the young.

Along the Plaza's south side begin the older high-rise apartment buildings, which have always contained an uncommon number of pretty young women, many being airline stewardesses. And west of these are other, and larger, older buildings. Some of the more well-fixed retirees have settled in this area. Behind them, up the hill, tall new apartment structures with outside porches offer a commanding, and often expensive, view.

One local wag, noted for cynicism, has concluded that, "The Plaza has cornered the world market on little old ladies with blue hair." One may wince at the cynicism more than the data. In a similar vein, one is reminded that in one luxury apartment building there is an elevator with chairs in it.

South of the Plaza is the Loose Park neighborhood. Again there is a mixture of old-line residents of means who like the area—and of younger families, many attracted by the roominess of the old homes, the comfortable feel of the neighborhood with its big trees and nearby park, and the accessibility of good schools. This section has more than its share of doctors, lawyers, and other professional types.

From here on out through the Southwest High School environs the feel of the neighborhoods is middle and upper class. It is a section of the city where Republican precinct workers have more bounce in their stride. Like Johnson County a good portion of this neighborhood—from the south rim of the Plaza to Gregory Boulevard (some twenty-three blocks)—proved its Republican faith in the ultimate test; it went for Barry Goldwater in 1964, something only two wards in the entire city managed to do.

"More recently," according to one knowledgeable former Republican legislator, Ray James, "this area has tended to be more independent. Because it is psychologically middle class it responds well to Republican appeals. But no Republican is safe in that section, anymore, if the Democratic opponent is clean and honest. It isn't the liberalism of Democrats that turns them off; it is that they tend to reject any Democrat with the least tarnish."

In any case, as Johnson County, Kansas, is the good life suburban style, this part of Kansas City, Missouri, is the good life urban style. And at its best, by that standard, would be the special life style of Ward Parkway. Along this spacious artery—with a median strip wide enough for mirror pools, fountains, and flower gardens—there is not so much a feeling of neighborhood as there is of people looking at each other from castle to castle. Here are some of the largest mansions in Kansas City, one or two to a block from the Plaza to Meyer Boulevard. Even before Mission Hills and Leawood were, Ward Parkway was; and today with very little real erosion, Ward Parkway still is. It could be said of many of Kansas City's affluent areas that you could probably live there for a while without money, and fake it. On Ward Parkway such a thing would be inconceivable.

Instead a drive along Ward Parkway reveals some great solid mansions. One wonders what it is like to live there. Like viewing scenes from old movies having a real life enactment inside, there is perhaps the elegant gentleman in his smoking jacket saying, "Gentlemen, will you join me in the drawing room for brandy?" Or there is the beautiful young woman who reeks of good schooling and understated elegance, standing there in her riding outfit while her mother advises, "You little fool, don't you know he's playing you along for your money?" But when these late show images fade, one remembers that these are Ward Parkway rich people. Without violating those sacred precincts to see for themselves, the authors would be willing to wager that in all of upper-class Kansas City there is not one English butler. About French maids and Filipino houseboys they are less certain. In any case the Ward Parkwayites cannot blame the rest of society for speculating about what they are really like. Because after all, they are never to be seen out in the yard. The nearest one gets is the sight of the Mercedes or the Rolls in the driveway. The drive south down Ward Parkway provokes the idea that in Kansas City the farther south one goes the richer things get. But there is an end. Somewhere out there past Seventy-first Street the tides of affluence break against the rocks of dear old Waldo.

This was another world of its own when Kansas City came out to meet it. Waldo made it as a commuter stop in the days of streetcars and interurbans. In its center, where there is now a parking lot—what else?—there once stood a red brick depot where the commuters gathered for morning coffee and to crowd onto the tram for downtown. Those who liked fresh air could catch the Dodson streetcar which went winding off into the southern sticks where a collector of vacant lots could find all he wanted. Those who did probably turned a nice profit later as the city swept on into the Seventies, the Eighties, and ultimately to 150th Street, the present southern city limit.

Waldo really has character. No matter what anybody does, it still has the feel of being a small town in the middle of a city. The merchants would like to call it a shopping center but it is really more. Side by side are things like a Western Auto store and an excellent Chinese restaurant; there is a TG & Y, but there is also an excellent shop for stamp and coin collectors. Waldo has a homey, old-fashioned bakery where people from all over town stand in line to buy yummy things; there is a Savings and Loan with, of course, the inescapable sign that flashes the time; there is an old neighborhood movie house which has become perhaps the finest dinner theater in America complete with an orchestra that comes up out of the pit just like old times. It's now called the "Waldo Astoria." And there is a superb Italian restaurant, Jasper's, where in Starlight Theater season one may run into Mitzi Gaynor having a midnight supper.

The neighbors take Waldo for granted, with its mixture of the homey things and the misplaced exotic spots. But the world is finding it out. Walt Bodine emerged one Sunday from a Winchell's doughnut place at Seventy-fifth and Wornall to find three Japanese tourists, complete with cameras, seeking directions. He decided then that the Japanese truly are everywhere.

But this is middle-class America—with a slight liberal leaning. It is the kind of place where candidates for office vie with each other to see who can put up the most yard signs. One can meet both Archie Bunker and Maude here, depending on which doorbell is rung.

Between Waldo (at Seventy-fifth) and Eighty-fifth Street there are some very modest areas of homes and a few blocks that have all the marks of near poverty areas; kids on the corners who look as if they aren't sure whose they are—and here and there a yard with several junk cars in it. The addresses of these few blocks would sound "good" downtown except to those who have stumbled into these forgotten sections.

Wornall Road, the main artery here, reminds people of some of the worst streets in Los Angeles. It is possible to walk up Wornall if one has any inclination, but sidewalks are spotty and the walk is mostly up and down over the driveways of TV repair places, filling stations, franchise eating places, liquor stores, and grocery stores. Worse, it is a visual nightmare—a fast-food Las Vegas. In the aggregate, Wornall is a blaze of unco-ordinated neon signs and a jumble of buildings irregularly set, with diagonal parking in makeshift lots in front of them.

Just east of Waldo is an area of nice older homes, twenty to thirty years old, with tree-lined streets and a look of pleasant comfortableness without pretense.

About a dozen blocks to the east is Troost Avenue, a busy street. In a city with lots of boulevards, all hostile to trucks, Troost Avenue is a teamster's dream. Its river of traffic is also a dividing line of life styles. On to the east the upward mobile black families have been moving in in large numbers. Many of the white residents have taken this as a signal to flee—as white residents will do. But in the Marlborough Heights section there are a fair number of white residents who have resisted the panic efforts of a few hungry real estate operators.

The rest of the southeast part of the city falls into that category known as a "changing neighborhood." Economic conditions have slowed down some of the changing, but the direction of the area is fairly clear. It will be a mixed section for some time to come. Fortunately, the racial uneasiness of past years seems to have subsided.

Completing the feeling tour of the core city, the authors head back north into the streets numbered in the Fifties and the Forties and come to the university area of the city. The University of Missouri at Kansas City, with a student body of 11,500, and Rockhurst College, with 1,200 students, set the tone here. It is a section of faculty homes and of student rooms and apartments. The UMKC students call the area from Troost Avenue to the Plaza in the Forties the "student ghetto."

This area and some of Westport contain the biggest part of the liberal vote in Kansas City. But it is a quiet kind of liberalism that talks about human needs and the quality of life more than it debates the sayings of Chairman Mao. The Paul Krassners, Angela Davises, and Jerry Rubins have all in their time come and gone—probably despairing over a rabble that will not rouse —and crowds that are a little too polite, seemingly gathered more in curiosity than in revolutionary fervor.

But that is how it is in River City. In the nervous 1960's, the high water mark was a Symposium on Dissent on the UMKC campus, some war protest picketing including a try or two at stopping morning traffic in a desperate attempt to see if this might be the elusive jugular of the body politic. It wasn't. A few tolerant cops turned up and got things moving. Some symbolic arrests were made and that was that. The Vietnam Veterans Against the War claimed a TV tower for a while, making all the local broadcasters nervous. And finally an authentic bearded bomber showed up to plant a few explosives and in time be apprehended on the Plaza.

Finally, the inner city. As mentioned above, Kansas City had one fair-sized riot in the wake of the murder of Dr. Martin Luther King, in 1968. And it scared the daylights out of almost everyone white and black, although it gave most blacks some kind of a feeling of self-assertion. When it was over, several blocks had been burned—all well inside the inner city; the National Guard had been called in—including a lot of Missouri country boys who had never seen the big city before. And the dead, eight in number, were all blacks. Several of the victims had wandered in innocence into the wrong place at the wrong time.

The black community, in the weeks following, was given the closest scrutiny it had experienced to date. The underlying thought was that if anybody acted up in that way the establishment had better find out what it was they really wanted. Rap groups abounded. Journalists tried to analyze who the real leaders were. Law officers kept a close watch on anyone who qualified as a militant. Businesses began to plan programs to enlarge black job opportunities. In other words, a more or less standard after-the-riot reaction.

Today the black community, in the central and southeast parts of town as well as in the ghetto areas east of downtown, is politically much more sophisticated. A population once led around by exploiting and patronizing white factional pols turned those rascals out. The black community has developed political leaders who can bargain with the *best* of them at City Hall and at the county, state, and national levels. The organization, Freedom, Inc., founded by the late Leon Jordan and now headed by Harold (Doc) Holliday, Jr., is the dominant force although not the only one. A city bond issue, a bid for the governorship, a school levy election; in all of these one of the early considerations of the white proponent is, "What will Freedom do?"

In addition to the practical political leadership in the inner city, the moral leadership appears to be built mostly around the churches. In black Kansas City as in white Kansas City, there seems to be a taste for moderation mixed with a dedication to further upward and outward growth.

The greatest lingering sore spot is in police and black relations. The city in general almost canonized Clarence Kelley at the time he was tapped by President Nixon to head the FBI. The lone dissenting voice came from Bruce Watkins of Freedom, Inc., who traveled to Washington to testify against Kelley's appointment before a congressional committee.

Kelley's successes were many, but building the confidence of the black community was not one of them. Nor was there any notable progress in his efforts to recruit black men for training as police officers, which is still at 6 per cent and holding.

When incidents occur involving allegations of police brutality, the result has been an instant polarization with the blacks believing the story of the black citizen who says he was brutalized, and the police believing that the actions of the officers involved were justified. The Office of Citizen Complaints, a pale facsimile of a police civilian review board, seems to the black community like a window-dressing operation under police control.

At the same time, many black citizens are concerned about crime. They point out that when black crime is discussed it often happens that the fact is omitted that blacks contribute out of proportion as victims of crime as well as criminals.

In summer, the black property owner, the middle-aged wage earner, and others are eager for city programs to occupy "the

youth". At the time of the Nixon cutbacks on many urban programs, Kansas City took strong steps to keep an effective summer work program in force for black youngsters.

One final area rounds out the Kansas City picture. It is a section that sends liberal politicians to the wailing wall and where
any politician had better know what he or she is doing before
making a move. It is the area often mentioned as "out Northeast." In New York terms, it might be considered the Queens of
Kansas City.

The Northeast is a large geographic area of Kansas City involving most of the northeast quadrant of the city other than the
black areas. Its people are hard working and the blue collar out-
numbers the white collar many times over. It has a tremendous
number of older people who live on the often mentioned "small
fixed income" and try to hold onto a little piece of property that
they can call home.

To the civic do-gooders downtown, some of whom haven't
been personally out Northeast in years, it seems like a foot-drag-
ging, contrary, and backward place. School levy proposals always run into the heavy artillery here. But it is understandable
when so much of the population is trying to survive on small incomes surrounded by big inflationary costs for everything.

In the Northeast the polls will turn up all kinds of negative attitudes. Not only are schools opposed for the economic hardship
of increased property taxes, but the complaints also take careful
note of every instance of vandalism at any school as evidence
that the kids aren't all that worthy anyway. People in the Northeast have a sneaking suspicion that they could really teach their
kids better at home anyway.

There are some strong resentments of federal programs like
Model Cities, which are seen as instances of taking the money of
hard-working people to help people who ought to pull themselves up, bootstrap style. This has not been helped any in some
border areas where a hard-up family of Northeast whites can see
an aid program assisting blacks in the next block, only to learn
that a boundary line excludes them from the area where such
help is available. Word of mouth conveys this kind of seeming
injustice over a wide territory.

For years the political thinking and action of Northeast Kansas City was shaped by the late William Royster. Royster, a high-born descendant of a pioneer Kansas City family, lived in a magnificent old mansion on Gladstone Boulevard, the Ward Parkway of the Northeast, until his death in 1973.

There his political lieutenants would gather, and deals were made to support this candidate or to dump that one.

Royster was a Democrat of the old ward boss school. He and his followers wasted no time discussing political ideology. The modern "issue-oriented" candidate sometimes seen in south Kansas City would have been in Royster's Northeast a wonder to challenge the two-headed hippopotamus. But Royster knew where his votes were and how to get them out. He knew where the jobs were and how to get them. And he knew when he was needed by the dudes downtown and he drove rock-hard bargains. In 1968, when Royster didn't think much of Presidential candidate Hubert Humphrey, his sample ballots simply began with Governor Warren Hearnes and went downward from there. In Northeast Kansas City, the Presidential ticket didn't exist.

As when any man of great power dies, a scramble ensued after the death of Royster. It was not a blatant scandal. His followers knew that even in death Royster wouldn't stand for that. But ever since his departure a lot of games of grabbies have been going on, and it seems likely that no one will really be the "new Bill Royster."

As exasperating as the Northeast can be in political and community efforts, there is a certain kind of middle American dignity about it. To the southsider who drives out for a look it has a substantial old-fashioned appearance. It looks, in fact, like a detached segment of St. Louis more than part of the physical body of Kansas City, Missouri. But it is home to a lot of good people. And that is not said to patronize them. Good people, however obstinate they can sometimes be, are not in oversupply in this world.

And that is the emotional terrain of the city at the heart of the metropolitan area. And even though this viewpoint has its negative spots, let it be added that it is the view of two people who look at dear old River City "through love-tinted glasses."